PRAISE F(

Sodomy II: The Trial of Anwar Ibrahim

"... A well written and readable account of extraordinary events that are of significance to Malaysia, its laws and politics."

The Hon. Michael Kirby,

Former Justice of the High Court of Australia

"Mark Trowell exposes sharply the flawed prosecution of Anwar Ibrahim — an absolute read for every one interested in understanding how and why this happened."

Rogier Huizenga,

Head Human Rights Programme,
Inter-Parliamentary Union, Geneva

"The charges against Anwar Ibrahim for the offence of carnal intercourse against the order of nature, the criminal trial that followed and the strictures with respect to pre-trial disclosure, show us two things: it is high time such an offence is expunged from our statute books, and trial by ambush has no place in the criminal justice system. This book is a timely reminder that justice is a global concern."

Christopher Leong,

President, Malaysian Bar

THE PROSECUTION OF ANWAR IBRAHIM

The Final Play

MARK TROWELL QC

Marshall Cavendish
Editions

Published by Marshall Cavendish Editions
An imprint of Marshall Cavendish International
1 New Industrial Road, Singapore 536196

This new edition is based on *Sodomy II: The Trial of Anwar Ibrahim*, first published 2012.

Other Marshall Cavendish Offices
Marshall Cavendish Corporation. 99 White Plains Road, Tarrytown NY 10591-9001, USA • Marshall Cavendish International (Thailand) Co Ltd. 253 Asoke, 12th Flr, Sukhumvit 21 Road, Klongtoey Nua, Wattana, Bangkok 10110, Thailand • Marshall Cavendish (Malaysia) Sdn Bhd, Times Subang, Lot 46, Subang Hi-Tech Industrial Park, Batu Tiga, 40000 Shah Alam, Selangor Darul Ehsan, Malaysia.

Marshall Cavendish is a trademark of Times Publishing Limited

National Library Board Singapore Cataloguing in Publication Data
Trowell, Mark, author.
The prosecution of Anwar Ibrahim : the final play / Mark Trowell, QC. – Singapore : Marshall Cavendish Editions, [2015]
pages cm
ISBN : 978-981-4561-61-7 (paperback)

1. Anwar Ibrahim, 1947- – Trials, litigation, etc. 2. Trials (Sodomy) – Malaysia. 3. Trials (Political crimes and offenses) – Malaysia. 4. Judicial process – Malaysia. I. Title.

KPG41.A58
345.595102536 – dc23   OCN899707186

Printed in Malaysia

To the memory of my late mother,
Patricia Aileen Powell.

This book is also dedicated to my friends
Datuk David Yeoh Eng Hok,
the late David Kingsley Malcolm AC QC
and the late Datuk Michael Bong Thiam Joon

Contents

Foreword

THE HON. MICHAEL KIRBY AC CMG[1]

This is a revised and updated edition of a book on the saga of Dato' Seri Anwar Ibrahim, a Malaysian leader of political skills, personal gifts and charismatic attraction. New sections have been added to an earlier edition, to bring the Anwar saga up to date. A new final chapter tells the dramatic story of the outcome of his appeal against a second conviction of the crime of sodomy. In February 2015, the Federal Court of Malaysia affirmed a decision of the Court of Appeal of Malaysia. That Court had taken a step, unusual in legal process, of setting aside an acquittal entered by the judge in Anwar Ibrahim's second sodomy trial and substituting a conviction of the crime. Judicial lightning could, it seems, strike twice. As he was led to commence serving his sentence of five years' imprisonment (which would prohibit him from political engagement for a further five years after his release), Anwar Ibrahim reminded his supporters: "I will again, for the third time, walk into prison. But rest assured my head will be held high. The light shines on me."

---

1 Former Justice of the High Court of Australia (1996–2009); member of the Eminent Persons Group on the Future of the Commonwealth of Nations (2010–11); UNDP Global Commission on HIV and the Law (2010–12); past President of the International Commission of Jurists (1995–98); and Chair of the United Nations Committee of Inquiry on the Democratic People's Republic of Korea (2013–14)

A number of international observers watched the Federal Court proceedings, as indeed they had the earlier appellate and trial hearings following the successive charges of sodomy. One such observer was the distinguished former Australian judge, the Hon. Elizabeth Evatt AC, a commissioner of the International Commission of Jurists (ICJ). As reported, she was critical of the intermediate court's reversal of the acquittal at trial, stating that it "adopted an approach wherein the burden was on Anwar Ibrahim to prove that he had a credible defence, rather than raising reasonable doubt as to the prosecution's case". Other international bodies had their own observers watching proceedings, including Human Rights Watch and Amnesty International. This book is written by Mark Trowell QC, of the Western Australian Bar. His mandate came from LAWASIA, the Law Council of Australia and the Inter-Parliamentary Union. Whilst all of the observers were critical of aspects of the judicial proceedings, Mr Trowell has turned his experience into this book. It is, at once, gripping, readable and disturbing.

Trial observers constitute a rare, but important, breed. In the 1990s, I had their usefulness brought to my notice in a direct way. At the time I was the chairman of the Executive Committee of the ICJ in Geneva. Following the first multi-racial elections conducted in South Africa, after the much delayed enfranchisement of all its citizens, I was invited to Pretoria to witness the inauguration of Nelson Mandela as the country's first black president. On 27 April 1994, under the shadow of the impressive Union Buildings, at the centre of Afrikanerdom, I watched the new president take his oaths of office.

President Mandela had invited me to attend the inauguration because he had particular reason to be appreciative of the ICJ. In August 1962, whilst he was serving a sentence for leading a workers' strike, he was charged, in the Rivonia Trial, with the capital crime of sabotage. Equivalent to treason, it was a charge easier for the prosecution to prove. Nelson Mandela stood at peril of his life. His lawyers' task was not made easier by the fact that he insisted on admitting the specifics of the several allegations involving conspiracy with the African National Congress and the South African Communist Party to use explosives to destroy water, electrical and gas utilities. In his statement from the dock, at the opening of the defence case, Mandela laid out the reasons why he had taken to violence. All of this brought him to the shadow of the gallows. It was a fact that he recognised by acknowledging that "if needs be, [my] ideal [is one] for which I am prepared to die".

The ICJ had arranged for Nelson Mandela's trial to be observed by a distinguished Australian barrister, Edward St. John QC of the New South Wales Bar. The trial judge afforded him the facility of attending throughout. Mr St. John regularly reported to the Commission in Geneva and to his colleagues in Australia, waiting anxiously for news.

In the end, all but one of the accused, including Nelson Mandela, were found guilty. However, they escaped the gallows. On 12 June 1964, they were sentenced by the trial judge to life imprisonment. Nelson Mandela considered that the simple vigilance of the observers at his trial had enhanced the fairness of his proceedings. It had also contributed to avoiding the imposition of the death penalty.

Ted St. John had died by 1994. That is how the invitation to President Mandela's inauguration fell to me. As I watched the ceremonies, and observed the rainbow flag of a newly freed nation unfold, I reflected on the growth of the international scrutiny of contested laws in every country, including my own. And on the utility of outside observers watching sensitive national trials. Occasionally, trial observance has helped those on trial. At the very least, it can serve to remind the judge of the basic principle, oft repeated in the common law, that judges, when performing their duties, are themselves on trial. This is why the principle of open justice is so important. It is why, in today's world of global news, the commitment to open justice often demands the opportunity for outside scrutiny, lest local passions add to the dangers of miscarriage and to the risks of injustice. (In his trial observance, Mark Trowell has sought to continue in the high tradition performed by Ted St. John years earlier.).

There were, of course, differences in the circumstances that the observers faced. Malaysia is not an apartheid state. Its Internal Security Act had lately been repealed. However, the law of sedition was still used against those accused of disturbing the "racial and cultural harmony" desired by government and officials. Sedition was often a feature of the late imperial laws of the British Empire, including South Africa. Despite promises, later withdrawn, sedition has neither been repealed nor reformed in Malaysia.

The second trial of Anwar Ibrahim, between July 2000 (when he was arrested and charged) and January 2012 (when he was acquitted by the trial judge) (Sodomy II) captured world attention. It had all of the ingredients likely to entrance and sustain global attention. There had already been an earlier trial in 1998–99 (Sodomy I). In that trial the accused had been convicted of sodomy and sentenced to nine years in prison. This conviction appeared to destroy the political career of a man who had earlier been viewed as heir apparent to the office of Prime Minister of Malaysia, at the time held by Tun Dr Mahathir Mohamad.

The fallout between these two successful and gifted politicians, and the exotic nature of the sexual offence of sodomy alleged, ensured an international fascination for each of the trials, and for the legal processes they involved, that more mundane allegations of corruption, fraud or gambling offences would not have done. Here was the stuff of infotainment — the apparent fall from grace of a brilliant exponent of the political arts, in a country to whose economic advancement the accused had apparently made significant contributions. A shattered political, and almost filial, affection, mixed with charges of the "abominable crime", said to be "against the order of nature", delivered a news cocktail that international media could simply not resist. Satellite television, rapidly enlarged by the advent of the Internet, blogs, informal media, social networks and the rumour mill, presented the world with a mouth-watering story of politics wrapped in sexual passion. Moreover, it was a story that came with a sequel.

When the first conviction of Anwar Ibrahim in Sodomy I was set aside on appeal, in September 2004, and he returned to an increasingly successful role in national politics, the initiation of a second trial for the same offence seemed to hard-nosed editors too good to be true. One can only imagine them at their desks, the pundits and commentators in broadcasting studios and the associated advertised gurus all salivating at the thought of another round of the media merry-go-round of sodomy and politics.

The author of this book has told the story of the two legal proceedings, but particularly the second. He has done so in the generally dispassionate way expected of a neutral observer who is a senior advocate in Australia, one of Her Majesty's Counsel learned in the law. Towards the close of the book, he admits that he was surprised by the outcome of the second sodomy trial which was announced by Justice Zabidin on 9 January 2012. He explains his reaction by reference to "the several key rulings made during the trial, all of which were against the accused, but importantly the judge's ruling on the no case submission". He admits: "I was absolutely wrong. Like many others, I was completely surprised by the acquittal."

Yet, because it is impossible normally to get into the mind of a judge, every experienced advocate is aware of the fact that the way a decision will fall out is quite often unknown, including to the judge personally, until just before the decision is announced. What may appear to be an adverse signal given by a judge (including in legal rulings) might be no more than ideas blowing in the wind, so that even the judge may not, at the time the signals are given, be certain of how things will finally pan out.

I have known very experienced advocates to swear that they can predict with total accuracy how a jury, say, will respond to an accusation or a judge or bench of judges to the evidence and the advocate's submissions. But as one who was on the receiving end of such submissions for 34 years, I have always been sceptical of such assertions. Especially because I was often myself uncertain, when reserving a decision, as to how I would ultimately decide a case. Or perhaps I had a strong conviction at the end of submissions that it would be resolved one way, only to find (on further study, reading and reflection) that my initial inclination had to be abandoned. Intuition and overall assessment may be useful to human decision making. However, the judicial process is expected to be more analytical and painstaking. Especially where another person's liberty, reputation, public office and human potential are at risk. As was the case with Nelson Mandela (whose life was on the line). And as was the case with Anwar Ibrahim in both of his judicial ordeals.

Many of the broad contours of the Anwar court proceedings are generally known by lawyers and other members of the international audience who consumed the two sagas over the years that they processed through the courts of Malaysia. However, the value of this book is that it recounts the two proceedings in a compendious way. It affords a well written and readable account of extraordinary events that are of significance to Malaysia, its law and politics. But they are also important to countries in the region and to the world that has looked with admiration at the advances in Malaysia's economy and its standards of living. With this admiration has come occasional anxiety about the political and legal scene that, to outsiders, has sometimes appeared to be locked in a time warp that has failed to permit the nation to enjoy the full fruits of its economic progress by permitting a greater freedom in politics, religion and civil society. In short, Malaysia has sometimes seemed a country that is surprised by its own material advancement yet unwilling to loosen the inherited colonial restraints that would permit a more vibrant political and social life to flourish as the counterpart to (and product of) its economic 'miracle'. Amongst some foreigners, there was occasionally a hope that Anwar Ibrahim might prove to be a catalyst to help Malaysia to resolve this paradox of its material success and domestic uptightness that made his successive judicial proceedings so fascinating and noteworthy.

Over the years, I have had the privilege of knowing some of the *dramatis personae* described in this book. I have had the pleasure, on many occasions, in my own country, in the region and in Malaysia itself, of receiving hospitality from the judiciary and legal profession of Malaysia, and public courtesy from Malaysian politicians, past and present. By and large, Australians get along well with Malaysians. We have many links of history, law, military and economic interests. And we also share an irreverent sense of humour that sets us apart from more solemn societies.

There have, of course, been moments of tension. I do not refer only to the unhappy relationship that arose between Prime Ministers Mahathir and Keating, when the latter described the former as 'recalcitrant', although this was a comparatively mild epithet in Paul Keating's lexicon, when deployed against his fellow Australians. For me, the worrying events involved in the removal of the then Lord President of the Federal Court of Malaysia, Tun Mohamed Salleh Abas, was enough to persuade me to write an earlier foreword, published in Tun Salleh's biographical reflection *May Day for Justice* (1989), after he was removed from judicial office. On that occasion, I shared the pages of that book with the founding prime minister and independence leader of Malaysia, Tunku Abdul Rahman Putra Al-Haj. But that was an incident in the past. By the late 1990s everyone hoped that it was largely behind us.

I do not intend, on this occasion, to make inappropriate comments on the conduct of the Anwar proceedings, as revealed in this book. I will leave any comments to him and to those quoted in these pages. This revised edition concludes with the outcome of the judicial process in Sodomy II in February 2015. Apart from everything else, this book shows that Malaysians sometimes pursue their litigation with inordinate vigour.

During the saga, Anwar Ibrahim and his lawyers left few, if any, litigious stones unturned, as this book demonstrates. Others may, even now, still be in the offing, despite the fact that litigious fortune sometimes runs out for any litigant. Still, courts are not always the best venues for politicians to fight battles that will often be more prudently waged in the legislature chamber, the media or at the hustings. Litigants, rightly, have no control (and only limited opportunities to influence) the outcomes of litigation. My own involvement at the Bar, and in many judicial posts, has taught me that to resort to law should generally be seen as a final option — to be avoided wherever possible and brought to conclusion as quickly as can be. The central character in the drama described in these pages sometimes appears to outsiders to be a great curial risk taker. Whilst risk taking can be a great strength in a politician, it can sometimes be unwise in a litigant. Nonetheless, in his appeal to the Federal Court in Sodomy II, following reversal of his acquittal at trial, Anwar Ibrahim really had no option left. He had to venture if he was to walk free. This book tells how his hopes, and those of his supporters, were to be dashed.

The last chapter in this revised edition on the saga recounts the adverse judgement of the Federal Court and the fiery speech that Anwar made, before being led away to prison. The chapter painstakingly analyses the issues that had to be resolved by the Federal Court. It explains certain suggested defects in the Federal Court's reasons, complained of by Anwar's supporters. The reliance by appellate judges on a complainant whose testimony did not persuade the trial judge (with the advantages he enjoyed). The failure to deal adequately with the astonishing evidence that the complainant had purchased KY lubricant before visiting Anwar. The reliance placed by the Federal Court on the complainant's knowledge of homosexual acts, which any young person would know is readily available from plentiful pornography. The failure to deal with the complainant's personal relationship with a member of the prosecuting team. The reliance on DNA evidence collected 54 hours after the alleged offence, with respected experts asserting that it was unreliable, risky and flawed. The acceptance of the complainant, supposedly a devout Muslim, that he had not washed himself for 54 hours after the intercourse.

Every appeal on factual grounds is problematic. But that is a reason why appellate courts are always highly respectful of the overall assessment of the trial judge. This is not because he or she has magic powers to tell truthful witnesses from false. It is because the trial judge sees and hears all of the evidence in sequence, whereas appellate judges are heavily reliant on the passages that the competing advocates choose to emphasise. If the accused had not been the Leader of the Opposition, who came within a whisker of government in the 2013 elections and who had already been subjected to one sodomy trial that eventually failed, little attention would have been paid to this decision of the Federal Court. But because of the offices of state that the accused had held, and those that were possibly in prospect, this was no ordinary litigation. Years hence, lawyers and other citizens will be pouring over the Federal Court's reasons and the angry assertion of the prisoner that he was innocent "of this foul charge". "The incident never happened. This is a complete fabrication coming from a political conspiracy to stop my political career: ... [A] ... murder of judicial independence and integrity [occurring in a] sea of falsehood and subterfuge".

However all this may be, there is a final and important observation that this book calls forth. It was mentioned, but not elaborated, in a statement issued by the Malaysian Bar Association in welcoming the decision of the trial judge to acquit Anwar Ibrahim at the end of his second trial. In that statement, the Bar, speaking from its high tradition of robust independence and scepticism of authority, observed [p.201]:

> "The charge against Datuk Seri Anwar Ibrahim, *which is based on an archaic provision of the Penal Code that criminalises consensual sexual relations between adults* [emphasis added], should never have been brought. The case has unnecessarily taken up judicial time and public funds."[2]

Of course, if the complainant's assertions in the second trial were believed, the charge against Anwar Ibrahim, based on section 377A of the Malaysian Penal Code, was not an instance of 'consensual sexual relations'. It was one of a forced and unwelcome intrusion upon the dignity and privacy of another human being. Nonetheless, the singling out of particular sexual activity, with specified body parts; its description in the law as an 'unnatural offence' and one deemed to be "against the order of nature"; its appellation by reference to the obscure Biblical term of 'sodomy'; and the assignment to it of condign punishment, all present elements designed to raise a special public horror and stigma about the case. Such a charge is bad enough in the case of any individual. But it is specially damaging when the

---

2   www.malaysianbar.org.my, Lim Chee Wee, Press Release: 'Acquittal on charge of consensual sex between adults is in accord with evidence', 9 January 2012

accusation is made against an important public figure. Indeed, against the alternate head of government of a nation.

Following scientific research by Dr Alfred Kinsey in the 1940s and 50s in the United States of America, steps were taken in the United Kingdom that led, in 1967, to the repeal of the sodomy offence in most cases and, ultimately, to its being subsumed in categories of sexual offences of general application. This development led to legislative and judicial reforms of the penal codes bequeathed by the British colonial administrators to the old dominions of the Crown (first Canada, then New Zealand and finally Australia) and to judicial decisions in post-Mandela South Africa and in the Fiji Islands. Later, in an important decision of the Delhi High Court in India, in *Naz Foundation v Union of India* [2009] 4 LRC 838, the judges confined the application of section 377 of the Indian Penal Code (upon which the later Malaysian provision was based) solely to cases concerned with underage sexual offences. Although that decision was later reversed by a two-judge bench of the Supreme Court of India in the *Koushal* appeal [2014] 3 LRC 555, a curative petition has been filed. That decision is basically inconsistent with enlightened later decisions on transgender rights decided both in India and Malaysia in 2014. It would have been open to the Federal Court of Malaysia, in a proper case, to prefer the Delhi High Court's approach. However, unfortunately, beyond a small collection of the older overseas possessions that were once the British Empire, little progress has been made to rid the statute book of this unlovely relic of the past.

In 41 of the 54 countries of the Commonwealth of Nations, the sodomy offence remains in force. In the contemporary world, this is a particular tragedy. The offence, with the stigma that its name, description and other features attracts, impedes the educative and other efforts to reduce the contemporary scourge of HIV/AIDS. This is why leaders of the United Nations, notable scientists and important citizens (including in Malaysia) have proposed that the offences, like 377A, should be repealed and subsumed in more generic crimes. As they have been elsewhere for reasons of legal principle and also current epidemiological prudence.

By chance, between the first and second sodomy trials of Anwar Ibrahim, I had the privilege of meeting him at a seminar of lawyers that he attended on the Gold Coast in Queensland, Australia. It was my task to chair his session. It provided an occasion to reflect on the lessons to be derived up to that time, for Malaysia and other countries, from the course and outcome of his first trial.

I took the occasion to urge upon the distinguished Malaysian visitor the need for him to advocate the repeal, or at least significant reform, of the sodomy offence in 377A of the Malaysian code. I urged this course so, as I put it, that some good should come out of his ordeal. As long as the offence remained in the books, it would be available to be deployed to the scandal of the public, the titillation of the media and the destruction of personal reputations in the future. The fact that any such offence would ordinarily take place behind closed doors and be easy to allege but difficult to disprove, made it important to remove it, lest it continued to afflict Malaysians and their body politic. Whilst my listener afforded me a polite hearing, he was noncommittal. Little did I imagine that so soon after our conversation, he would once again face a charge of sodomy. And that a second bandwagon of litigation and media attention would begin its journey to a contested outcome.

In the course of this book, Mark Trowell has ascribed to the current prime minister of Malaysia, Dato' Sri Najib Razak, a conviction that Anwar's second trial, on a further sodomy charge, was an "unwelcome distraction from the serious business of running our country in the interests of the Malaysian people."[3] [p.199]. However that may be, it became a distraction, in part at least made possible by the survival of the peculiar and exotic features of the sodomy offence. And by the deep wells of prejudice that this offence is designed to conjure up.

By a further irony of history, I was later to take part in two international bodies that, more recently, have examined the persistence, mainly in countries of former British rule, of the sodomy offence and its unfortunate consequences for the urgent task of HIV/AIDS prevention in our world. One of these bodies, which reported to the Secretary-General of the United Nations in July 2012, was the Global Commission on HIV and the Law initiated by the United Nations Development Programme. The other was the Eminent Persons Group of the Commonwealth of Nations. It reported in October 2011 to the Commonwealth Heads of Government Meeting in Perth, attended by Prime Minister Najib. Each of these reports urged prompt attention to the reform and repeal of provisions such as S377A. Specifically, the latter report pointed out that Commonwealth countries "comprise over 30% of the world's population and over 60% of people living with HIV. There is still no cure for, or vaccine against, HIV/AIDS. Providing the anti-retroviral medicines that palliate against the 32 million people infected in our world has become more difficult with the Global Financial Crisis." All countries must take their own urgent steps to make it easier to advance education and to prevent the spread of infection. Unanimously, the Eminent Persons Group went on:

> "These laws [sodomy] are a particular historical feature of British colonial rule. They have remained unchanged in many developing countries of the Commonwealth despite evidence that other Commonwealth countries have been successful in

reducing cases of HIV infection by including repeal of such laws in their measures to combat the disease. Repeal of such laws facilitates the outreach to individuals and groups at heightened risk of infection. The importance of addressing this matter has received global attention through the United Nations. It is one of concern to the Commonwealth, not only because of the particular legal context, but also because it can call into question the commitment of member states to the Commonwealth's fundamental values and principles including fundamental human rights and non-discrimination."

The people of the Commonwealth are still waiting for an effective (or any) response to these recommendations by the member governments, leaders and officials. But it is important to notice that the Chair and leader of the Eminent Persons Group that made these recommendations unanimously was himself a former prime minister of Malaysia, mentioned in these pages, Tun Abdullah Ahmad Badawi. As is revealed, he was to succeed Prime Minister Mahathir. And he played a moderating role in the Anwar affair, described in this book, that gained the approbation of the author and of many others.

Some good should surely come out of the unhappy story recounted by Mark Trowell. Of course, it is impossible to expunge the sensational headlines, the pain to Anwar Ibrahim's wife, family and friends, the distraction to the Malaysian nation, and the words said at home and abroad about its politics, judicial and legal system. Yet, good would come for the proper boundaries of criminal law, for a scientific approach to sexual offences, and for a reduction of discrimination, stigma and disease in the world, if offences such as that in section 377A were removed and replaced by modern provisions that concentrate on elements of the age of a complainant, the private or public character of the event, and the presence or absence of consent. These considerations, rather than the particular organs of the human body, gender of the actors and special features of an antique offence, prone to whip up sensational tabloids, seem to be the way forward. The sodomy offence does damage that renders even the highest in the land extremely vulnerable, in ways that can never be fully repaired.

The postulate of the prosecution case against Anwar Ibrahim in Sodomy II was that he had committed sexual intercourse, by way of anal penetration, upon the complainant. It was always the accused's assertion that nothing of the kind ever happened. Those who alleged it were "wallowing in filth and foulness". In short, the controversy was a simple one between act or non-act. However, just imagine, for the purposes of argument, that there was such an act as the prosecution claimed. But that it was consensual: an event between two undoubtedly adult persons, happening in private, occurring in a fleeting space of time but subsequently blown up into a crime having a horror name; a criminal charge specially damaging in politics; a peculiar affront to devout religious supporters; and a litigious ordeal and distracting media circus. If that were so, it would still be a tragedy for an accused like Anwar Ibrahim. There would be some evidence, at least, to support such a postulate, although he always denied it. The secluded venue of the events. The opportunity that was afforded. And the still remarkable and poorly explained fact that the complainant came to the fateful meeting armed with lubricant, admitting to have contemplated the possibility of sex. In Sodomy II, everyone was locked into a denial of these postulates at the least because the consent and adult years of the actors and the private occasion of the act were no defence under section 377A. With a name like 'sodomy', evoking religious horror, Anwar Ibrahim could scarcely embrace such a postulate, even if it had been true. Counterfactuals are now big business in history studies. If this counterfactual were imagined, it would only emphasise the more nuanced tragedy that faced this accused. The defence he could never raise because (in law) it was unavailable and (in politics) it was fatal to his political ambitions. No accused person in Malaysia should be faced with such a dilemma. Even one who, like Icarus, had risen so high as to risk a mighty fall from grace and favour as he approached the sun of triumph.

Those who do not learn from the lessons of history are condemned to repeat its mistakes. The greatest lesson from the Anwar trials, I would suggest, is the need in the criminal laws of Malaysia to capture the same energy, dynamism and activism that has been so evident in that country's remarkable economic growth. And to modernise the statute book in the way the landscape and beautiful country of Malaysia has been re-created since *Merdeka*. It is in the hope that this book by Mark Trowell will contribute to a thoughtful reflection that produces this resolve in the judiciary, the legal profession and the political process of Malaysia, that I commend the author for presenting this story. Truly, the Anwar trials have been a distraction. But in a sense, it has been a distraction of Malaysia's own making. That is a vital lesson of this book. But is it a lesson that will now at last be heeded?

Michael Kirby
Sydney, 18 March 2015

Preface

On the sultry and overcast morning of Wednesday, 3 February 2010, Malaysia's opposition leader Datuk Seri Anwar Ibrahim sat in the dock in the High Court of Malaysia to stand trial for the criminal offence of carnal intercourse against the order of nature. He was alleged to have sodomised a young male member of his staff 18 months earlier at a private condominium in Kuala Lumpur.

Anwar claimed that the accusation was false and part of a political conspiracy to discredit him. Many feared that it was simply a replay of the police investigation and criminal trials of 1998, which resulted in his imprisonment for six years until released on appeal, and another attempt to finish him politically.

Following his convictions for sodomy and corruption, many observers within Malaysia and from the international community expressed significant concern that the proceedings were patently unjust and tainted by significant errors of law. The prosecution maintained Anwar was not above the law and it was doing no more than bringing to trial allegations of a serious crime.

It was a long trial lasting almost two years. The trial was subject to many delays while Anwar's lawyers lodged several appeals relating to issues which they claimed affected the fairness of his trial. These included the prosecution's refusal to disclose a list of the witnesses it intended to call at trial and evidence it would rely upon to prove its case. The defence also challenged the trial judge's refusal to strike out the prosecution for what it claimed was an obvious abuse of process and his refusal on two occasions to disqualify himself from hearing the trial because of actual bias. None of the defence appeals succeeded.

During the trial many events occurred which, although not directly relevant to the proceedings, illustrated that the political impact and ramifications of the trial were complex and significant. It was at times portrayed as a contest between the government and the opposition. It also brought into sharp focus the Malaysian justice system and, particularly, whether the judiciary could act in an impartial and independent way.

Finally, on the morning of Monday, 9 January 2012, Justice Datuk Mohamad Zabidin Mohamad Diah delivered his decision to a packed courtroom on the fifth floor of the High Court complex at Jalan Duta. In a few brief sentences, he announced that he was not satisfied the charge had been proved and he acquitted Anwar.

Very few had anticipated an acquittal. Anwar told the large contingent of media outside the court complex that he welcomed the decision, declaring he was "vindicated at last". He added that "a decision to the contrary would have put Malaysia in a disastrous light". The government was quick to claim that the verdict confirmed judicial independence.

Some commentators saw the verdict as a potential 'game-changer' in the forthcoming national election. It nearly proved to be so when the opposition led by Anwar almost defeated the government at the polls on 5 May 2013 taking 50.87 per cent of the popular vote. The government narrowly scraped back into power taking 60 per cent of parliamentary seats even though it won only 47.38 per cent of the popular vote.

It was a devastating result for the government and it was only widespread gerrymandering that kept it in office. Anwar had proved to be a formidable opponent and capable of toppling the ruling party.

But Anwar's legal struggle was far from over. The prosecution immediately challenged the acquittal. The appeal process was to last more than another three years until the Federal Court finally delivered its decision on Tuesday, 10 Feburary 2015. It upheld the verdict of the Court of Appeal convicting Anwar of the offence of sodomy and sentencing him to a term of five years' imprisonment.

This is the story of how that all came about, documenting the dramatic and often sensational twists and turns as the trial and appeal process played out in the courts.

Mark Trowell
March 2015

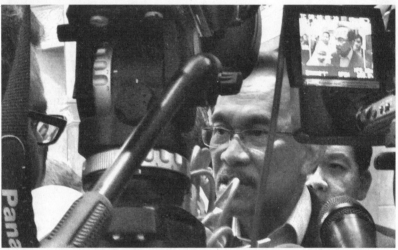

Timeline of events

Sodomy I

1993–98 • Anwar Ibrahim, deputy prime minister of Malaysia.

2 Sep 98 • Prime Minister Mahathir Mohamad dismisses Anwar as deputy prime minister and finance minister.

20 Sep 98 • 30,000 people rally in streets of Kuala Lumpur to protest Anwar's dismissal from office. Anwar arrested by police at his home under the Internal Security Act and taken into custody. Held in solitary confinement for nine days during which he was assaulted by the Inspector-General of Police Rahim Noor (Rahim later convicted of Anwar's assault).

29 Sep 98 • Anwar charged with sodomising his wife's driver and for corruption in attempting to interfere with the police investigation of the sodomy allegation. Appears in Sessions Court to answer charges showing visible signs of physical injury. Denied bail and remanded in custody to stand trial.

Nov 98–Apr 99 • Corruption trial. Anwar convicted and sentenced to six years in jail.

Jun 99–Aug 2000 • Sodomy trial. Anwar convicted and sentenced to additional nine years in jail.

2 Sep 04 • Anwar successfully appeals sodomy conviction and released from prison.

15 Sep 04 • Anwar's appeal against corruption conviction rejected.

Sodomy II

2008

8 Mar • National elections. Opposition parties make unprecedented gains depriving Umno-led Barisan Nasional of its two-thirds majority in parliament. Mohd Saiful Bukhari employed by Anwar soon after.

26 Aug • Anwar wins by-election for the parliamentary seat formerly held by his wife and becomes de facto leader of Pakatan Rakyat (PR).

24 Jun • Mohd Saiful meets Deputy Prime Minister Najib Razak at his home.

25 Jun • Mohd Saiful meets a senior police officer in a room at the Concorde Hotel, Kuala Lumpur.

26 Jun • Date of alleged sodomy in a KL condominium.

28 Jun • Mohd Saiful goes to the private Hospital Pusrawi claiming to have been sexually assaulted 48 hours before; examined by Dr Mohd Osman. Four hours later, he is examined by three doctors at Hospital Kuala Lumpur (HKL); rectal swabs taken and no injuries consistent with forcible anal penetration found. Mohd Saiful lodges police report.

29 Jun • Deputy Superintendent of Police Jude Pereira collects swabs from HKL and keeps them in a filing cabinet in his office. Sends swabs to Chemistry Department for analysis 43 hours later. Anwar seeks sanctuary at Turkish Embassy claiming to be in fear of his safety.

15 Jul • Anwar arrested and kept in police cell overnight. Refuses to provide DNA sample fearing it will be misused as it was in 1998. Police seize items used by Anwar in cell for DNA testing.

7 Aug • Anwar charged in Sessions Court for the offence of sodomy and released on bail.

2009

10 Mar • Sessions Court transfers case to High Court.

Mar–Jun • Case pending in High Court waiting trial listing.

15 Jul • Defence applies to have charges struck out for abuse of process on basis that there was no medical evidence of anal penetration. Judge reserves decision, but rejects application on 1 Dec.

16 Jul • Trial judge orders prosecution to supply documents and witness list to the defence. Prosecution immediately appeals decision. Court of Appeal overrules judge's decision on 21 Dec.

2010

29 Jan • Federal Court upholds Court of Appeal's decision refusing pre-trial access to prosecution documents and witness list. Judge orders trial to start on 3 Feb.

TRIAL COMMENCES 3 FEBRUARY 2010

4 Feb • Mohd Saiful called to testify. Judge orders part of testimony to be held in camera and court visits the condominium where the alleged sexual act took place.

5 Feb • Malay language newspaper publishes in camera evidence. Judge refuses Karpal Singh's request that he cite newspaper for contempt.

8 Feb • Defence applies for judge to disqualify himself from hearing the case for not citing the media for contempt.

12 Feb • Fifty Australian MPs lodge formal protest and call for the sodomy charge to be dropped.

16 Feb • Senator John Kerry, Chairman of US Senate Foreign Relations Committee, releases statement calling for a fair trial for Anwar.

18 Feb • Judge refuses to disqualify himself from presiding at trial for not citing media for contempt and adjourns case to 25 Mar. Defence appeals refusal, but later withdraws it on 25 Mar.

1 Apr • Inter-Parliamentary Union at 186th Session in Bangkok passes a 7-point resolution recording its concerns about Anwar's trial.

10 May • Trial resumes. Judge refuses a second application by defence for disclosure of prosecution witness list and Mohd Saiful's police statement. Defence appeals decision, but Court of Appeal refuses to intervene.

3 Jun • General surgeon Dr Mohd Razali Ibrahim of HKL testifies confirming penile penetration had taken place based on chemist's report which indicated the presence of semen on four swabs taken from Mohd Saiful.

4 Jun • Defence requests disclosure of all medical notes and reports, but trial judge later refuses.

23 Jul • Allegations of affair between junior counsel in prosecuting team Farah Azlina Latif and Mohd Saiful surface on Raja Petra's blog, Malaysia-Today. The Attorney-General removes her from prosecution team.

2 Aug • Anwar files police complaint against Mohd Saiful and junior prosecutor alleging they have violated the Official Secrets Act by exchanging prosecution documents.

26 Oct • Dr Mohd Razali cross-examined. Reveals another set of undisclosed proforma examination notes prepared before the July 13 Medical Report, but refuses to refer to them so that they cannot be tendered into evidence. Prosecutor says defence should not be allowed access to the proforma notes.

2 Nov • Hillary Clinton visits Malaysia and calls for the case to be "conducted fairly and transparently".

23 Nov • Dr Siew Sheue Feng cross-examined. Clashes with Karpal over his proforma notes and is seen reading them outside courtroom. Judge orders immediate disclosure, but refuses to cite him for contempt.

24 Nov • Defence applies to judge to disqualify himself for bias because of "intimidating" remarks he made to Karpal. Judge refuses application.

16 Dec • Anwar expelled from parliament for six months over his comments that a government unity policy was inspired by an Israeli initiative.

2011

16 Feb • Government scientist Dr Seah Lay Hong testifies that she found two unknown male DNA profiles in Mohd Saiful's rectum, one of which she calls "Male Y" (prosecution claims "Male Y" is Anwar's DNA).

8 Mar • Judge excludes DNA analysis of samples taken from three items in Anwar's cell as forensic evidence. Prosecution objects, and applies for judge to review decision and compel Anwar to provide a DNA sample. Judge adjourns trial to hear submissions.

20 Mar • Prime Minister Najib Razak publicly comments on leaked submissions saying that Anwar should provide a DNA sample.

21 Mar • Defence asks judge to cite the PM for contempt of court but retracts.

23 Mar • Judge reverses ruling and allows DNA analysis of samples to be produced as evidence on basis that arrest was lawful, but refuses to force Anwar to provide a DNA sample.

24 Mar • Prosecution completes its case tendering three items taken from Anwar's cell for DNA analysis. It has called 27 witnesses.

4 Apr • Three men reputed to have links with Umno and who the media dub "Datuk T" release a video featuring a man resembling Anwar having sex with a woman who appears to be a prostitute. Anwar says it is a fabrication and another attempt to smear him.

25 Apr • Prosecution case closes. Defence submits there is no case for accused to answer.

16 May • Judge rules prosecution case 'credible' and there is a case for Anwar to answer. Orders defence case to commence on 6 June.

6 Jun • Defence fails in third bid to disqualify judge for bias on account of his no case ruling. Judge dismisses application. Appeal to Court of Appeal dismissed. Case adjourned to 13 July.

8 Aug • Judge allows defence to interview prosecution witnesses on the condition that they are willing to be interviewed. Defence calls for PM Najib

and his wife to be interviewed. Both refuse. Defence issues witness summons requiring them to attend court, which is later set aside.

22 Aug • Defence case begins and Anwar makes his statement from the dock.

24 Aug • Defence calls forensic expert Professor David Wells to testify. He is critical of the investigation questioning the integrity of the rectal swabs taken from Mohd Saiful and findings of the government chemists.

26 Aug • Defence calls DNA expert Dr Brian McDonald to testify. He rejects entire prosecution DNA extraction process as being faulty and findings as inconsistent with the known medical history. Case adjourned until 19 Sep.

6 Oct • Defence calls spinal surgeon Dr Thomas Hoogland to testify. He says poor condition of Anwar's back precluded him from performing the sexual act described by Mohd Saiful. Prosecutor says Dr Hoogland did not examine Anwar in 2008 and so could not know whether he was physically incapable of doing the act.

23 Nov–13 Dec • Parties make final written and oral submissions. Judge adjourns trial to 9 Jan 2012 for verdict.

2012

9 Jan • Judge acquits Anwar giving brief oral reasons.

20 Jan • A-G's Chambers file notice of appeal against the acquittal.

28 April • Bersih 3.0 rally. Anwar later charged with civil disobedience for his part in rally.

22 May • Former trial prosecutor Datuk Mohd Yusof joins Anwar's legal team.

8 Jul • Judge's written reasons for acquittal published.

10 Jul • Prosecution files grounds of appeal against the judge's decision.

Anwar and lead counsel Karpal Singh conferring over a matter in court.

2013

5 May • Government wins 13th General Election.

17 Sept • Defence successfully applies to disqualify Justice Tengku Maimun Tuan Mat of the Court of Appeal from hearing the prosecution appeal.

18 Sept • Defence fails to disqualify prosecutor Tan Sri Muhammad Shafee Abdullah on basis that his appointment was invalid. Federal Court upholds decision.

6 Dec • Defence fails in second application to disqualify Shafee Abdullah based on Mat Zain's statutory declaration.

2014

12 Feb • Court of Appeal refuses defence application to call DSP Jude Pereira as witness in proceedings.

21 Feb • Karpal Singh convicted of sedition. Sentencing deferred.

28 Feb • Case management hearing to list appeal before Justice Aziah Ali instead of court Registrar.

3 Mar • Defence fails in third application to disqualify Shafee Abdullah on basis that he is not a fit and proper person to prosecute and because of conflict of interest. Federal Court upholds decision.

6 Mar • First day of hearing appeal before the Court of Appeal.

7 Mar • Second day of hearing appeal before the Court of Appeal. Anwar convicted of sodomy and sentenced to five years' imprisonment. He is granted bail.

11 Mar • Karpal sentenced for sedition and fined RM4,000. Nominations close for state parliamentary seat of Kajang.

25 Mar • Federal Court rejects Anwar's application to expunge reference to "homosexual acts" from the 2004 Appeal Judgement.

17 Apr • Karpal is killed in motor vehicle accident.

18 Aug • Anwar's lawyer N. Surendran is charged with sedition.

16 Oct • Malaysian Bar Council members march in protest against sedition laws.

28 Oct • Federal Court appeal begins with Datuk Seri Gopal Sri Ram leading the defence team.

8 Nov • Appeal hearing ends. Decision reserved by Court.

27 Nov • Prime Minister 'flip-flops' on promise to repeal sedition laws.

2015

10 Feb • Federal Court upholds sodomy conviction and Anwar is sentenced to five years in prison.

Key players in the prosecution of Anwar Ibrahim

Sodomy II Trial

Datuk Seri Anwar Ibrahim — the accused

He was deputy prime minister of Malaysia from 1993 to 1998 when Prime Minister Mahathir Mohamad dismissed him from office following allegations of sodomy and corruption. Although tried and convicted of both charges and sentenced to nine years in prison, he was ultimately convicted of the corruption charge and imprisoned for six years. In 2008 he was again elected to parliament and became de facto leader of the three-party opposition alliance Pakatan Rakyat.

Mohd Saiful Bukhari Azlan — the complainant

Joined Anwar's staff as a volunteer and later became his private assistant. He was 23 years old when he accused Anwar of sexually penetrating him several times in 2008.

Datuk Mohamad Zabidin Mohd Diah — trial judge

A High Court judge since 2006. Before the Anwar trial, he was neither well known nor associated with high profile cases or controversial judgements. A gruff and taciturn judge, he frequently locked horns with an often belligerent Karpal Singh, the lead defence counsel.

Datuk Mohamed Yusof Zainal Abiden — chief prosecutor

Deputy prosecutor at Anwar's sodomy and corruption trials in 1998–99, and at Anwar's appeal to the Federal Court in 2004. Appointed Solicitor-General II on 5 January 2009, he officially retired less than a month after Anwar was acquitted. A few months later, he accepted Anwar's invitation to join his legal team. A good humoured advocate who handled a difficult prosecution brief adeptly.

Tan Sri Abdul Gani Patail — Attorney-General

Formerly Senior Federal Counsel for Sabah, he has been A-G of Malaysia since 1 January 2002. He was chief prosecutor at Anwar's corruption and sodomy trials in 1998–99 and also chief counsel at Anwar's appeal against conviction at the Federal Court in 2004.

Karpal Singh — lead defence counsel

One of Malaysia's most prominent lawyers and a controversial figure both in the law and politics. Karpal represented Anwar at both his sodomy trials until his untimely death in a car accident in April 2014.

Dato' Param Cumaraswamy — defence lawyer

A high-profile Malaysian lawyer with an international reputation. His quietly spoken and polite manner masks his steely determination and resolute commitment to human rights. He was Chairman of the Malaysian Bar Council (1986–88); President of LAWASIA (1993–95); Commissioner, International Commission of Jurists (1990–2000); and the United Nations Special Rapporteur on the Independence of Judges and Lawyers by the United Nations Commission on Human Rights (1994–2003).

Sankara Narayanan Nair — defence lawyer

Sankara Nair is the principal of the firm of S.N. Nair. He was with Anwar from the time of Anwar's sacking in 1998. A cheerful character with a keen intellect, he was the motivating force of the defence team who acted as Anwar's spokesman to the media.

Ramkarpal Singh — defence lawyer

Ramkarpal is the third son of Karpal Singh and a senior lawyer in his father's law firm. He specialises in litigation law and was responsible for handling the complex and difficult DNA evidence at Anwar's second trial and at each of the appeals.

DSP Jude Pereira — chief investigating officer

Served the arrest warrant on Anwar. At the trial, he was severely criticised for ignoring strict procedures regarding chain of custody of forensic exhibits and the storage of the exhibits.

Farah Azlina Latif — junior deputy public prosecutor

During the trial, Farah Azlina was reported to be having an affair with Mohd Saiful. The A-G did not admit the existence of any romantic relationship between them but nevertheless removed her from the prosecution team, he said, to "avoid any negative public perception on the prosecution team".

Dr Mohamed Osman Abdul Hamid

The doctor who first examined Mohd Saiful on 28 June 2008 at the private hospital Pusat Rawatan Islam. He testified at the trial that Mohd Saiful had complained of pain in the anal region and claimed to have been anally penetrated by a "VIP". He found no evidence of injury.

Dr Mohd Razali Ibrahim — general surgeon

One of the three doctors at the government Hospital Kuala Lumpur (HKL) who examined Mohd Saiful on 28 June 2008. He took samples from the complainant's body and clothing for analysis.

Dr Seah Lay Hong — government chemist

A key prosecution witness whose evidence was capable of corroborating Mohd Saiful's claim of having been sodomised by Anwar. She was the chief chemist from the government Chemistry Department who analysed samples which she believed had come from Mohd Saiful's rectal swabs for the purpose of identifying DNA. She concluded that Anwar's DNA was present in his rectum.

Dr Brian McDonald — expert witness

The key expert witness for the defence. His expert opinion was critical in discrediting the process by which the forensic samples were taken from the complainant, and then stored and analysed by police investigators and government scientists.

Professor David Wells — expert witness

A recognised expert in handling sexual assault cases. He was critical of the way in which the findings of Mohd Saiful's medical examination at HKL were recorded. He was also highly critical of the collection, storage and testing of the forensic samples for DNA. He told the court that the samples tested by the government chemist were unlikely to have survived and that after 72 hours it would be "hardly worthwhile to test for DNA".

Dr Thomas Hoogland — expert witness

The orthopaedic surgeon who first examined Anwar in 2001 when he was in prison and later performed spinal surgery on him at his clinic in Munich in 2004. He reassessed Anwar's medical condition in 2011. At the trial, he testified that it was "very, very unlikely" for Anwar to indulge in "fast and vigorous" sex as described by Mohd Saiful.

Mohd Najwan Halimi — the complainant's friend

Claimed to have known Mohd Saiful since 2003. He testified that he thought Mohd Saiful was pro-Barisan Nasional when they were students at Universiti Tenaga Nasional. His testimony raised the prospect that Mohd Saiful's accusations were part of a political conspiracy to frame Anwar.

Sodomy II Appeals

Datuk Seri Muhammad Shafee Abdullah — chief prosecutor

Appointed by the A-G to prosecute the Anwar appeals in the Court of Appeal and Federal Court. Regarded as Umno lawyer and advisor, and confidant to Prime Minister Najib Razak.

Datuk Mat Zain Ibrahim — former CID chief

Police investigator of what is known as the "black eye" incident relating to the assault of Anwar while in custody in 1998. He made serious allegations of corruption against the A-G Gani Patail and deputy prosecutor Shafee Abdullah.

Sivarasa Rasiah — defence lawyer, prominent opposition politician and human rights activist

Co-founder of Suara Rakyat Malaysia or Suaram (a human rights NGO) and vice-president of the opposition Parti Keadilan Rakyat (PKR/People's Justice Party). An important member of Anwar's legal team.

Defence lawyers Sivarasa Rasiah (left) and Sangeet Kaur

Datuk Seri Gopal Sri Ram — lead defence counsel at the Federal Court appeal

A former Federal Court judge who retired from the bench in 2010. He controversially took over the lead role as senior defence counsel at the Federal Court appeal. Possesses a razor-sharp intellect, and is witty, blunt and persuasive.

Sangeet Kaur Deo — defence lawyer

Counsel at the Federal Court Appeal who dealt with the tricky issue of the admissibility of the DNA samples taken from items seized by the police from a cell where Anwar had spent the night after his arrest. She is Karpal Singh's only daughter.

Christopher Leong — Chairman, Bar Council of Malaysia

Also Vice-President of LAWASIA, he led the protest march of Malaysian lawyers on 16 October 2014 agitating for the repeal of the Sedition Act 1947, which had been used to charge several opposition members of parliament, journalists and student activists.

SODOMY I
1998 – 2004

CHAPTER 1
Sodomy I:
The first episode

Anwar Ibrahim was deputy prime minister of Malaysia from 1993 to 1998. In September 1998, then Prime Minister Mahathir Mohamad dismissed him after he was charged with allegedly sodomising his wife's driver and acting corruptly by attempting to interfere with the police investigation. Anwar was convicted and imprisoned, but released when Malaysia's Federal Court overturned the sodomy conviction in September 2004.

In May 2004, I observed the hearing of the appeal at the Federal Court in Putrajaya on behalf of the Australian Bar Association and the International Commission of Jurists (ICJ).

In my report to those organisations, I briefly outlined some of the history of the events leading up to Anwar's arrest in 1998 and conviction in 1999. To put this second trial in context, it is worth repeating some of that history, but also to update it by recounting the events since Anwar's release from prison.

The political crisis of 1998

Anwar was Dr Mahathir's political protégé and favourite to succeed him as prime minister. He was seen as the moderate and progressive voice of Islam. However, his political fortunes ended abruptly when, on 2 September 1998, Dr Mahathir — who had by then been in power for 17 years — dismissed his heir apparent from the positions of deputy prime minister and finance minister.

There had been tension between them for some months. For the most part, it seemed to concern the issue of how best to respond to the growing Asian Financial Crisis, but increasingly as Dr Mahathir's public popularity fell the real possibility of a leadership challenge became apparent. Anwar had become the prime minister's chief rival and was seen as the natural successor to the premiership. He was popular and highly regarded internationally as Malaysia's finance minister. Some, in fact, preferred to credit him with the management of the "financial miracle" that had transformed the country.

It seemed abundantly clear that Dr Mahathir was convinced Anwar was moving to replace him, but he was not ready to leave office. The smear campaign against Anwar started in the Malaysian newspapers only days after his sacking. Traditionally favouring the government, the media headlined that Anwar had been implicated in acts of sodomy with others. It is difficult to imagine that such allegations would have been made against the wishes of Dr Mahathir or that the police investigation and subsequent decision to prosecute Anwar would have taken place without his approval.

The public response to Anwar's sacking was immediate. A series of public demonstrations occurred, culminating on 20 September 1998 with a rally of more than 30,000 people led by Anwar through the streets of Kuala Lumpur protesting his dismissal and demanding the prime minister's resignation. The protests confirmed that Anwar was not about to leave public office quietly. The massive crowd of demonstrators that had gathered in Merdeka Square in the heart of the capital must have been viewed as a serious threat to Dr Mahathir's rule.

Dr Mahathir justified his decision to dismiss Anwar on moral grounds, saying Anwar was "morally unfit to lead the country". He argued the dismissal was based on allegations of sexual misconduct, tampering with evidence, bribery and threatening national security, and had nothing to do with disagreements over IMF plans for economic recovery.[1] He was quoted as saying: "He has hoodwinked the whole nation and appeared to be very religious. If he becomes prime minister, God help this country ... We cannot have a leader who is easily swayed by his lust ... We cannot accept a leader who has strange behaviour."[2]

He went on to allege that Anwar had wanted to topple the Malaysian government. Anwar counterclaimed that he was a victim of a high-level conspiracy to prevent him from revealing corruption and cronyism within the government.

Anwar's arrest and the "black eye" incident

On the evening of 20 September 1998 after the rally in Merdeka Square, when Anwar was in the middle of a press conference with local and international media, a contingent of 250 armed and masked security police forced their way into his home, smashing doors and manhandling a large number of supporters who had gathered there.

Anwar was immediately arrested under the Internal Security Act and taken from his house. He was kept in solitary confinement in police custody for nine days, interrogated and severely beaten.

He was brought before a court on 29 September 1998 and charged with several offences of corruption and sodomy to which he pleaded not guilty. When he appeared, it was obvious that he had been assaulted as there were bruises to his left eye and temple. He was photographed entering the courthouse with his right arm raised in defiance.

---

1   *The Straits Times*, Singapore, 12 October 2004

2   Agence France-Presse, 25 September 1998

He told Judge Hasnah Hashimin that he was "asked to stand up and I was boxed hard on the left temple and the right part of my head. I was hit very hard on the left part of my neck. I was then slapped very hard left and right, until blood seeped from my nose and lips."[3]

Anwar described to me the events of that night. He said he was handcuffed and blindfolded, then savagely kicked and punched and left unconscious on the lockup floor. Eventually, some junior police officers took pity on him and assisted him; he said some were even tearful as they helped him. Without their help, he believed he might have died from the assault. He added that his repeated requests for medical attention were ignored.

The police denied inflicting the injuries, claiming they were self-inflicted. However, in March 1999, the Inspector-General of Police (IGP) Tan Sri Rahim Noor admitted to a Royal Commission of Inquiry that he assaulted Anwar while he was in police custody. In April 2001 he pleaded guilty to the assault, and was fined RM2,000 (US$525) and imprisoned for two months. Anwar's lawyer Karpal Singh described the sentence as "manifestly inadequate".[4] In 2005, Rahim Noor publicly apologised for the "pain and hurt" caused to Anwar and his family.[5]

The police assault of Anwar in 1998 would become relevant to events a few years later. On 1 July 2008, Anwar lodged a police report at the Selangor police contingent headquarters claiming that information concerning the assault on him by Rahim Noor in 1998 had been falsified. He alleged that the persons involved were the investigating officer Musa Hassan (who was by then IGP) and then Senior Deputy Public Prosecutor at the corruption

3   Asian Human Rights Commission, Report, 5 October 1998

4   BBC News, 1 March 2000

5   BBC News, 3 August 2005

trial Abdul Gani Patail (now Attorney-General).[6] Musa Hassan rejected the allegations and threatened to sue Anwar for making the allegations against him.[7] Musa resigned his commission on 13 September 2010.

The basis for this police report can be traced to an open letter written in September 2001 by former chief of the Criminal Investigation Department Datuk Mat Zain Ibrahim to the current IGP Tan Sri Ismail Omar. In the letter, Mat Zain claimed that Musa Hassan and Abdul Gani fabricated forensic evidence obtained from Anwar on 26 October 1998 to produce three other medical reports that would show that Anwar "injured himself" in the "black eye" incident — this was ostensibly in a bid to protect the police from prosecution for the assaults on Anwar. He also claimed that according to Dr Zahari Noor of Hospital Kuala Lumpur, Musa Hassan and former Malacca police chief Mohd Rodwan Mohd Yusof took some of Anwar's blood samples, which later led to complaints that the DNA evidence was fabricated.

Convicted after trial

In April 1999, after a lengthy trial, Anwar was convicted for acting corruptly — using his office to interfere with the police investigation of the sodomy allegations — and sentenced to six years' imprisonment.

And at the culmination of another trial on 8 August 2000, he was convicted of various acts of sodomy allegedly committed on his wife's driver. For this he was sentenced to an additional term of nine years' imprisonment. Both trials attracted considerable international attention.

---

6   Bernama, 14 July 2008

7   themalaysianinsider.com, 'Mat Zain: Musa, Gani duped Dr M into sacking Anwar' by Shannon Teoh, 12 September 2011

Release from prison

Anwar has always maintained his innocence. In September 2004, he was partially vindicated when the Federal Court, by a majority of 2:1, upheld his appeal against conviction on the sodomy offences and ordered his immediate release from prison. The majority found the complainant Azizan bin Abu Bakar, who was the Anwar family driver and on whose testimony the prosecution was based, to be an unreliable witness. Given the various inconsistencies and contradictions in his testimony, the judges concluded that it was not safe to convict on the basis of his uncorroborated testimony alone. They found that Anwar should have been acquitted without having to enter a defence.

Weeks later, the same court refused to reverse an earlier decision by it to uphold the convictions on the corruption charges.

Still, for Anwar, the court's decision was the culmination of a six-year struggle for justice after pleading his innocence through the various tiers of the Malaysian court system. During his six years of incarceration, Anwar became the symbol of political opposition to the Mahathir regime. Amnesty International declared him to be a prisoner of conscience, stating that he had been arrested in order to silence him as a political opponent.

Dr Mahathir was later to say: "I have always been able to stand up against the people who challenge my leadership and I have won. And I believe that even against Anwar, I would have won."[8] He also said that he had sacked Anwar for moral reasons and the sacking had nothing to do with disagreements over IMF plans for economic recovery.[9]

---

8   Bernama, 14 July 2008

9   *The Straits Times*, Singapore, 12 October 2004

Was Anwar's appeal controversial?

The ICJ and the Australian Bar Association appointed me as their observer at Anwar's appeal against his convictions for sodomy heard by the Federal Court of Malaysia in May 2004. The primary objective of my report was to record my observations of the proceedings. The appeal was not particularly controversial insofar as the conduct of it was concerned. At the conclusion of proceedings, I told journalists that:

> "I make no complaint as to the conduct of the appeal proceedings. The judges acted with courtesy, patience and apparent interest in the submissions made by counsel.
>
> However, the fairness of this appeal will be judged by the final decision of the Federal Court. Whether the court has been fair and just shall be assessed by its response to the process of the original trial...
>
> The international community has a clear perception that the original trial was patently unfair and contained many errors of law. That perception can only be overcome by the court acting objectively and dealing with the appeal on its merits without regard to any extraneous factors. Malaysia's reputation as a modern and democratic nation governed by the rule of law will be assessed by how the judges deal with this appeal."[10]

The lingering perception of the original trials was that the judges, when dealing with Anwar throughout his court hearings, had failed to act independently from the executive arm of government that for the most

---

10   Al-jazeera.net, 22 May 2004; Associated Press, 22 May 2004;
       The China Post, 24 May 2004

part was identified with the interests of Prime Minister Mahathir. There was no direct evidence of political interference despite the many claims, but undoubtedly this perception was influenced by past events.

In the late 1980s, the executive government acted firmly to curtail judicial independence. It was then that Dr Mahathir stamped his authority firmly on the judiciary by dismissing the Lord President (now Chief Justice) and other justices thought hostile to the government or, at least, considered to be unwilling to comply with its will. Following that intervention, the judiciary in Malaysia was criticised for lacking the capacity to independently and impartially determine politically sensitive cases. In fact, for many years thereafter, there was open hostility between the judiciary and the Malaysian Bar Council because of the perception that the judiciary lacked independence.

In Anwar's case, substantial complaints had been made against the legal process, including the use of the infamous Internal Security Act[11] (ISA) to arrest and isolate Anwar and other persons in custody for extended

---

11   The ISA was enacted after independence from the British in 1957 to curb the activities of communist insurgents then active in Malaysia. It allowed for the detention without criminal charge or trial for a period not exceeding two years where it was "necessary to prevent any person acting in a manner prejudicial to the security of Malaysia" (Section 73(1)). In reality, the period of detention could be indefinite as the two years could readily be extended indefinitely by increments of two years. Successive governments for more than 50 years used the ISA, together with the Sedition Act of 1947, as political instruments of the state against political opponents. On 15 September 2011, the Malaysian government announced its intention to repeal the ISA and replace it with new legislation to safeguard peace and order. The ISA was replaced in April 2012 by the Security Offences (Special Measures) Act and by amendments to the Penal Code, the Criminal Procedure Code and the Evidence Act. The new legislation allows for the detention of a person suspected of a security offence for a period of 28 days for investigation purposes.

periods of time before charging them with substantive offences, the use of violence by police to interrogate Anwar and his alleged accomplices to obtain confessions, the use of tactics by the judiciary and prosecution to intimidate Anwar's counsel during his trial by bringing charges of contempt and sedition against them, the many unfair rulings made by the presiding judges at the trials, and the admission of obviously inadmissible evidence against the accused during those proceedings.

Some critics claimed that in Anwar's case, the judiciary simply failed to respond fairly and impartially to his complaints until such time as the influence of Dr Mahathir had been lifted from it by his departure from office in October 2003. It seemed to them that only then was it possible for the abuses and injustices of past legal proceedings to be rectified.

There is no doubt Anwar's struggle for justice exposed fundamental issues confronting the Malaysian justice system, including judicial independence, police brutality and corruption and the use of the draconic ISA in prosecuting alleged offenders.

A return to judicial independence?

One question posed in my 2005 Report was whether it could be said that the Federal Court decision to uphold Anwar's appeal represented a change of direction for the judiciary. In other words, was it an independent and impartial decision made without any political interference? I concluded there was probably little doubt the Federal Court decision would not have been possible under Dr Mahathir's regime given his considerable influence over the judiciary. Then Prime Minister Abdullah Badawi made it perfectly clear in media interviews he would not seek to influence the court decision, emphasising it was entirely a matter for the judges.

Anwar's assessment of the result was clear. He told reporters on his release that he was grateful to PM Badawi for not imposing his will on the judiciary: "You've got to recognise the fact that his predecessor [Mahathir Mohamad] wouldn't have made this judgement possible."[12]

Badawi was at the time keen to distinguish his style of governing from that of his predecessor. He had early in his term authorised prosecutions against politicians and businessmen for corruption and spoke constantly of the need for the government to be accountable.

Critics of the government suggested his approach was no more than window dressing, claiming the prosecutions were few and selective. They also took the view that his public statements about judicial independence carried little weight, given they were made at a time when Anwar was no longer a political threat.

However, I thought at the time there were signs that the system was changing. For example, in May 2005, the Royal Commission appointed to inquire into the Royal Malaysian Police Force delivered its report. The Commission found that the police had abused powers of preventative detention and recommended that the police should no longer be able to use internal security laws to sidestep courts and lock up suspects.

I commented in my report that foreign observers regularly took the view that the Malaysian judicial system should not be congratulated for doing what it should do and that is to decide cases based on the principles of law rather than be influenced by political considerations, but the court's decision to uphold Anwar's appeal seemed to me to be a positive indication of a change of attitude.

I suggested the Federal Court decision perhaps indicated a shift in direction for a judiciary that for some 20 years had been subject to executive government influence, and that by this decision the judiciary had shown itself capable of now acting in a more independent and impartial way. I concluded that whether the Anwar appeal decision was the turning point for the Malaysian judicial system was yet to be seen.

But again, Anwar and his supporters have claimed that his second prosecution was politically motivated. Whether that is true or not, it cannot be denied that ultimately he was acquitted. Was it as Rais Yatim, Malaysia's Minister of Information, Communications and Culture, said, that "this verdict proves that the government does not hold sway over judges' decisions"?[13]

Was the verdict the impartial decision of the trial judge made without any political influence? That is almost impossible to say because ultimately the verdict of acquittal was the correct decision in the face of the insufficiency of the evidence at the trial.

There were just too many factual inconsistencies to justify a conviction. Of course, commentators will suggest various scenarios. For example, that Anwar might be more troublesome if imprisoned because he would be able to portray himself as a political martyr. That the trial judge's decision may have been exactly the result the government wanted because it was concerned to avoid a greater loss of electoral support. That the prosecution served as a useful political tool because it disrupted Anwar's political efforts and focus by obliging him to fight criminal charges for almost four years.

Some Malaysian lawyers in private conversation express the view that High Court judges are increasingly prepared to act independently. However, they do not believe that is the case of the more senior appeal judges who they characterise as being decidedly pro-government and susceptible to political influence. If their assessment is correct, then perhaps the best test of impartiality and independence will be how the Court of Appeal decides Anwar's appeal.

---

13 *New York Times*, Liz Gooch, 9 January 2012

THE *REFORMASI* MOVEMENT

Although Anwar enjoyed considerable international support, his criminal convictions effectively removed him from the Malaysian political stage as well as from the dominant political party, Umno (United Malays National Organisation).

He became the titular head of a small opposition grouping formed around him which called itself the National Justice Party (Parti Keadilan Nasional). Parti Keadilan Nasional would later become Parti Keadilan Rakyat (PKR) after merging with Parti Rakyat Malaysia (PRM) in 2003.

Popularly known as Keadilan, the party sprang out of the *reformasi* movement. However, its membership and influence increasingly dwindled over the next few years. Keadilan suffered a severe defeat in the national elections of March 2003, losing four of its five seats in parliament, with Anwar's wife, Dr Wan Azizah, barely winning the seat her husband held before his downfall.

Dr Mahathir's successor, Abdullah Badawi, on the other hand, led his party to a resounding victory by defeating the country's fundamentalist Muslim opposition party, known as PAS, or Parti Islam Se-Malaysia, in one or two states it controlled and widening Umno's majority in parliament.

Prevented by legislation from returning to parliament until April 2008, Anwar was still considered by many as having the potential to become prime minister of Malaysia.

The ruling party, Barisan Nasional — a coalition comprising Umno, the Malaysian Chinese Association and the Malaysian Indian Congress — called an early election for 8 March 2008, which some commentators observed was an attempt to prevent Anwar from returning to parliament. The election was a disaster for Barisan Nasional. Opposition parties seized over a third of parliamentary seats and five states in the worst ever showing for the coalition that had ruled Malaysia for half a century.

Anwar's political return in 2008

Dr Wan Azizah, who for a time had been Malaysia's first female opposition leader, had declared that she would resign her Permatang Pauh parliamentary seat and force a by-election.

On 26 August 2008, Anwar won the by-election with a majority of more than 15,000 votes, returning to parliament as leader of the three-party opposition alliance known as Pakatan Rakyat (PR).

After being sworn in as a member of parliament, Anwar kept up a relentless attack upon the government, threatening to topple the ruling coalition party from office. Although he struggled to gain a majority in parliament to fulfil his promise of a transition of power to the opposition, the opposition has made gains in the states of Sarawak and Terengganu in a series of by-elections.

Following his election to parliament, Anwar consistently taunted the government by calling for such things as emergency sessions of parliament, issuing threats to meet the Yang di-Pertuan Agong (the King) to stake his claim to government, and has made claims of attempts by Barisan Nasional officials to bribe PR members of parliament to defect to the ruling party.

In June 2009, Prime Minister Badawi resigned his office in favour of his deputy Dato' Sri Najib Razak. Some commentators suggested that Badawi had paid the price for the ruling coalition's loss of a two-thirds majority in parliament.

The new prime minister was the target of a sustained attack by the opposition alliance a few months before taking office. It organised a petition urging the Yang di-Pertuan Agong to delay his appointment as prime minister until his reputation had been cleared by an independent commission appointed to consider his alleged involvement in the murder of a Mongolian national by two police officers.

However, tensions soon emerged in the opposition alliance to the extent that in March 2010 several parliamentary members of PKR quit the party, including the Penang Deputy Chief Minister Mohammad Fairus Khairuddin who applied to join Umno. Most of the problems related to regional conflict in the party's control of the administration of Penang.

Barisan officials were quick to predict the demise of the opposition alliance, but Anwar responded saying the resignation of Fairus was not a surprise as he had been a "poor performer". He saw no reason to dissolve PR just because the component parties could not agree on a few issues.[14]

Since then, the opposition alliance has lost several members and Prime Minister Najib continues to exploit the tensions saying that people have lost faith in PKR and that it is not fit to lead the country. During a speech at the launch of Yayasan Kelana Ehsan at Felda Sungai Tengi on 4 April 2010, Najib said: "If its inner circle is losing faith one by one and leaving the party, with some joining us, what kind of message is that?"[15]

The political pressure on Anwar also increased following an allegation that he had committed an act of sedition by apparently telling PR leaders that the King and the Chief of the Armed Forces had endorsed his move to take over the government on 16 September 2008. The allegation, made by former PKR MP Datuk Seri Mohd Zahrain Hashim, was immediately referred to the Attorney-General to decide whether to prosecute. Several police reports were lodged against Anwar for allegedly using the names of the King and the armed forces chief to instigate a takeover of the government.

14   *The Star*, 2 March 2010

15   *The Star*, 4 April 2010

Datuk Seri Nazri Aziz, Minister in the Prime Minister's Department, said at the time that any legal action would only come after investigations were completed. However, he said that in his view using the name of the King and armed forces to endorse a plan to overthrow the Barisan Nasional government was a criminal act. He told reporters in parliament following the revelation:

> "I strongly feel that these words are seditious. So I would suspect that action could be taken against him under the Sedition Act, because when you mention the King and the armed forces, it means you are instigating people to topple the existing government. If you look at the Act, it actually covers what Anwar has done, but this depends on the court to decide." [16]

So Anwar's political fortunes, at least in the last decade, have very much been bound up in his continuing legal battles within the justice system. His struggle provides some insight not only into the development of the justice system under the considerable influence of Dr Mahathir over the 22 years of his rule, but also in the years following the latter's departure from office.

16 Free Malaysia Today, 'Sedition Act for Anwar?' by Rahmah Ghazali, 23 March 2010

THE SODOMY II TRIAL
September 2008 – January 2012

Reporters eagerly waiting to speak to Anwar Ibrahim outside the High Court in a photo taken in 2012.

CHAPTER 2
Sodomy II:
Anwar charged again

Just before the national elections in March 2008, a young man by the name of Mohd Saiful Bukhari Azlan was invited by a friend, who was employed by Anwar Ibrahim, to work in the opposition leader's office.

Mohd Saiful, then aged 23 years, was unemployed, having left his electrical engineering studies at Universiti Tenaga Nasional because of poor academic performance. He joined Anwar's office as a volunteer, but later became a paid member of staff as Anwar's private assistant.

On 28 June 2008, Mohd Saiful lodged a police report claiming that Anwar had sodomised him on the afternoon of Thursday, 26 June 2008 in a condominium. He also claimed that Anwar had sexually assaulted him some eight or nine times against his will over the previous two months.

The next day, the non-government news website Malaysiakini reported that an aide of Anwar had lodged a police report claiming that he had been sodomised by Anwar.

On 30 June 2008, despite rumours he was soon to be charged with sodomy, Anwar issued a statement insisting he would fight a by-election later that year — for the Permatang Pauh parliamentary seat vacated by his wife and PKR President Dr Wan Azizah Wan Ismail — and form a new government.

That same day, Malaysiakini reported that police investigations into the sodomy complaint against Anwar had been completed and that the papers had been delivered to the Attorney-General's Chambers for further action. It further quoted senior opposition party officials as saying that Anwar might be arrested within 48 hours, saying that it was to stop him contesting the by-election.

Anwar charged with criminal offence

At 1 pm on 15 July, a police team stopped Anwar's car along Jalan Segambut and arrested Anwar. Overseeing the arrest was the Inspector-General of Police Musa Hassan who had been a key witness for the prosecution of Anwar in 1998.

Anwar was kept overnight in a police cell, released the next day and told to report back to the police within 30 days. He was asked to provide a DNA sample, but had refused claiming that it could be misused to fake evidence against him.

No charges were filed over the accusations made by Mohd Saiful two weeks earlier. Instead the prosecution chose to charge Anwar only with the last act allegedly committed at the Desa Damansara Condominium on 26 June.

After his release, Anwar said that the allegation was a high-level conspiracy to prevent him from entering parliament, adding that he had refused to give his DNA as he did not believe in the system: "It should not be used as a personal vendetta against me. I was questioned for 5½ hours, I was stripped naked including the examination of my private parts. Why treat me like a major criminal and a public enemy?[1]

Anwar added that Musa Hassan harboured a grudge against him for lodging a report on 1 July 2008 with the Malaysian Anti-Corruption Commission saying that the police chief had fabricated evidence against

1   ITN Source, 17 July 2008

him in the investigation into his beating while in police custody 10 years earlier.[2]

Anwar's claim of corruption was later corroborated by a former police officer who had led the investigation into the "black eye" injuries inflicted on Anwar by police chief Rahim Noor in 1998. On 12 September 2011, former city criminal investigation chief Mat Zain Ibrahim claimed in an open letter to the then Inspector-General of Police Bakri Omar that Musa, who was at the time assistant criminal investigation chief and under the direction of the then prosecuting officer (now Attorney-General) Gani Patail, had in 1998 fabricated evidence against Anwar by stealing his DNA to ensure he would be convicted of sodomy.[3]

With Anwar in the midst of a political comeback, many of his supporters viewed the sodomy charge as a desperate attempt by the government to cling to power. The timing of the charge, they suggested, was just too coincidental with his return to politics.

Mohd Saiful's allegation of sodomy

Mohd Saiful alleged that on 26 June 2008, he was asked by Anwar to meet him at a private condominium not far from the centre of Kuala Lumpur to discuss work-related matters and deliver documents.

He alleged that he arrived at about 2.45 pm. He stopped at the security gate and gave the password "Mokhtar", which he claimed Anwar had told him to use to enter the compound. Video cameras at the security gate recorded his arrival and departure. Security cameras also monitored the public areas of the apartment complex.

---

2   Reuters, 17 July 2008

3   themalaysianinsider.com, 'Mat Zain: Musa, Gani duped Dr M into sacking Anwar' by Shannon Teoh, 12 September 2011

He parked his vehicle, took the lift to the fifth floor and entered the apartment where he found Anwar seated at the dining table. He said that Anwar asked him to have sex with him, and being "angry and frightened" he complied with the demand and went into the bedroom where the alleged offence took place.

Mohd Saiful medically examined

Two days later, on 28 June, Mohd Saiful went to the private Hospital Pusrawi on Jalan Tun Razak to be medically examined.

He told general surgeon Dr Mohamed Osman Abdul Hamid that his anus had been painful for the past few days and that a "plastic" item had been inserted into it. A proctoscopy examination showed no physical signs of penetration and a normal anus and rectum. After the examination, Mohd Saiful told the doctor that he had been sodomised by a "VIP". Because of the allegation of sodomy, Dr Mohd Osman advised Mohd Saiful to be re-examined at a government hospital.

More than two hours later, Mohd Saiful arrived at Hospital Kuala Lumpur (HKL), which was close to Hospital Pusrawi. Three specialist doctors examined him that night, but found no evidence of injury. They said there were "... no conclusive clinical findings suggestive of penetration to the anus and no significant defensive wound on the body of the patient."[4]

They took various swabs from Mohd Saiful's body for scientific analysis. These included swabs taken from his tongue, nipples, body, perianal region and private parts. High and low rectal swabs and blood samples were also taken for DNA profiling. For some reason, the samples did not reach the chemistry laboratory for analysis until two days later.

Later that night, Mohd Saiful lodged a police report.

---

4   Hospital Kuala Lumpur Medical Report, 28 June 2008

Anwar charged again

Anwar was finally charged in the Sessions Court on 7 August 2008 under section 377B of the Penal Code. The charge alleged that he committed the offence of sodomy against Mohd Saiful on 26 June 2008. Anwar pleaded not guilty to the charge. The charge (translated from the Malay) reads as follows:

In the High Court of Malaya in Kuala Lumpur
Criminal Case MTJ3-45-9-2009
Public Prosecutor v Datuk Seri Anwar bin Ibrahim

Charge
That you, on 26th June 2008 at about 3.01 pm to 4.30 pm, at Unit 11-5-1, Desa Damansara Condominium, No. 99 Jalan Setiakasih, Bukit Damansara, Kuala Lumpur, in the Federal Territory of Kuala Lumpur intentionally committed carnal intercourse against the order of nature with Mohd Saiful Bukhari bin Azlan by inserting your penis into his anus, and thereby committed an offence punishable under section 377B of the Penal Code.

Punishment: If found guilty, you shall be punished with imprisonment for a term which may extend to twenty years and shall also be liable to whipping.

Dated 2nd February 2010
With the power of the Public Prosecutor
Datuk Mohd Yusof bin Zainal Abiden
Senior Deputy Public Prosecutor

Allegation of political conspiracy

There were some interesting twists in Mohd Saiful's testimony at the trial, which began some 17 months later on 3 February 2010.

For example, he revealed that several days before the alleged sexual assault on 26 June 2008, he had met with the then Deputy Prime Minister Najib Razak and a senior police officer, Senior Assistant Commissioner Mohd Rodwan Mohd Yusof. This confirmed what the defence had all along suspected — that Mohd Saiful was somehow connected to the DPM.

Soon after Anwar's arrest, Mr Najib told reporters that he was not involved in the case at all and denied knowing Mohd Saiful. But when the opposition alliance produced a photograph showing the complainant with a staff member at the DPM's office, he said that the photograph was taken three months earlier on the occasion of Mohd Saiful's visit to his office to apply for a government scholarship.[5]

Three days later, however, Najib admitted that several days before the alleged incident, Mohd Saiful had in fact met with him at his residence, at which time he revealed he had been sodomised by Anwar. At a press conference held at his parliament office, the then DPM said: "I received his visit in my capacity as a leader and he as an ordinary citizen who wanted to tell me something ... I don't (sic) know him before this."[6]

Najib denied he had advised Mohd Saiful to lodge a police report.

It further emerged that the day before the alleged incident with Anwar, Mohd Saiful met with SAC Mohd Rodwan in Room 619 of the Concorde Hotel in Kuala Lumpur. Mohd Rodwan had played a key role in the police team in Anwar's earlier trials in 1998. He is particularly remembered for allegations against him of illegally using Anwar's blood sample for DNA

5   *The Star*, 30 June 2008

6   Bernama, 3 July 2008

testing and allegations of planting fabricated DNA samples on the mattress brought to court.

When asked about the meeting with Mohd Saiful, Mohd Rodwan refused to comment to the media. Anwar's supporters saw this as further evidence of a conspiracy to discredit the opposition leader.

Anwar maintained throughout the proceedings that "...this is a malicious, trumped up case and shouldn't have started in the first place."[7] In the weeks leading up to the commencement of the trial in early 2010, Anwar told the media he intended to subpoena Prime Minister Najib and his wife as witnesses at his trial.[8]

---

7   Reuters, 26 March 2010

8   *New Straits Times*, 3 February 2010

Malaysian Penal Code
applying to "Unnatural Offences"

Homosexuality or homosexual acts are not defined in the Malaysian Penal Code. They are described by reference to "unnatural offences" deemed to be "against the order of nature" and are punishable by up to 20 years imprisonment and whipping.

SECTION 377A OF THE PENAL CODE STATES:

"Any person who has sexual connection with another person by the introduction of the penis into the anus or mouth of the other person is said to commit carnal intercourse against the order of nature."

SECTION 377B OF THE PENAL CODE STATES:

"Whoever voluntarily commits carnal intercourse against the order of nature shall be punished with imprisonment for a term which may extend to twenty years, and shall also be liable to whipping."

SECTION 377D OF THE PENAL CODE STATES:

"Any person who, in public or private, commits, or abets the commission of, or procures or attempts to procure the commission by any person of, any act of gross indecency with another person, shall be punished with imprisonment for a term which may extend to two years."

In addition, under Sharia law in several Malaysian states, homosexual acts between Muslims are illegal and can result in terms of imprisonment of up to three years as well as mandatory whipping.

CHAPTER 3

The international reaction

Anwar's convictions and imprisonment in 1998 provoked a significant international reaction. The police investigation and trial were viewed as being highly suspect and politically motivated to prevent him becoming prime minister of Malaysia.

The Malaysian government underestimated his international influence and reputation. When he was charged again in 2008 after having just returned to parliament to lead the opposition, many international observers saw it as another attempt by the government to manipulate the legal system to drive Anwar out of national politics.

Australian MPs lodge formal protest

On 12 February 2010, 50 Australian politicians — comprising MPs and senators from both major political parties — lodged a formal protest urging Malaysia to drop the sodomy charge against Anwar. They warned the charge would hurt the country's image and dropping it would build confidence in the impartial rule of law in Malaysia. The protest letter said:

> "Many friendly observers of Malaysia find it difficult to believe that a leading opposition voice could be charged with sodomy a second time, and so soon after his party made major gains in national elections. It should be made known to the Malaysian government, that in our opinion, global esteem for Malaysia will

be affected by these charges against Mr Anwar. We hope that Malaysia's authorities will not pursue these charges."[1]

The response in Malaysia to the Australian MPs' protest was immediate. Deputy Foreign Minister A. Kohilan Pillay said the MPs should respect Malaysian law: "The case is still pending in court and we should not be commenting on it."[2] He stated the Malaysian High Commissioner in Australia would brief the Australian MPs about what was happening in Malaysia.

Deputy Minister in the Prime Minister's Department Datuk T. Murugiah said the trial was Malaysia's internal affair: "The MPs should not interfere in our judiciary and other internal matters." Barisan Nasional backbenchers joined the chorus of those calling on foreigners not to interfere.[3]

Pakatan Rakyat announced the following day that it also would send its own representatives overseas to explain what was happening in the Anwar case and to counter the lies that were being spread about it.

The protest letter led to hundreds of demonstrators from Barisan Nasional Youth and Malay rights group Perkasa protesting outside the Australian High Commission in Kuala Lumpur.

John Kerry issues statement

On 16 February 2010, United States Senate Foreign Relations Committee Chairman John Kerry added to calls for a fair trial for Anwar after meeting

---

1   ABC News, 12 February 2010

2   Muslim World News, 8 February 2010

3   *New Sunday Times*, 14 February 2010

him over the weekend at the US-Islamic World Forum in Doha, Qatar. He released the following statement:

> "I call on the government of Malaysia, and specifically on Prime Minister Dato' Sri Najib Razak, to ensure a fair and equitable resolution of the legal proceedings currently underway against former Deputy Prime Minister Anwar Ibrahim.
>
> It has been over a decade since Anwar's first trial, on charges that were later overturned by the Federal Court. The current charges closely mirror the ones levied years ago, and have been brought soon after Mr Anwar's resumption of his role as elected Member of Parliament and leader of the parliamentary opposition. I urge the Malaysian government to accord Mr Anwar every legal protection to which he is entitled as a Member of Parliament and as a citizen — and to settle his case in a manner that builds confidence in the impartiality and credibility of the Malaysian judicial system."[4]

Deputy Foreign Minister Pillay responded to Senator Kerry's comments saying the US Senate could send its representatives to monitor the case, which had been open to and followed daily by several local and foreign interest groups.[5]

Foreign Minister Datuk Seri Anifah Aman, speaking in reference to Senator Kerry's comments, responded by saying:

---

4   www.kerry.senate.gov, 16 February 2010

5   *New Straits Times*, 20 February 2010

"Our system honours and respects the independence of our courts to find facts and to apply the law impartially ... our system has the obligation to proceed with this trial, not because the accused is a prominent political figure, but because it has the responsibility to protect all Malaysians under the law, to seek justice and to avoid any form of prejudice regarding any of the parties involved in a trial."[6]

In the week that followed, Law Minister Datuk Seri Mohamed Nazri Abdul Aziz led a group of Malaysian legislators on a five-day visit to the United States to meet senior US officials, Congress members and senators, ostensibly to discuss issues on export control, the Malaysia-US Free Trade Agreement and counter-terrorism.

Mohd Nazri also invited Attorney-General Abdul Gani Patail and former chief justice Tun Abdul Hamid Mohamed, now chairman of the Malaysian Anti-Corruption Commission's Advisory Board, to take part in a seminar themed "Governance and Rule of Law and Malaysian Legislative Initiatives" and organised by the Center for Strategic and International Studies.

Anwar supporters claimed there was little doubt the invitation for these men to join the delegation was designed to counter criticism by Senator Kerry's press release and because of fears that the significant trade relations between the two counties might be damaged because of unfavourable media coverage of the Anwar case. However, according to news reports, the so-called high-profile seminar had, at the last minute, become a closed-door event with the session going 'off the record'.

---

6   Ibid.

No explanation was provided as to why the seminar went 'off the record' or why the media was not given access to the session. It is not known whether the decision was made to limit the public discussion of the Anwar case to avoid embarrassment to the Malaysian government or whether the minister simply thought it inappropriate to publicly comment on a trial that was then proceeding before the courts.

Allegations were made by various blog-sites in Malaysia that the government had paid US$20 million to Washington lobbyists to clear its image. Mohd Nazri dismissed the allegation as baseless. He further said the Anwar issue was not mentioned during his meetings with US legislators and officials, but it was raised during the seminar. He thought the case was "too small to affect the relations with the US".[7]

Resolution of the Inter-Parliamentary Union

The Geneva-based Inter-Parliamentary Union is an international organisation of the parliaments of 157 sovereign states with permanent observer status at the United Nations. The Governing Council of the IPU was also quick to respond to the situation, adopting a resolution at its 186th Session in Bangkok on 1 April 2010.

After having noted that the fresh sodomy trial had been "widely criticised as a bid to wreck Anwar Ibrahim's political career", it went on to resolve that it was deeply concerned about aspects of the trial, including that it seemed to "suffer from flaws similar to those of the first sodomy trial" and that the absence of physical signs of penetration meant that the charges "should now be dismissed". It was also critical that the defence had been denied access to prosecution evidence.

---

7   Bernama, 28 February 2008

CHAPTER 4

Pre-trial skirmishes and start of trial

Criminal trials are, more often than not, preceded by various procedural applications from the parties. For the most part, it is to gain a tactical advantage, but applications may also be made to ensure the trial is conducted fairly. Anwar's trial was no different. His lawyers made pre-trial applications over three matters:

1. Transfer of the case to the High Court. They complained that the Attorney-General Abdul Gani Patail should not have transferred the prosecution to the High Court for trial because of his involvement in Anwar's first trial as prosecutor.
2. To strike out the charge for abuse of process on the basis that there was no physical evidence of anal penetration.
3. Disclosure of evidence. They complained that the prosecution was acting unfairly by not making proper disclosure of the evidence it was to rely upon at trial. The trial judge agreed, but his ruling ordering the prosecution to disclose material was overturned on appeal. This was a continuing complaint made by the defence throughout the entirety of the trial.

Prosecution transfers case to High Court

On 5 March 2009, Anwar's case was transferred to the High Court on a Certificate under section 418A of the Criminal Procedure Code (CPC) signed by the Attorney-General in his capacity as public prosecutor. That provision of the CPC enables the A-G to transfer any matter from a subordinate court to the High Court.

One of the first complaints made by Anwar's legal team concerned the transfer of the proceedings to the High Court. They argued that Abdul Gani should not have transferred the proceedings as he was biased against Anwar because of allegations that he had fabricated evidence against Anwar (to protect those involved in the "black eye" incident) at the first sodomy trial when he was chief prosecutor. They also relied on then Prime Minister Abdullah Badawi's public pledge in July 2008 that the A-G would have no part in Anwar's trial while he was under investigation by the Malaysian Anti-Corruption Commission (MACC).[1]

Similar allegations were made at Anwar's appeal to the Federal Court in 2004, but these have never been proved.

On 11 March 2009, the MACC, with a three-member panel acting as deputy public prosecutors, found that Abdul Gani did not fabricate evidence in the police assault of Anwar in 1998. Immediately following that finding, the Malaysian government brushed aside accusations that Abdul Gani and a senior police officer, Senior Assistant Commissioner Mohd Rodwan, had conspired against Anwar ahead of his trials in 1998.[2]

Some four months earlier, on 7 November 2008, Judge Komathy Suppiah of the Sessions Court dismissed the prosecution's application for the case to be transferred to the High Court after ruling that the transfer certificate signed by Abdul Gani was invalid.

---

1   Human Rights Watch, Malaysia, 'Politics Drive Upcoming Anwar Trial', 13 July 2009

2   The Press Trust of India, 'Malaysian police chief, top lawyer cleared of political plot', 11 March 2009

First, Judge Komathy found there was a legitimate expectation arising from the public promise made by Mr Badawi that Abdul Gani would not be involved in the case, which was further bolstered by the "Clients Charter" of the Prosecution Division of the Attorney-General's Chambers and the United Nations "Guidelines on the Role of Prosecutions" adopted by Malaysia in 1990. The certificate under section 418A was personally signed by Abdul Gani, which the judge ruled amounted to a breach of the legal expectation that he would not be involved in the case.

Second, the judge rejected the submission that Abdul Gani was exercising an administrative function in respect to the transfer, finding he was exercising a quasi-judicial function when he signed the transfer certificate. As such, he was acting in a position of conflict (or perceived conflict) of interest and the rule against bias would disqualify him from issuing the certificate. Judge Komathy concluded: "...it is evident that any involvement by the Attorney-General in this case would seriously undermine public confidence in the administration of criminal justice."[3]

The prosecution filed for a revision of the decision three days later on the ground, among others, that Abdul Gani was only carrying out an administrative function, not a judicial or quasi-judicial function, when he signed the certificate as he was not judging any dispute between parties.

The High Court in *Anwar Ibrahim v PP* — comprising Judges of the Court of Appeal Justices Abdul Hamid Embong, Abu Samah Nordin and Jeffrey Tan Kok Wah — agreed with the prosecution submissions and unanimously overruled Judge Komathy's decision. Justice Embong delivered the court's decision:

---

3   *Pendakwa Raya v Datuk Seri Anwar bin Ibrahim* No. 62-407-2008,
    KL Sessions Court, per Komathy J. at [43]

52. In signing this certificate, the PP cannot be said to be exercising a quasi-judicial function, but merely an administrative one, and one that only he can exercise.
(see *PP v Oh Keng Seng* [1976] 2 MU)

53. In this case, we are of the considered opinion that the rule that a person under a suspicion of bias should not act as an adjudicator is not applicable to the act of the PP in signing this certificate. We would apply the exception that natural justice may be overridden by a statutory provision as enunciated in *Franklin & Ors v Minister of Town and Country Planning* [1948] AC [87], an exception which is applicable in both administrative and legislative process.

54. We rule that, in this instance, despite the allegations of bias and conflict of interest against him, the PP being the specific and only officer authorised by law to sign the s 418A certificate, may do so. His act cannot be impugned by reason of the imputed bias or conflict of interest. (see *Mohd Zainal Abidin bin Abdul Mutalib v Mahathir Mohamed, Minister of Home Affairs and Anor* [1989] 3 MU 170)

The case was accordingly transferred to the High Court.

Defence applies to strike out sodomy charge due to lack of physical injuries

On 1 December 2009, Anwar's lawyers applied to the trial judge, Justice Datuk Mohamad Zabidin Mohd Diah, to strike out the charge for abuse of process.

Karpal Singh, lead counsel for the defence, submitted there was no evidence of anal penetration because the medical examinations found no injury to the anus or rectum. He argued that on the basis of the medical reports alone, the charge should be struck out as oppressive and vexatious.

Deputy Prosecutor Mohd Yusof Zainal Abiden opposed the application, saying that clinical tests alone were insufficient to show there had been no penetration. He submitted that the medical reports were only part of the evidence, and to prove penetration the prosecution would present not only Mohd Saiful's direct testimony but also forensic, circumstantial and documentary evidence. He said there would be scientific evidence to show that semen found in Mohd Saiful's anus matched Anwar's DNA. On that basis, he concluded, the prosecution would establish a *prima facie* case of anal penetration.

Justice Zabidin accepted the prosecution submission and refused to strike out the sodomy charge.

On 3 February 2010, the first day of the trial, the defence asked the judge to stay the proceedings pending an appeal to the Court of Appeal against his refusal to strike out the charge. But Justice Zabidin ruled there were no special circumstances[4] to stay the trial and ordered it to commence the next day. However, it was adjourned to 8 February when Karpal applied to the judge to disqualify himself for actual bias for failing to cite the media for contempt for publishing articles commenting on the trial. More about this is covered on pages 86–90 of this chapter.

---

4   When applying to stay or suspend a trial pending appeal, the applicant must show
      special circumstances as to why such an order should be made. The court has an
      absolute discretion to refuse or grant the stay. Special circumstances, as the phrase
      implies, must be special under the circumstances as distinguished from ordinary
      circumstances. It must be something exceptional in character, something that
      exceeds or excels in some way.

The Court of Appeal heard the appeal on 12 February before a panel of three justices comprising Datuk Wira Abu Samah Nordin, Datuk Sulaiman Daud and Datuk Azhar Izhar Ma'ah. At the appeal, Karpal submitted that the sodomy charge should be struck out because the three doctors from Hospital Kuala Lumpur (HKL) had found "no conclusive clinical findings suggestive of penetration to the anus". He said that proof of penetration was an essential fact to be proven in a sodomy charge and that notwithstanding Mohd Saiful's claim to have been anally penetrated, there was no physical evidence of it.

In reply, Mohd Yusof submitted that the medical report alone could not be relied upon as the trial judge needed to hear the testimony of the witnesses adduced in court before deciding whether there was sufficient evidence of penetration.

The Court of Appeal did not deliver its decision until 17 February. In a unanimous decision, it rejected Anwar's appeal to strike out the charge.

Justice Abu Samah dismissed the appeal saying that Anwar had not shown that the charge or the prosecution against him to be oppressive or an abuse of process, and the court would not use its inherent power to strike out the charge purely on the medical report. "We agree with the prosecution that the medical report [from HKL] is not conclusive and the only evidence," he said, adding it was only corroborative of what the doctors might say in court. He said that the prosecution had by affidavit confirmed that the case would be based on oral testimony and forensic evidence, and not solely on medical reports.

Was there any basis to strike out the charge?

In circumstances where it has been alleged that forcible penile penetration had occurred, it is understandable the defence would focus on the absence of physical injury to Mohd Saiful's anus and rectum.

The application to the trial judge to strike out the charge was based on the absence of physical injury. Anwar's lawyers submitted that in that circumstance, it was oppressive and vexatious to continue the prosecution. There were two obvious difficulties with that submission.

First, it is accepted by most medical doctors experienced in examining victims of sexual assault that the absence of anal trauma neither confirms nor excludes sexual penetration. Injuries would be more likely to occur following non-consensual anal penetration, which Mohd Saiful alleged, but that alone would not be conclusive of the fact that it did not happen.

Second, the submission was premature. When Justice Zabidin came to consider the ultimate question of whether he was satisfied beyond a reasonable doubt that anal penetration had occurred, he would need to consider all of the evidence. However, at that early stage of the proceedings, not all of the prosecution evidence was before him.

The absence of anal trauma may arguably have been inconsistent with anal penetration, but there was also evidence submitted by the deputy prosecutor that was to the contrary, which included the proposed testimony of the complainant and scientific evidence of Anwar's DNA extracted from material found in his rectum.

If the trial judge accepted that the DNA evidence was reliable, then it would certainly be strong evidence of penetration and something that would corroborate Mohd Saiful's testimony.

Defence applies for pre-trial disclosure of prosecution documents and materials

Dissatisfied with the prosecution's lack of response, the defence filed an application by way of an originating motion, dated 10 June 2009 pursuant to sections 51 and/or 51A of the CPC, for an order to compel disclosure and inspection of various documents and materials, including all CCTV recordings taken at the Damansara apartment complex; DNA samples and all scientific papers; all doctors' notes and reports; any material that would not be used by the prosecution at trial; and a list of prosecution witnesses.

Shortly after the application was filed, the prosecution provided to the defence the following documents and materials: a CD with a copy of the alleged CCTV recording only for 26 June 2008; copies of the electropherogram of the alleged DNA samples tested; notes of the doctor (as opposed to a report) from Hospital Pusrawi; and a clearer copy of Mohd Saiful's statement.

On 16 July 2009, Justice Zabidin ordered the prosecution to disclose to the defence various other items including such things as the security CCTV recording from the condominium where it was alleged the crime occurred; DNA samples, the worksheets and case notes of the chemist who conducted the DNA testing and analysis; all witness statements; and the medical notes of the complainant's physical examination at HKL.

He also ordered that copies of all documents to be tendered at trial as part of the prosecution case and a Statement of Facts favourable to the defence are to be supplied to the accused pursuant to sections 51A (1)(b) and (c) of the CPC.

The judge ruled that certain items did not fall within the scope of his order, namely CCTV recordings at other locations within the Desa Damansara Condominium complex, the original DNA samples and the police witness statements of other witnesses not named by Anwar made under section 112 of the CPC. No order was made in regard to the production of the electropherogram on certain identified DNA samples since it had already been supplied to Anwar. Finally, he made no order in respect of the video recording of Mohd Saiful's statement since his section 112 police witness statement had already been provided.

In reaching his decision, Justice Zabidin took into consideration both sections 51 and 51A. He addressed his mind to the philosophy underlying section 51A, which in his view had changed the prosecutorial process to be one that was more transparent and fair according to the circumstances of the case. He reasoned that it would be fair to allow the accused access to these documents and materials so he would know the case against him in advance of trial and be better able to prepare his defence, rebuttal evidence, cross-examination and to avoid any postponement.[5]

The disclosure of prosecution material had become an issue very early in the proceedings. Soon after he was charged in the Sessions Court, Anwar, through his lawyers, made numerous requests to the public prosecutor for documents and materials to be disclosed. These included the prosecution list of witnesses and any evidence the prosecution would reply upon at the trial. Each of these requests was refused.

The law relating to the disclosure and inspection process in criminal proceedings is to be found in sections 5, 51 and 51A of The Criminal Procedure Code (Act 593). Section 51 provides that when any court considers that the production of any document is necessary or desirable for the purposes of any trial, it may issue a summons for the production of that document. Section 51A was introduced in 2006; it requires the prosecution to supply to an accused person the first offence report made under section 107 of the CPC, a copy of any document it intends to tender at trial as part of the prosecution case and any statement of facts favourable to the defence.

---

5   *Pendakwa Raya v Datuk Seri Anwar bin Ibrahim* No. 05-145-2009;
    Datuk Seri Anwar bin Ibrahim v Pendakwa Raya No. 05-144-2009;
    Federal Court, at [30]

Prosecution appeals judge's disclosure order

Not satisfied with the disclosure order, the prosecution immediately appealed the judge's decision to the Court of Appeal. The appeal was made on two grounds, namely:

1. The trial judge wrongly applied section 51 of the CPC by reading it conjunctively with section 51A and giving it too wide an ambit.
2. The trial judge erred in ordering disclosure of documents pursuant to these provisions when he had no jurisdiction to do so.

The defence also filed an appeal against that part of the trial judge's order that barred them from having access to various documents and materials.

Before the hearing of the appeal, the prosecution complied with section 51A by providing the defence with a copy of the offence report and copies of documents it would tender at trial. They also provided several other documents including an electropherogram of the DNA samples, medical report from Hospital Pusrawi, CCTV recording dated 26 June 2008 and a copy of the complainant's police statement dated 28 June 2008.

As the prosecution did not consider there were any facts favourable to the defence, no statement was provided to that effect.

Court of Appeal upholds prosecution appeal

The core issue at the appeal was whether Justice Zabidin correctly ordered the various documents and materials to be supplied to the accused.

Anwar's counsel Karpal Singh submitted that the documents and materials described in the originating motion were important for the preparation of the defence case, particularly since the main points of the defence were alibi, the credibility of the complainant, political conspiracy and tampering with evidence.[6]

DPP Mohd Yusof submitted that the trial judge had been wrong in taking too liberal an approach in interpreting the relevant provisions of the CPC and that the two provisions were distinct and specific. He further submitted that the judge had no jurisdiction to make such an order.

On 21 December 2009, the Court of Appeal, having rejected an objection to its jurisdiction to hear the appeal, overruled the findings of Justice Zabidin and, except for the orders made under sections 51A(1)(b) and (c) of the CPC, set aside all the orders made by him.

The Court of Appeal agreed that sections 51 and 51A were separate and distinct provisions and should not be read together. It found that while section 51A imposed an obligation upon the prosecution to supply specific documents and material, section 51 gave the court the discretion to allow for discovery only in specific instances.

The Court of Appeal ruled that each application had to be considered on its merits and that different considerations may apply to each category of application in deciding whether to order the production of documents or materials. In this case, Justice Zabidin chose to rely on section 51 of the CPC, rather than section 51A.

The Court of Appeal adopted a narrow interpretation of section 51. It considered that the object of section 51 is for limited access and that its scope was restricted in law. It stated that the so-called liberal philosophy behind section 51A should not affect a court's interpretation of section 51, which before the commencement of a trial was confined to documents or materials only specified or referred to in the charge. It considered that a general demand should not be entertained. After the commencement of trial, the court needed to consider whether the documents or materials

6 *Pendakwa Raya v Datuk Seri Anwar bin Ibrahim* No. MTJ3-44-99-2009, Court of Appeal at [16]

were relevant to an issue for adjudication.[7]

Finally, the Court of Appeal rejected some of the requests for documents and materials as no more than a fishing exercise by the defence.

Federal Court also upholds prosecution's appeal

Having been refused in the Court of Appeal, Anwar's lawyers took the appeal to the Federal Court.

On 29 January 2010, the Federal Court upheld the Court of Appeal's decision, agreeing that the provisions of the CPC limited an accused's entitlement to disclosure before trial. It adopted the Court of Appeal's narrow interpretation of the legislation rather than supporting the more liberal approach taken by Justice Zabidin. It also emphasised the distinction between disclosure "at the pre-trial stage" and "in the course of the trial". It found the trial judge had improperly exercised his discretion to order disclosure to the extent that he did.

The Federal Court's 'Review of Decision'

On 25 February 2010, I was at the Federal Court in Putrajaya to observe Anwar's motion to review the Court's decision to uphold the prosecution's successful appeal against the pre-trial disclosure order. The critical issue was jurisdiction, namely whether the Federal Court had jurisdiction to review a decision made by another bench of that court.

Karpal Singh submitted that the Federal Court by its own rules (Rule 137) had the jurisdiction to correct a decision that was wrong and thereby remove a real injustice and ensure public confidence in the administration of justice.

---

7   *Pendakwa Raya v Datuk Seri Anwar bin Ibrahim* No. MTJ3-44-99-2009, Court of Appeal at [31]

Alternatively, he argued, if Rule 137 could not be relied upon, then the Court had an inherent jurisdiction to review the decision. He submitted that before the Court could review a decision, it needed to be satisfied that an injustice had occurred that was obvious on the face of the record and that there were exceptional grounds for it to intervene.

Karpal argued that each of these requirements existed. There was injustice, he said, "because the prosecution is conducting trial by ambush by withholding documents, including the witness list." He further argued the Federal Court was in error when it accepted that the trial judge's decision was reviewable and, in doing so, it had misinterpreted the law on the discretionary power of a trial judge to order disclosure.

Mohd Yusof submitted in reply that the Federal Constitution did not expressly confer on the Federal Court the power to review its own decisions nor did the rules of court confer jurisdiction to do so. He submitted that once the Federal Court had disposed of a matter — which it had done by its earlier decision — that was the end of it. Mere disagreement with the reasoning of another bench of the court was not sufficient to warrant intervention.

The Federal Court comprised Justices Datuk Zulkefli Ahmad Makinudin, Datuk Wira Mohd Ghazali Mohd Yusof and Datuk Heliliah Mohd Yusof. After hearing final argument, they delivered an *ex tempore* decision, which in summary was as follows:

1. Rule 137 of the Federal Court Rules does not confer jurisdiction on the Federal Court to review its own decision.

2. Even if it did, the Court was not satisfied there were exceptional grounds to justify the review.

3. It was not a suitable case for review and there needed to be some finality to proceedings.

Trial begins and defence asks judge to disqualify himself for actual bias

The trial began on 3 February 2010 with the prosecution calling Mohd Saiful to testify. The complainant told how he had been an "Anwar fan" and that he was employed by Anwar as a member of his staff in March 2008.

He claimed that on 26 June 2008, he was instructed to take some documents to Anwar at a condominium located not far from the centre of Kuala Lumpur. He alleged that when alone with Anwar in the condominium, he was asked in "coarse language" to have sex with him, saying in English: "Can I fuck you today?" He told the court: "I refused his request. I said I don't want to. Anwar got angry and asked me why. I said I wasn't willing to do it." He claimed that Anwar then ordered him to go into the master bedroom. There, Anwar drew the curtains, turned the lights off and told him to wash himself. Mohd Saiful said there was still light coming from the bathroom and filtering through the curtains. He said he obeyed and came out wearing only a towel around his waist. Anwar was also wearing only a towel, he said, and was standing near the bed. Anwar asked him to come near to him and then he hugged him.

At that point, the defence requested Justice Zabidin to allow the remainder of Mohd Saiful's testimony to be recorded in camera without members of the media and public being present due to its explicit nature. The judge agreed but allowed international observers to remain in court.

In general terms, Mohd Saiful described Anwar instructing him to use lubricant he had been asked to bring with him. Anwar was then alleged to have penetrated Mohd Saiful's anus with his penis from behind in what he said was a "fast and rough" manner.

As Mohd Saiful was testifying and describing what took place, Deputy Prosecutor Mohd Yusof handed him a tube of KY-Gel, which Mohd Saiful identified as the tube he had used at the time. Until then, the defence was not aware that the tube existed or that lubricant had been used. Mohd Saiful said that he had been asked by Anwar to bring the lubricant. The sexual act alleged on 26 June was not the only occasion on which it was alleged that sexual acts occurred between them, but it was the one Anwar was charged with.

I thought the fact that Mohd Saiful had brought the lubricant made nonsense of his claim that he did not anticipate what happened. The defence was reluctant to canvas the other occasions when sex was alleged to have happened, most probably because it may have made the narrative more sensational and graphic — and have a greater impact on a conservative public. It was a matter for the defence, but it seemed to me that was a risk worth taking because it made the complaint less credible and provided an opportunity for the defence to test the reliability and truthfulness of Mohd Saiful's account and maximise the opportunity of exposing more contradictions.

The judge also interrupted the proceedings during Mohd Saiful's testimony to enable the court to view the alleged crime scene at the Desa Damansara Condominium. The visit to the condominium was also to be held in camera. The media was barred from entering the apartment, but photographs were taken outside and in the public areas of the complex.

On 5 February 2010, the Malay daily *Utusan Malaysia* published an article on the front page with a heading "*Tak Rela Diliwat Lagi*" ("Not Willing to be Sodomised Again") and on page three, the heading "*Berhenti Kerana Tidak Mahu Diliwat Lagi*" ("Resigned Because Not Willing to be Sodomised Again").

Karpal asked the judge to cite the newspaper for contempt, not only because it had defied his in-camera order, but also because the published material was intended to show Anwar in a bad light. He added that the newspaper was owned by the political party Umno, of which then

Prime Minister Badawi was the president, and the material was therefore politically motivated. "The headings are to put Anwar in a bad light. Saiful did not, in his testimony, say he was sodomised repeatedly," Karpal said, adding that the headings were false, mischievous and improper.

Justice Zabidin refused to cite the newspaper for contempt.

The next day, *Utusan Malaysia* published another article on the front page. It came with a photograph taken at the condominium with a caption stating that the alleged victim had pointed to a bed in the master bedroom where Anwar sodomised him.

Karpal again submitted that the court must act as the newspaper was becoming bolder. He submitted that the judge should at least caution the newspaper, claiming that Mohd Saiful's evidence on where the alleged sodomy took place was in closed-court proceedings and that the report was misleading as the alleged offence did not take place on the bed.

Justice Zabidin said that evidence in relation to a bed in the condominium had been given in open court. He ruled that the newspaper had not broken reporting restrictions.

Anwar consistently denied the charge, saying it was part of a political conspiracy against him. "We can't even get a decent judgement over a basic issue like that," Anwar told reporters after the trial adjourned.[8]

On 8 February 2010, as the trial entered its fourth day, Karpal applied for Justice Zabidin to disqualify himself from further hearing the trial. He submitted the judge's refusal to cite *Utusan Malaysia* for contempt for its reporting of the view at the condominium demonstrated bias on his part. Karpal maintained that the visit to the bedroom and condominium was, in fact, part of the in-camera proceedings. He submitted that:

---

8   Reuters, 5 February 2010

"... there is nothing in the notes of proceedings or audio before this court to show that this detail was ever mentioned in open court. With much respect, Your Lordship did not tell the truth and that translates into Your Lordship has lied. You lied and it can and has been proven that you are not being honest in court. You can't be impartial and you can't be unbiased. On those grounds, you have no alternative but to step down. It is not a mere perception, but a reality. You can stand down by your own ruling."

In response, DPP Mohd Yusof said the defence was being "insulting", insisting that the bed had been mentioned in public hearings. He told the court: "To say Your Lordship has lied is a very strong word. Lawyers can defend their client without fear or favour, but to use strong language against the judge is unacceptable."

Justice Zabidin ordered the case to be adjourned until 18 February to allow him time to consider the arguments over whether he should recuse himself as the presiding judge. When court resumed, Justice Zabidin refused to disqualify himself and ordered the trial to continue. He said:

"If I recuse myself in such circumstances, it will mean that I am running away from my responsibility as a judge. A judge who has taken an oath of office should not avoid carrying out the duty which has been entrusted to him. There must be facts to show that a rational person would think that there was a possibility that the judge will make his decision over the tried issues not based on the evidence adduced in court, but on other considerations."

Anwar Ibrahim at the Federal Court Building, Putrajaya, immediately
after an appeal to the Federal Court on 12 February 2010.

Karpal informed the court that the defence would appeal the recusal
ruling.

The judge then granted a stay pending the appeal on the recusal
ruling and set 25 March 2010 for mention. He said: "It is important for a
higher court to decide on this matter to avoid any violation of principles.
If the Court of Appeal decides that my ruling on the recusal application is
erroneous, then as stated by the case law, it will only make the proceedings
nugatory."

However, when proceedings resumed on 25 March, Anwar's lawyers
advised the judge that the defence had withdrawn the appeal against his
ruling. They gave no explanation for doing so, but they may have considered
the appeal was unlikely to succeed and that it was not worth the effort given
the limited nature of the complaint. They may also have believed that the
message to the media was clear and understood, that is, that there was a risk
the trial judge would cite them for contempt should it happen again. Justice
Zabidin adjourned the trial to resume on 10 May 2010.

CHAPTER 5

Continuing fight for disclosure during trial

The prosecution successfully blocked disclosure to the defence before the start of the trial. Although Justice Zabidin had agreed with the defence that the prosecution should provide substantial pre-trial disclosure, his order was overruled on appeal.

The appeal decision did not suggest that the judge did not have the power to order disclosure during the course of the trial, but for some unfathomable reason it seemed from his remarks that he believed he lacked the discretion to make such orders.

The prosecution did disclose what it claimed was relevant material, but it did not make it any easier for the defence by refusing to disclose materials that modern justice systems accept as being essential to ensure a fair trial , which included amongst other things the prosecution witness list and the complainant's police statements.

Prosecution plays hardball on disclosure of witness list and Mohd Saiful's police statements

The prosecution refused to disclose the prosecution witness list despite repeated requests by the defence to do so. When the trial resumed on Monday, 10 May 2010, Karpal Singh applied to the judge to order disclosure "in the interests of justice", but was refused.

The veteran defence lawyer replied he had never before been denied access to a witness list and told the judge: "...you always supply the list. In fact, the court is supplied the list together with the defence. What is there to hide?"

Justice Zabidin again refused, saying his ruling was in line with an earlier Federal Court decision.

Karpal went on to say: "There is a political conspiracy to eliminate Anwar from the political scene. The prime minister is involved. There is no doubt about that."

He then applied to the judge to order the prosecution to supply the defence with Mohd Saiful's witness statements first recorded during the police investigation. Mohd Saiful had claimed that the sexual act was committed without his consent, he submitted, and yet the charge was framed on the basis that the sexual act was consensual. There was a conflict between what he claimed to have happened and the offence charged, which suggested a direct contradiction that the defence needed to explore.

Karpal submitted that the defence had the right to have Mohd Saiful's witness statements for the purpose of impeaching him by showing he had changed his story.

Deputy Prosecutor Mohd Yusof in reply submitted there was no basis for the court to direct the prosecution to supply copies of the statements to the defence. He said whether the allegation was consensual or non-consensual did not alter the charge of sodomy. "As such," he said, "there is no basis for this court to direct the prosecution to supply the statements." He said the Attorney-General had the discretion to bring a lesser charge against Anwar, which was what had happened in this case.

Justice Zabidin adjourned the proceedings for 48 hours to consider the application.

When the trial resumed on 12 May, Justice Zabidin said that he would not order the prosecution to provide copies of the complainant's witness statements because he saw no contradiction in them. He also said the defence could not demand the police documents on a mere hunch and that a lesser sodomy charge framed against the accused did not make the evidence given by Mohd Saiful contradictory.

The defence requested a stay of proceedings to challenge the judge's ruling to the Court of Appeal. Justice Zabidin refused. He ruled that his decision to dismiss the application was procedural and could not be appealed, and in any event the defence could not show special circumstances for the stay to be granted. He said the applicant (Anwar) must show malicious intent, which he had not. The judge ordered the cross-examination to continue. However, after further argument, he relented and the proceedings were adjourned to allow the appeal to be heard.

Superior courts refuse to order disclosure

The Court of Appeal upheld the judge's refusal to order disclosure of Mohd Saiful's witness statements. The defence argued that the disclosure of the statements was critical to an assessment of the complainant's credibility and if proved right, the prosecution's case would collapse.

The prosecution responded saying that whatever the witness might say happened, it was the public prosecutor who decided the appropriate charge in the circumstances of each case.

The Court of Appeal refused to intervene to overrule the trial judge's decision, as it did not consider the decision a final order or an issue an appeal court could review. Justice Datuk Sulong Matjeraie said the High Court's ruling to dismiss Anwar's application to obtain the witness statements did not come within the meaning of a "decision" in the Courts of Judicature Act 1964.

This decision was taken on appeal to the Federal Court, which heard submissions on 19 August 2010 before a bench comprising the Chief Judge of the High Court of Malaya Tan Sri ArifinZakaria, Tan Sri James Foong and Datuk Raus Sharif. The Court unanimously refused the appeal also finding that it had "no jurisdiction" to intervene because the trial judge's decision was not a final order, but an interlocutory order made during the course of a trial.

Prosecution repeatedly refuses to disclose materials to the defence

The superior courts in Malaysia ruled that Justice Zabidin's pre-trial order requiring the prosecution to disclose a range of materials to the defence went beyond what was allowed by the relevant legislation. In doing so, the courts adopted a conservative view of the Act, ruling that at the pre-trial stage disclosure was limited to the few documents specified in the legislation.

Of course, these rulings related only to pre-trial orders made by the judge and did not affect his discretion to order disclosure during the trial. Justice Zabidin retained an overall discretion to order the prosecution to disclose material that was relevant to the defence and if he thought it should be disclosed as a matter of fairness.

During the course of the trial, the defence had, on more than one occasion, applied for orders of disclosure for such things as the prosecution witness list, the complainant's police statements and other materials. Anwar's lawyers argued that the materials were critical to the preparation of his defence. In each case, Justice Zabidin refused to order disclosure of material that he originally thought was relevant and, as a matter of fairness, should be disclosed to the defence.

The approach taken by the superior courts in this case was quite correct for in most legal systems, except for some express statutory exceptions, there are no interlocutory appeals in criminal matters. The statutory right of appeal is against conviction or what is regarded to be a "final order".

The intention of the 'final judgement rule' is to avoid inefficient pre-trial litigation and piecemeal appeals.

The appeal courts adopted the 'final judgement rule' not only on rulings on matters of disclosure, but to all of the rulings made by the trial judge. For instance, on 21 September 2010, the Court of Appeal refused to hear an appeal against the trial judge's refusal to strike out the charge because of the revelation of an affair between a junior member of the prosecution team and the complainant. The application was made on the ground that the integrity of the prosecution team led by Mohd Yusof had been compromised as a result of the alleged affair. Anwar's counsel submitted to the Court of Appeal that the application for the charge to be struck out was based on there being an abuse of the court process and therefore it was not procedural, but substantive. The Court of Appeal rejected that submission.

Nevertheless, there were many practical difficulties for the defence during the trial. Anwar's lawyers repeatedly asked the prosecution to provide a copy of its witness list, but these applications were flatly refused. The trial judge also refused to order the prosecution to provide the material. As such, the defence only had a general idea as to who would be called by the prosecution to testify.

In Malaysia, witness statements are not provided to the defence so that an accused person has no more than a limited idea as to what any witness will say.

Should witness statements be treated as privileged?

A month before the trial began in February 2010, I met with the Attorney-General Abdul Gani Patail at his Chambers in Putrajaya. When we met, I took the opportunity to ask him why witness statements were treated as privileged and not disclosed to the defence.

He denied that it was intended to deprive the defence of the tactical advantage of cross-examining a prosecution witness about any prior inconsistent statement. He explained that, sometimes, statements do not accurately reflect verbatim what the witness had said, but rather was more likely to be a police officer's interpretation of the account given by the witness.

That may well be so, but one would expect that a witness would have the opportunity to confirm the accuracy and truthfulness of his statement taken by the police. In fact, that is the case in many legal systems. When a statement is completed, the witness is asked to read it carefully and to adopt its contents by signing it. If something is inaccurate, the witness can ask for it to be changed so that it reflects what was intended. The witness then signs it, declaring it to be true and correct to the best of his or her knowledge and belief.

The practice of not disclosing witness statements in Malaysia may not be so oppressive where medical and scientific witnesses are required to provide reports, but there is an obvious forensic disadvantage with other witnesses. It is difficult for the defence to adequately prepare the cross-examination of a witness when it only knows what the witness will say when he or she testifies. It is also extremely difficult for the defence to challenge the credibility of a witness if it is not able to impeach that witness by using any prior inconsistent statement made by that person to another or taken from a statement given by the witness to the police.

The forensic disadvantage

The forensic disadvantage to the defence was obvious. For example, Mohd Saiful's police statements were significant. They could potentially refute the central plank of the prosecution case with respect to the alleged act of anal penetration. The prosecution case was heavily dependent on the reliability and truthfulness of the complainant. The trial judge would need to accept his testimony to convict Anwar, and if proved, the DNA evidence would corroborate his allegation.

So the proper testing of the complainant's police statements by cross-examination was an essential tool in casting doubt on his account. If any of that evidence was proved to be unreliable or untruthful, it would give rise to a reasonable doubt that anal penetration had actually occurred.

Disclosure is always a critical issue in determining whether a trial has been fair or not. In Malaysia, an accused person is entitled to the disclosure of a limited range of material before trial. That may not prejudice an accused, because after the trial begins it falls to the judge to decide in his or her discretion whether relevance and fairness justifies ordering further disclosure of materials in the possession of the prosecution.

It must be said that Justice Zabidin's refusal during the trial to order disclosure of certain prosecution materials was not only inconsistent with the liberal approach he took before the trial, but was also inconsistent with general principles of fairness that usually operate in criminal trials.

The Malaysian appeal courts strictly applied the 'final judgement rule' in refusing to intervene in a trial before it is concluded. That was entirely consistent with legislation that distinguishes between procedural and substantive orders made during a trial. However, whatever rulings may be made at trial, an accused will not be deprived of the right to appeal a guilty verdict where a miscarriage of justice has occurred.

Did Anwar get a fair trial?

Whether Anwar obtained a fair trial cannot be judged simply on the result. A trial may also be judged by whether the actual process has been fair. It must be said that some of the trial judge's rulings were questionable. In some respects, the judge was limited by the legal procedure that operates in Malaysia, but in other instances there were matters fully within his discretion to decide.

Anwar's trial demonstrates that the failure to properly disclose evidence can disadvantage an accused person so that it makes it more difficult to meet the prosecution case which is a fundamental human right. Minimum human rights standards relating to procedural fairness and the rights of an accused are contained and enshrined in the United Nations Declaration of Human Rights and incorporated into the European Convention of Human Rights.

Anwar had limited access to prosecution witness statements (protected under a claim of privilege) and also to some documents which the prosecution did not intend to use at trial. He was not provided with the prosecution witness list and it seemed his lawyers could only speculate who might be called in support of Mohd Saiful's complaint. Deputy Prosecutor Mohd Yusof did tell the defence the number of witnesses the prosecution would call and gave some idea of who those witnesses were, but this was by way of informal disclosure rather than some formal process.

It is expected that the failure to disclose this type of material may cause difficulties for the accused, for example, if the accused wants his own forensic experts to be present in court when the prosecution experts testify. Each of Anwar's experts was resident overseas and it was necessary to give them sufficient notice to travel to Malaysia.

The medical reports detailing the physical examination of the complainant and DNA reports were disclosed to the defence pursuant to section 51A of the Criminal Procedure Code (CPC). However, access was denied to the materials on which the reports were based.

While accepting that, sometimes, circumstances may limit direct access to DNA samples, there does not appear to be a valid reason not to disclose material on which the findings were based — if the material is available. If it isn't possible to provide forensic samples for independent analysis, then at least the materials on which expert opinion is based should be disclosed. The failure to disclose this material would make it almost impossible for forensic experts engaged by the accused to properly assess the adequacy and accuracy of the prosecution expert's methodology and conclusions and to properly question these expert witnesses at trial.

The prosecution and defence view of the obligation to disclose evidence

It seemed appropriate during the trial to ask the defence and prosecution to comment on the issue of disclosure on the understanding that their responses would not be published until the trial was over. That was a reasonable request. I asked each to explain how they saw the situation and the effect that disclosure — or the lack of it — had upon the trial. Understandably, each party took a different view.

The defence took the view that Anwar was denied due process. They said this clearly affected his ability to adequately prepare his defence. They claimed the trial judge was simply not interested in their several applications and stays were only granted under extreme pressure.

Anwar's lawyers considered the disclosure legislation to be adequate, but that it should be interpreted more liberally by the superior courts to ensure that accused persons are not disadvantaged and receive a fair trial.

They considered that the trial judge's refusal to order disclosure of Mohd Saiful's police statements prejudiced the defence by depriving it of material critical to challenging his claim of sexual assault. Complaints were also made that the prosecution's refusal to disclose its witness list made trial preparation difficult.

The prosecution had refused to also provide the material on which the prosecution experts based their opinion. "How are the forensic and DNA experts able to provide proper opinions without all of the scientific evidence being provided to them so they may assess it?" said defence lawyer Sankara Nair.

The prosecution was also asked to respond. It took the view that the legislation concerning disclosure was properly interpreted and applied by the superior courts. The prosecution said it complied with the legislation and provided what it was required to disclose to the defence. It also took the view that the decision of the superior courts did not affect the trial judge's discretion to order disclosure of more material once the trial had commenced. 'Of course', said DP Mohd Yusof, "that discretion would be subject to the rules of relevance and general admissibility."

The refusal to disclose Mohd Saiful's hospital records

General surgeon Dr Mohd Razali Ibrahim was one of three doctors at Hospital Kuala Lumpur (HKL) to medically examine Mohd Saiful on the night of 28 June 2008. The other doctors were emergency care specialist Dr Khairul Nizam Hassan and forensic pathologist Dr Siew Sheue Feng.

Dr Razali was the first to testify and completed his testimony for the prosecution on 14 June 2010. He confirmed that "even without clinical injuries"[1] he believed that penile penetration had taken place because the chemist's report indicated the presence of semen on rectal swabs taken from the complainant. That statement was later challenged by the defence on the basis that his expertise didn't extend to analysing DNA material and that he should confine his testimony to what he observed at the physical examination.

Before cross-examining Dr Razali, Karpal applied to inspect the complete history of the medical examination of Mohd Saiful conducted at HKL, including any clinical notes, reports and specimens taken by

---

1   *Taipei Times,* 4 June 2010

the examining doctors as well as their qualifications and experiences. In particular, he wanted access to the primary hospital notes recorded during Mohd Saiful's examination. He had seen a composite medical report dated 13 July 2009, but not the notes on which it was based (called at trial the 'proforma notes').

He told the court that the proforma notes were critical in assessing Dr Razali's credibility, particularly if there were contradictions between his testimony and Mohd Saiful's recorded medical history. He maintained this was "more than a hunch".

Finally, he submitted that since Dr Razali was giving expert testimony, any material which formed the basis of his opinion should be disclosed to the defence. He accepted that it was not automatically admissible into evidence, but that the court could call for its production so that it may be tested under cross-examination.

Deputy Prosecutor Mohd Yusof responded saying that the proforma notes or, indeed, any clinical notes could only be admissible if Dr Razali used the documents to refresh his memory, which he had not in the course of his examination-in-chief. It was for the prosecution to decide what it wanted to tender as evidence. He concluded saying that the defence was acting on no more than a "hunch" that there was some discrepancy to be found in the material.

Justice Zabidin ruled that he would not order the prosecution to produce the proforma notes to the defence, although he did accept that the defence would be entitled to see the notes if the witness refers to them, but at that stage he had not done so.[2]

---

2   The law requires that should any witness refresh his or her memory from a document when testifying, the document must be produced to the other party to enable it to cross-examine the witness if it chooses.

Karpal commenced to cross-examine Dr Razali during which the doctor admitted that he could not remember everything that transpired during the three-hour examination. He was repeatedly asked if he wanted to refer to notes made at the time of the examination, but on each occasion he declined to do so. It was obvious that Karpal was attempting to trap the witness into using the notes to refresh his memory. If the witness referred to them for that purpose, Karpal could then compel the document to be produced. Dr Razali was too cagey to fall for that trick, saying he just could not remember the details.

When the hearing commenced the next day, Karpal told Justice Zabidin that he wanted to make further submissions concerning the disclosure issue. He said there might have been a misunderstanding as to what the defence was actually seeking from the prosecution. "What we want are the clinical notes. The preliminary medical report is not an issue," he said.

He submitted that Dr Razali had been an "evasive" witness for refusing to refer to his notes to refresh his memory. "What he said at various points made no sense, and even if it did, he persistently refused to refer to the notes so as not to give the defence an opportunity and a right to access his notes," said Karpal.[3]

Justice Zabidin responded by saying he had been clear in his ruling and he would not order the production of any hospital notes.

3　My view is that Karpal Singh was effectively speaking about the same thing, but using different terms. He seemed to be subtly changing emphasis from the proforma notes, to what he now called "clinical notes". Essentially, the proforma notes were no more than the notes taken at the time of the medical examination. That was surely what he was referring to when he cross-examined Dr Razali. Anyway, it did not get him very far.

Defence applies the second time for trial judge to disqualify himself for actual bias

On Tuesday, 23 November 2010, Karpal submitted to Justice Zabidin that he should disqualify himself from presiding over the trial because of intimidatory comments the judge had made, which Karpal said indicated bias against Anwar.

The comments referred to by Karpal were made during the legal arguments relating to the disclosure of the proforma notes. When making his submissions, the veteran lawyer reminded the trial judge that the world was watching the events unfolding at the trial. "Your Lordship is under scrutiny and Malaysia's legal system is on trial as a result of this case," he said, citing US Secretary of State Hillary Clinton's call for Anwar to be given a fair trial and the presence of US embassy officials in the courtroom as proof. In view of this, he said, if there was real danger of bias, the judge must recuse himself.

Justice Zabidin responded immediately saying that Karpal was "responsible for whatever instructions" given by his client and that he could be cited for contempt. Then there was this exchange between them:

> **Karpal:** "Just that remark, to threaten us with contempt at this stage is entirely misplaced."
>
> **Justice Zabidin:** "I am not saying that is contempt."
>
> **Karpal:** "For this threat of contempt is entirely unwarranted. To intimidate counsel is a very serious matter. We observed the court as much as Your Lordship ... This threat of contempt, Yang Arif should withdraw that. Not proper."
>
> **Justice Zabidin:** "Okay, I withdraw. Is not proper."

Karpal Singh with Solicitor-General II Mohd Yusof. Seated in the foreground is Karpal's son, Ramkarpal Singh.

It was not until the next day, 24 November, that the defence filed a notice of motion for the recusal application and the hearing was listed before the trial judge for Friday, 26 November.

At the hearing, Karpal submitted that the judge should disqualify himself from hearing the case. He referred to the affidavit filed by Anwar. In it, Anwar supported the recusal application saying that by his remarks, Justice Zabidin had intimidated his counsel by suggesting that his application to disqualify the judge could amount to contempt of court. As such, he had serious concerns that he would not get a fair trial if the judge were to continue to preside over the trial.

He further said that even though the judge had withdrawn the comment, there was a real danger of bias if the judge continued to hear his case. He added: "The fact that Your Lordship backtracked and withdrew [that remark] does not mean that the bias and prejudice in Your Lordship's mind is erased. It is there."

In response, Deputy Prosecutor Mohd Hanafiah Zakaria said the judge was only commenting on the law, which did not amount to intimidation. He said the defence was applying to disqualify the judge to buy time and that it was a "delay tactic". He added that the defence had resorted to disqualifying the judge because there were instances when the judge made rulings against Anwar. He also said that the defence's reasoning to disqualify the judge had been inconsistent.

This was the second time Anwar had filed an application to recuse Justice Zabidin. The first application was in March 2010, when Anwar accused the judge of bias for not initiating contempt action against the Malay daily newspaper *Utusan Malaysia* for being mischievous and causing disruption to a fair trial. That application was refused by the trial judge and ultimately withdrawn by the defence.

After hearing submissions, Justice Zibidin adjourned proceedings until 6 December 2010 to enable him to decide on the recusal application. He also ruled that should he decide not to disqualify himself, the trial proper would resume on that day.

Trial judge refuses to disqualify himself

When the court assembled again on Monday, 6 December, Justice Zabidin delivered his decision. I was present at court to observe the proceedings on behalf of the Inter-Parliamentary Union.

In summary, the judge incorporated the transcript of the proceedings, which included the so-called 'threat' made by him, so he said, as to "understand the proper context in which those words were spoken".

Having read the transcript, Justice Zabidin concluded:

> "I think a reasonable man who reads those words in its proper
> context would not have the impression that there was a real

danger of bias, just because there was an exchanged (sic) of those words between a counsel and a trial judge. Therefore this application is dismissed."

The defence then asked for, and was granted, an adjournment so it could file appeal papers to challenge the trial judge's decision. Consistent with its earlier rulings, the Court of Appeal dismissed the appeal, ruling it had no jurisdiction to hear it.

Should the judge have disqualified himself from hearing trial?

Justice Zabidin's refusal to disqualify himself from hearing the trial was a judgement for him to make. He conceded his remark was improper and immediately withdrew it. He accepted that he had spoken of contempt, but he found that it was part of an exchange of words between counsel and judge that a reasonable person would not consider indicated bias.

At times during the trial, there were robust exchanges between the judge and counsel. Heated verbal exchanges are hardly unusual in criminal trials. Karpal Singh is a vigorous and fearless advocate. He had said things to Justice Zabidin that were often inflammatory and even offensive at times. It is difficult to accept that Karpal would have felt 'intimidated' by the threat of contempt.

CHAPTER 6
The affair

While the fight for disclosure of Mohd Saiful's medical records was being waged with the doctors who had examined him at Hospital Kuala Lumpur, (HKL) the hearing was interrupted by an extraordinary revelation — that Mohd Saiful was having an affair with a member of the prosecution team. It raised the question of whether the prosecution should be discontinued.

The allegation had first surfaced in late July 2010 when fugitive blogger Raja Petra Kamarudin alleged in his blog, Malaysia-Today, that Junior Deputy Public Prosecutor Farah Azlina Latif was having an affair with Mohd Saiful. Farah Azlina was part of an eight-person prosecution team.

Attorney-General removes junior prosecutor from trial team

The Attorney-General Abdul Gani Patail reacted immediately and removed Farah Azlina from the trial team. In doing so, he made no admission that there was any truth in the allegation. He said:

> "The Attorney-General's Chambers cannot compromise on any issue that can tarnish the image or credibility of the department and we are looking at such matters very seriously. This can be very difficult for us but any personal matter, if it can have any

implication in whatever form on the department, will be handled very seriously."[1]

Abdul Gani told the media at a press conference at his office that Farah Azlina had to be dropped, not because she was found guilty, but to avoid any negative public perception of the prosecution team. "This move is also to ensure that the smooth running of the case is not affected," he said.

He also added that Farah Azlina had very limited involvement in the case, pointing out that she only assisted in recording all notes on the proceedings. "She had no access at all to the investigation papers or any confidential information that the prosecution has."[2]

Reaction of the Malaysian Bar Council

The disclosure of the relationship prompted a response from the Malaysian Bar Council. Its president, Ragunath Kesavan, said that being romantically linked to a key witness in a prosecution was "definitely an ethical matter, as prosecutions are done in the interest of justice. You are there to put your case before the court in the interest of justice. As there is no client here, there should be no relationship between prosecutor and complainant."[3]

Defence files to strike out sodomy charge

On Monday, 2 August 2010, Anwar filed a complaint with the police against Mohd Saiful and Farah Azlina. He said the defence was concerned that Farah Azlina might have passed court documents to Mohd Saiful, and he wanted the police to investigate whether the two had violated

---

1   The Associated Press, 27 July 2010

2   *The Star*, 28 July 2008

3   *The Sun*, 28 July 2010

the Official Secrets Act. The next day, his defence team filed an application to strike out the sodomy charge on the basis that the integrity and impartiality of the trial had been compromised because of the revelation of the affair.

The defence team had been scheduled to cross-examine Dr Mohd Razali from HKL, one of the doctors who had physically examined Mohd Saiful and taken samples for analysis from his body and clothing. However, lead defence counsel Karpal Singh urged the court to hear the application to strike out the sodomy charge before cross-examination of the doctor.

Karpal said that as a result of the alleged affair, the integrity of the prosecution team had been attacked. "Following this, the entire prosecution team should step down and Solicitor-General II [the lead prosecutor Mohd Yusof] should be blamed with regard to the allegations," he said.

Mohd Yusof responded saying that claims of an affair were but "mere allegations without any substance". Furthermore, Farah Azlina's role in the case was limited to taking notes on the proceedings. He said that she was a junior member of the team with no access to confidential information.

Anwar told reporters outside the court that the alleged affair was evidence of a conspiracy against him. "It just supports our contention right from the beginning that this is all a farce, a politically motivated trial, trumped-up charges," he said. "This is an additional fact or evidence to support our case, to show the prosecution is not and cannot be impartial."

At the hearing of the application, Karpal told Justice Zabidin that Farah Azlina, by virtue of being a part of the prosecution team, would have been privy to investigation papers and other key documents in the case. "There is a strong likelihood that Mohd Saiful had access to all documents, including the statement by Datuk Seri Anwar," he submitted, adding that both would have committed an offence under section 8(1) and (2) of the Official Secrets Act 1972, as investigation papers were classified under the Act.

Section 8(1) of the Act relates to any person who has in his possession or controls any official secret, and communicates it, while section 8(2) relates to any person who receives any official secret.

Karpal also challenged the pair to deny the affair by filing affidavits. However, the only affidavits filed were from other members of the Attorney-General's Chambers (AGC), namely deputy prosecutor Mohamad Hanafiah Zakaria and investigating officer Jude Pereira. Their affidavits did not deal with the truth or otherwise of the alleged affair, and merely detailed Farah Azlina's role in the prosecution team.

Defence fails to strike out the sodomy charge

Justice Zabidin dismissed Anwar's application to strike out the sodomy charge, saying that the defence had failed to show the prosecution had abused the court process.

In his judgement, which he read to the court on 16 August 2010, he said the prosecution had not denied or confirmed the existence of an affair between Farah Azlina and Mohd Saiful, but had merely stated in affidavits that Farah Azlina had been dropped from the prosecution team to prevent any negative perception. However, he accepted that the allegation of an affair was true.

Nevertheless, he accepted statements in the prosecution affidavits that Farah Azlina had no access to investigation papers and other key documents, and that she had a minor role in the prosecution team. He said: "She was not involved in any briefing with regard to strategies adopted by the prosecution in conducting the case. The conduct of the case is not determined by Farah. She is not a deputy public prosecutor who examines witnesses."

The judge went on to say that he accepted that Mohd Saiful had no influence over Farah Azlina as she was not the public prosecutor who decided to frame the charge against Anwar. As such, he concluded, the issue of prejudice against Anwar and the question of whether he would get a fair trial did not arise.

Defence applies to stay proceedings pending appeal

Immediately after Justice Zabidin delivered his reasons, Karpal said there was an apparent inconsistency in his ruling and applied to stay the proceedings to allow the defence to lodge an appeal against his refusal to strike out the charge.

Karpal told the judge that he knew the defence, in making the application to stay the proceedings, must have before the court a motion supported by affidavit evidence showing special circumstances, but that he needed some time to do that.

The prosecution opposed the adjournment and Justice Zabidin refused to adjourn.

Karpal continued to argue the point. He told the judge that Anwar was entitled to a fair trial and part of that was the right to appeal. He said, "I am not going to sit back and see an injustice perpetrated," which prompted a warning from the judge that his comments were too provocative.

Justice Zabidin ordered the trial to proceed, but Karpal again asked him to adjourn the hearing, this time so that he could take instructions from Anwar. The judge attempted to impose conditions on the adjournment, insisting that if he agreed to adjourn, Karpal should undertake to cross-examine the witness (Dr Mohd Razali) immediately after the resumption of the hearing. Karpal refused to be bound by the condition saying it would depend on the defence case strategy. The judge finally agreed to adjourn for a brief period.

When the proceedings resumed, Karpal renewed his application for a stay. He asked the judge, "Why was there this unholy haste?" He reminded Justice Zabidin that he had previously granted a stay in similar circumstances and so had set his own precedent. On the assurance that the appeal papers would be ready that afternoon, Justice Zabidin adjourned the trial until after lunch.

When proceedings resumed after lunch, Justice Zabidin agreed to order a stay pending appeal, accepting that the defence had made out special circumstances. "If I carry on with the trial," he said, "and if the appeal is allowed later, much of judicial and prosecutorial time will be wasted. There will also be a waste of public funds." He said that it was more appropriate for the Court of Appeal to make a ruling since the striking out application affected the integrity of the prosecution.

The trial was then adjourned for mention to 20 September 2010.

Should the sodomy charge have been struck out?

Justice Zabidin was rightly concerned with the issue of whether Anwar suffered any actual unfairness arising from the affair between the complainant and the junior prosecutor. However, his analysis should have gone further and taken into account the appearance of unfairness.

(A) PROSECUTION DID NOT DENY THE AFFAIR

The prosecution did not address the allegation of an affair and somewhat disingenuously did not file affidavits either from Mohd Saiful or Farah Azlina in reply to Anwar's application.

Instead, the prosecution filed affidavits from Mohamad Hanafiah and Jude Pereira from the AGC that focused solely on the role of Farah Azlina within the prosecution team and the matter of her access to sensitive material. They downplayed her role, describing it as one of simply keeping notes at the trial, and explained that she had no access to any important documents and played no part in deciding prosecution tactics at trial.

Given that the prosecution had neither confirmed nor denied the existence of an affair between Mohd Saiful and Farah Azlina, the judge accepted that it was true. It was only appropriate that he did so in circumstances where the prosecution had simply ignored the allegation, rather than admit or deny it. However, whatever the reality of the situation, the fact was that a public perception had been created that the trial may have been compromised by their relationship.

(B) FARAH AZLINA HAD DIRECT ACCESS TO PROSECUTION MATERIAL

Farah Azlina would almost certainly have had access to all of the material comprising the prosecution brief, including medical reports, scientific reports, police reports and witness statements. Even if she were not part of tactical discussions, she would have been aware, if only in a general sense, of what was being planned and obtained some insight into the nature of the prosecution's case.

The prosecution claimed that she did not have access to the "investigation papers" or any "confidential information". What does that mean?

First, the expression "investigation papers" undoubtedly means police investigation notes, but it may also include witness statements prepared by the police. Witness statements in Malaysia are prepared by the police and form part of the prosecution brief, but they are classed as privileged and are not disclosed to the defence. Given that these documents form the essential part of the prosecution brief, it is highly unlikely Farah Azlina would not have had access to this material.

Secondly, the expression "confidential information" must include not only material disclosed to the defence by the prosecution, but it may also include material not disclosed because it is classified as being privileged.

Police witness statements are an example of privileged documents. There is no reason to think that even a junior prosecutor would not have access to all of this material. Farah Azlina was not just an employee of the AGC, but an actual member of the legal team prosecuting the case against Anwar.

(C) HOW WAS THE RELATIONSHIP ABLE TO DEVELOP?

What about her relationship with Mohd Saiful? How was it that she was able to develop a romantic relationship with the complainant during the course of the trial? It must be assumed that, unless they already knew each other, there was frequent contact between them to enable a relationship to develop. But that hardly seems likely if she was no more than a mere 'note-taker' at the trial.

It must also be assumed that, initially at least, any contact between them was solely for work purposes relevant to the trial, but it would also be relevant to know whether there were occasions when they met socially, away from the trial. These are important questions because they would explain the nature and extent of their relationship.

It is unlikely, however, that Farah Azlina would have proofed or prepared Mohd Saiful to testify as a witness at trial. A more senior member of the team would almost certainly have undertaken that task. Still, if they did communicate, they would undoubtedly have talked about the case. After all, it was the event that had brought them together and it was the principal focus of their lives at that time. Given that situation, therefore, it is highly likely that, in whatever context, the conversation between them would have drifted to the subject of the trial and his role in it.

(D) 'PILLOW TALK'

There is always the prospect of confidential information being spoken of in what the Americans call 'pillow talk'. This is not to suggest that there was a sexual intimacy between them, only that a romantic connection would have created a trust between them that may have led to some indiscreet remarks by the prosecutor about the trial.

Essentially, the necessary formality between prosecutor and complainant would have been absent. They may have discussed nothing of consequence, but critically the opportunity was there to do so. That situation should never have occurred. Farah Azlina's relationship with Mohd Saiful completely compromised the prosecution. Dropping her from the prosecution team did not solve the problem because the perception that the prosecution case had been compromised by the affair was inescapable.

It is a fundamental principle of natural justice that the mere appearance of bias is sufficient to overturn a judicial decision. It prompts the oft-quoted aphorism: "Not only must justice be done; it must also be seen to be done." It is worth quoting in full:

> "...it is of fundamental importance that justice should not only be done, but should manifestly and undoubtedly be seen to be done. The question therefore is not whether in this case the deputy clerk made any observation or offered any criticism which he might not properly have made or offered; the question is whether he was so related to the case in its civil aspect as to be unfit to act as clerk to the justices in the criminal matter. The answer to that question depends not upon what actually was done, but upon what might appear to be done."[4]

---

4   *R v Sussex Justices*, Ex parte McCarthy [1924] 1 KB 256, [1923] All ER 233 per Lord Justice Hewart

(E) PROSECUTION SHOULD BE A 'MODEL LITIGANT'

The prosecution must always be a model litigant. It must never be seen to have compromised its impartiality to the facts, albeit that it is prosecuting a case against an accused person. It must not be seen to have acted in any way that might suggest it has acted improperly or inappropriately. For that reason, the public perception of its role as a model litigant is critical to upholding the integrity of the justice system.

It was appropriate that Justice Zabidin assessed Farah Azlina's role at the trial and within the prosecution team to decide whether the trial had been compromised. Obviously, if she had a more senior role, his decision would almost certainly have been different but, whatever her status, she was nevertheless a member of the prosecution team.

Notwithstanding the reassurances of the AGC, she was, by reason of her membership of the prosecution team and the intimate nature of her relationship with the complainant, completely compromised, and that immediately created the perception that the prosecution itself had been compromised, even if in reality it had not.

For that reason alone, the trial should have been abandoned. In Malaysia, there are no means by which a judge can simply abandon or abort a trial, but the judge can strike out the charge. It would then be up to the Attorney-General to decide whether to charge the person again and appoint a new prosecution team to take the matter to trial.

Should the Attorney-General have discontinued the trial?

I am firmly of the view that the circumstances were such that the charge should have been struck out by the trial judge. I also believe that the conduct of the prosecution was sufficiently serious for the Attorney-General to halt the criminal prosecution.

First, if it is accepted that Mohd Saiful improperly obtained confidential information from Farah Azlina that enabled him to tailor his testimony to fit within the physical evidence, then the case had been compromised to the extent that Anwar could never obtain a fair trial. Even if Mohd Saiful did not gain confidential information from Farah Azlina, the perception that he did would taint any subsequent trial in the same way.

Secondly, this incident happened in a trial where there were serious allegations of political interference at the highest level. The prosecution of Anwar occurred within a context of the admitted involvement of Prime Minister Najib Razak and his staff, Attorney-General Abdul Gani and Senior Assistant Commissioner of Police Mohd Rodwan, and the bringing of a charge at a time when Anwar had just returned to parliament to challenge the ruling coalition when its fortunes were flagging.

Mohd Saiful admitted when cross-examined at the trial that he had met with Mr Najib (then deputy prime minister) at the latter's home and Mohd Rodwan in a hotel room only days before the offence allegedly occurred. The defence claimed these meetings, which occurred so proximate to the alleged offending behaviour, suggested contrivance.

The defence also complained of the involvement of Abdul Gani when he transferred the sodomy charge from the Sessions Court to the High Court in circumstances where it had been alleged that he fabricated evidence against Anwar at his earlier trial. Although the Court of Appeal accepted that Abdul Gani had merely acted administratively, it again brought into focus complaints of political interference.

The direct involvement of PM Najib, Abdul Gani and Mohd Rodwan allowed the defence to question their role in bringing the charge against Anwar. It was an issue that had the potential to bring into disrepute the Malaysian justice system, which surely was not in the public interest.

Thirdly, there was a sound basis to discontinue the prosecution against Anwar on public interest grounds. The prosecution had obviously been compromised even by the mere perception that a member of its team was guilty of wrongdoing. Removing Farah Azlina from the team did not solve the problem because her wrongdoing had tainted the entire prosecution team and the integrity of the trial.

For the purposes of exercising his discretion, it would also be relevant to have regard to the personal impact of continuing a trial upon the defendant in these circumstances. Anwar had been subject to intense personal stress, substantial legal costs and disruption to his daily life. If the prosecution was abandoned at that stage, it could not be said that it was because of anything that Anwar had done. The responsibility rested entirely with the prosecution to maintain the integrity of the justice system.

As the Court of Appeal noted in its decision concerning the disclosure of Mohd Saiful's police statement, the Attorney-General has a very wide discretion over the control and direction of all criminal prosecutions. Not only may he institute and conduct any proceedings for an offence, he may also discontinue criminal proceedings that he has instituted, and the court cannot compel him to institute any criminal proceedings that he does not wish to institute or to go on with any criminal proceedings that he has decided to discontinue.

The general principle that the Attorney-General must act in the public interest applies with particular force to his powers under clause 3 of Article 145 of the Malaysian Federal Constitution and section 376(1) of the Criminal Procedure Code, which states:

> "In deciding whether to institute or discontinue a prosecution against an accused the Attorney-General is always guided by

legal principles, but the public interest shall also be the paramount consideration."[5]

Given that the prosecution case had been completely compromised, the public interest justified discontinuing the proceedings. The Attorney-General chose not to do so.

By August 2010, when the affair between Mohd Saiful and the prosecutor was revealed, the trial had already drifted over a period of more than six months. Although the trial had started in February of that year, it was interrupted several times mostly because of appeals made by Anwar's lawyers against rulings made by the trial judge, which they claimed affected the fairness of the trial.

There was a substantial delay in March 2010 when the trial clashed with the opening of parliament and the parliamentary duties of Anwar and his lead counsel Karpal Singh (also a parliamentarian and National Chairman of the Democratic Action Party, which is a member of the opposition parliamentary alliance). Unfortunately, proceedings in August were again delayed when Karpal was suddenly taken ill with pneumonia.

5   Azmi bin Ariffin, 'Effective Administration of the Police and the Prosecution in Criminal Justice in Malaysia', UNAFEI Annual Report 2001, Deputy Public Prosecutor, State Legal Advisor's Office, Kelantan, p. 149

CHAPTER 7
Was it Anwar's DNA?

When Anwar Ibrahim was taken into police custody in July 2008, he was placed in a cell and kept there overnight. He was released the next day. The police retrieved physical items that he had used in the cell and submitted them for DNA analysis. The items seized were a toothbrush, a mineral water bottle and a hand towel.

Anwar's lawyers challenged the admissibility of the DNA analysis, submitting that the items from which samples of DNA were taken were improperly obtained. They argued that the items were taken without Anwar's consent and that it would be unfair to use them as evidence against him. The judge was asked to exercise his discretion to exclude the evidence on the basis of unfairness.

The defence also questioned the integrity of the DNA samples taken from Mohd Saiful's rectum. In October 2010, government chemist Dr Seah Lay Hong testified that she had found two unknown male DNA profiles around Mohd Saiful's anus, one of which she had earlier called "Male Y". Anwar's lawyers were concerned with those findings, citing the example of the first sodomy trial in 1998 where it was stated on record that Anwar's DNA profile was "abused" by the police. Anwar had refused to provide DNA samples in that trial for fear they could be manipulated. Those suspicions were not unfounded; in January 2010, former Kuala Lumpur CID chief Mat Zain Ibrahim claimed that DNA evidence was fabricated in Anwar's first sodomy trial.

Defence doubts integrity of DNA evidence

In his opening address on 3 February 2010, Deputy Prosecutor Mohd Yusof told the court: "The prosecution will also bring specimens of semen from Saiful Bukhari Azlan's anus which is verified by the chemistry department as belonging to the accused."

The prosecution claimed that the DNA sample extracted from Mohd Saiful's rectum corroborated his allegation and incriminated Anwar as it provided evidence of penetration.

Before the adjournment of the trial on 18 February 2010, Anwar's lawyer Sankara Nair announced that the defence had appointed foreign DNA and forensic experts to debunk the prosecution's claim of a DNA match. The experts were Dr Brian McDonald from Sydney, Australia, Professor Dr C. Damodaran from Chennai, India, and Associate Professor David Wells from Melbourne, Australia.

Even at that early stage of the proceedings, it was obvious this was to be the battleground on which the case would be fought. There were many unanswered questions concerning the prosecution's DNA evidence and the findings of the government chemistry department. For example, the prosecution refused to provide the defence with a sample of the material from which they claimed DNA was extracted so that it might be independently tested. In cases involving DNA analysis, there may be sound reasons for not providing samples. For instance, it may be that the sample size is too small to provide some of it to the defence for testing while at the same time preserving the integrity of the exhibit. Still, the prosecution simply refused to provide any material for analysis to the defence despite conceding that there was enough of the sample to do that.

Anwar's lawyers claimed that the prosecution's refusal to provide some of the sample to them for analysis disadvantaged their client by denying them the opportunity to challenge the opinions of the prosecution's experts.

They also questioned the chain of custody of the forensic samples taken by the doctors at Hospital Kuala Lumpur (HKL). The samples were not delivered to the laboratory for analysis for at least 48 hours after they were obtained by the doctors — which meant some 96 hours after the alleged sexual assault. Anwar's lawyers raised this issue because the delay affected the integrity of the samples that were finally analysed by chief chemist Dr Seah. They also claimed that the refusal by the prosecution to provide the notes made by Dr Seah in reaching her conclusion failed to exclude the potential for contamination of the samples.

Finally, Anwar's lawyers said it was highly unlikely that DNA could have been obtained from material taken from Mohd Saiful's rectum 48 hours after the act of penetration. Most experts confirm that the rectal cavity is an extremely hostile environment and semen degrades quickly so that it would be highly unlikely that DNA would survive in it after that period of time.

In any event, Anwar's lawyers claimed their client was not in the bedroom of the condominium where Mohd Saiful alleged he was sodomised but was, in fact, in another unit in the complex. They claimed that at the relevant time — 3.01 pm to 4.30 pm on 26 June 2008 — he was meeting with several other people, including the condominium owner.

Judge excludes DNA evidence obtained when Anwar was in custody

Anwar's lawyers had challenged the admissibility of the DNA findings on the basis that the material for analysis had been obtained from items improperly taken from the police lock-up.

Justice Zabidin delivered his decision on 8 March 2011. He upheld the objection finding that the items taken from Anwar's cell had been obtained through unfair means because Anwar had not been informed of their possible use against him.

Of course, this meant that any DNA evidence obtained from the items was also inadmissible. Without this evidence, the prosecution would now have to rely mostly on the testimony of Mohd Saiful, which made it a much weaker prosecution case.

Anwar told the media outside the courtroom: "I am grateful for the verdict and this just further supports what I have said, that I am being persecuted unfairly by the authorities in their bid to silence me."[1]

But the battle for the DNA evidence was not yet over. Following the close of the prosecution case, Mohd Yusof made two applications. First, he requested the trial judge to review his decision to exclude the DNA evidence obtained from the three items. Secondly, he asked the Court to use its powers under the Evidence Act to compel Anwar to provide a DNA sample for analysis.

The hearing was adjourned to enable the parties to provide written submissions to the judge outlining their respective positions.

Prosecution submissions leaked to media

Only days before the court was to hear these applications, the prosecution submissions were published in the *New Straits Times* and *Utusan Malaysia* dailies and the online portal Malaysia Today. The *New Straits Times* carried a page-4 exclusive entitled "New bid to get Anwar's DNA" which outlined details of Mohd Yusof's yet-to-be-presented submissions.

Anwar's lawyers were outraged at the publication of the prosecution submissions. Sankara Nair said they would likely push for orders of contempt of court. He told online news site The Malaysian Insider: "This is a repeat of 1998 where affidavits were leaked. Trial by media at its highest.

---

1   BBC News, 8 March 2011

It may be contempt [of court]. We will be discussing with our legal team before deciding, but most probably we will ask the court to stand down to discuss this. That is totally out of line. The A-G is behaving like a political arm of the government."[2]

At the hearing on 14 March 2011, lead counsel Karpal Singh urged the court to take action over the leaked submissions. "This is the first time in legal history where submissions of the A-G was in the Internet even before today," he said.

He also submitted that an article in *Utusan Malaysia*, which covered a rally by Perkasa in which there were demands that Anwar surrender his DNA samples, could affect the judge's ruling in the prosecution's latest application.

Karpal accused Mohd Yusof of leaking his own submissions over the weekend. "For my learned friend to have leaked out submissions to the Internet, Malaysia Today ... there's no point in filing an application. The court must call upon those who have leaked the report [over] contempt of court before my learned friend comes up with submissions that is already in public knowledge," he said.

In response, Mohd Yusof said that while he took full responsibility over the leaked submissions, he maintained that as lead prosecutor, he was not being "used by anybody". He said: "I do my battle in court, not outside. I have stated last Friday, we are going to make application [of the] mentioned section. I am not being used by anybody. I answer to no one except this honourable court. I don't think it's anything. Just that it [the submissions] came out earlier than when it should."

Justice Zabidin warned all parties not to do anything that could lead to possible contempt of court. "The trial is ongoing, [I must] remind parties

2   themalaysianinsider.com, 14 March 2011

... anything done in contempt of court, those responsible will face the music," he said.

Prime Minister Najib comments on DNA issue

A few days later, on 20 March 2011, PM Najib added to the debate publicly when he told the media that the opposition leader should surrender his DNA for analysis. His comments provoked an immediate response from Anwar's lawyers.

Karpal said the prime minister had gone against Justice Zabidin's warning to all parties not to publicly comment on the trial, and that doing so was tantamount to an act of contempt of court. He raised the issue when the court resumed on 21 March 2011. He submitted to Justice Zabidin: "... the prime minister should be hauled up here for comments ... in telling Anwar to provide DNA. Your Lordship should make a ruling for contempt of court for the prime minister. All parties concerned must not commit contempt of court."

But Justice Zabidin said that if the defence wanted to initiate such proceedings, it needed to first file a fresh application to the court. "If you really feel that way, then you can file an application to the court," said the judge.

Sankara Nair later told the media outside the court that the defence would not push for contempt proceedings against the prime minister for the time being, but would do so if he repeated his comments.

When the hearing resumed, Mohd Yusof, in support of his application for the trial judge to review his decision to exclude any evidence of DNA material taken from the items used by Anwar, submitted that while the judge could not ask Anwar to surrender his DNA samples, he could order someone else to obtain them from him. What was relevant, according to Mohd Yusof, was whether the DNA obtained from Mohd Saiful's rectum could be matched to the accused. He said that the trial judge should not be concerned with how evidence samples in the trial were obtained — "as long as it is relevant, it is admissible."

Who leaked the prosecution submissions — and why?

The leaking of the prosecution's legal submissions was highly unusual and unfortunate. If the leak was deliberate, it was an insult to Justice Zabidin who had yet to hear the application. If it was accidental, then it showed very lax security in the Attorney-General's Chambers (AGC) and was worthy of a top-level police investigation.

Curiously, the trial judge was never given an adequate explanation as to how the leak happened. All that Mohd Yusof could say was that he was not being used by anyone and that the submissions just "came out earlier than when it should".

Did Mohd Yusof's explanation mean the prosecution submissions had been released to the media by the AGC, but earlier than intended? If so, why was the AGC releasing its submissions to the media in the first place unless it wanted to publicly exploit the DNA issue against Anwar? These submissions should properly have been dealt with in court rather than argued in the media. It hardly seems appropriate for a prosecution service to conduct its case in this way.

It was also unfortunate that the prime minister made public statements to the media. Of course, this was a very political case, and the boundaries between the law and politics were often crossed, but the PM's remarks were contrary to the official government view that the courts must in this case act independently without any political interference. Fortunately, there was no jury to be influenced by the comments.

Judge reverses earlier order and allows DNA analysis of exhibits to be submitted

On 23 March 2011, Justice Zabidin reversed his earlier ruling and allowed the toothbrush, towel and mineral water bottle to be admitted as evidence at the trial. He said the ruling was made without the evidence of the investigating officer Deputy Superintendent Jude Pereira.

"In the light of the evidence of the IO and arresting officer [Superintendent Ahmad Taufik Abdullah] the arrest is lawful," said the judge, adding that the detention was for a lawful purpose. "Those items and all the evidences relating to the items are now admissible. My earlier ruling is reversed," he said.

Chief prosecutor Mohd Yusof said he would call chemist Nor Aidora Saedon and former Bukit Aman Crime Scene Investigation unit chief Amidon Anan to tender the exhibits.

...but refuses to force Anwar to provide samples of his DNA

The prosecution had asked the court to compel Anwar to provide a sample of his DNA for analysis. The judge could only make such an order under the provisions of the Evidence Act.

The Malaysian parliament had passed legislation in 2008 empowering the police to take DNA samples from suspects.[3] However, it did not apply in Anwar's case because it had no retrospective effect and so could not be used to compel Anwar to provide a sample of his DNA in his second trial.

When delivering his decision, Justice Zabidin said that he had read section 73 of the Evidence Act over and over again, but could find no legal authority for the court to force Anwar to provide samples of his DNA. (Section 73 deals with taking samples from a person for the purposes of

---

3   DNA Identification Act 2008

comparing handwriting and fingerprints.) He rejected an application by the prosecution to compel Anwar to give a DNA sample.

The case of the lubricant

The first mention of lubricant being used to assist penile penetration came up when Mohd Saiful was testifying for the prosecution. The prosecution produced a tube of K-Y Gel, which Mohd Saiful identified as the one he had been asked to bring to the condominium and which he said Anwar had used.

Mohd Saiful did not mention the tube of K-Y Gel or that lubricant had been used when interviewed by police on 28 June 2008. The police must have come into possession of the tube of lubricant sometime after that date and would have been aware of its existence and Mohd Saiful's claim that lubricant was used.

The police seized Mohd Saiful's clothing and the rug that was in the room on the night he claimed to have been anally penetrated. These items were sent for DNA analysis, but no forensic tests were conducted to confirm the presence of lubricant. Neither was there any request to test for lubricant. That may have been because DSP Jude Pereira was, at that point of time, unaware that lubricant had been used. Still, there was nothing to stop him requesting further tests once he knew about it. The presence of lubricant on these items would have corroborated Mohd Saiful's claim to having been sexually penetrated and may have explained why there were no injuries. It should have been done, but was not. It was sloppy police work.

The general lax attitude of the authorities to testing for lubricant is further illustrated by the answer given by forensic pathologist Dr Siew Sheue Feng. When asked by Sankara Nair why he did not conduct a lubricant test, he responded, "I did not think it was important."

The doctors who examined Mohd Saiful at HKL did not take samples to test for lubricant. It may be understandable given the fact that Dr Mohd Osman from the private Hospital Pusrawi who was the first to examine Mohd Saiful had used lubricant when inserting a proctoscope into his rectum. Obviously, it would not have been possible to distinguish between lubricant used in that medical procedure and lubricant used to facilitate penile penetration.

Did Mohd Saiful defecate before doctors examined him?

Whether Mohd Saiful had defecated or not before forensic samples were taken from his rectum on the night of his physical examination at HKL was a relevant factor in assessing the reliability of the DNA evidence. It was relevant because it may have affected the outcome of any DNA test. For example, if he had defecated before being examined, then it would be less likely that any cellular material would be found from which DNA could be extracted. That is because the motion of evacuating his bowels would almost certainly have flushed his lower rectum and anal canal. On the other hand, if he had not defecated, it meant that any traces of cellular material — including semen — had a better chance of surviving and providing a good source of DNA.

When he was being cross-examined at the trial, Mohd Saiful told the court he had informed the doctors examining him at HKL that he had not defecated or washed his anus since being anally penetrated 54 hours before. He said he did not wash because he wanted to "preserve the evidence".

This was a curious thing for a victim of sexual assault to do. It is well known that victims of sexual assault will, if they have the chance, almost always wash their bodies in an attempt to 'cleanse' themselves of the sexual contact. Very few have the presence of mind not to wash so as to preserve evidence of sexual contact. Mohd Saiful's explanation was also curious because he claimed to be a devout Muslim, which meant that he would need to wash himself before being called to daily prayers.

When Dr Razali from HKL testified, he said that he found Mohd Saiful's rectum to be empty, despite the fact that the complainant had said he had not defecated since the alleged sexual act. That was confirmed by a proctoscopy examination. When cross-examined, he said that even if Mohd Saiful had not defecated for two days, it did not necessarily mean there would be faeces in the rectum. He explained there might be faeces in the upper rectum, which would not reach the lower rectum where the swabs were taken as the lower rectum was only to facilitate defecation and not for storing faeces.

Dr Razali's explanation for not finding faeces in the lower rectum may not have directly contradicted the complainant's claim not to have defecated, but after 54 hours one would expect some evidence of faeces in that location. It was a potential inconsistency that directly affected the credibility and truthfulness of the complainant.

Was there presence of seminal fluids in rectum?

In any event, if Anwar's DNA was to be found inside the complainant's rectum, that would undoubtedly be persuasive evidence of sexual contact — if it could be proved.

One serious difficulty for the prosecution was the period of time that had elapsed between the alleged sexual penetration and the taking of the swabs to obtain specimens for DNA and seminal analysis.

Dr Razali told the court he examined Mohd Saiful's anus and took several rectal swabs. He said the examination took place 54 hours after the alleged act of penetration. He accepted that the likelihood of seminal fluids remaining in the rectum depended on a person's anal functions, or when a 'mass movement' occurs, but he maintained that despite the lapse of time, it was still possible that traces of semen could be found.

"In some cases, you can still get samples within the 72 hours as the anal canal is not straight," said the doctor. He also said it was possible for a person to pass motion and still retrieve seminal fluids from the rectum, as some samples may remain "stuck" there. "When I did the examination, I did not know what to expect or whether I would find any samples," he said.

"There can still be specimen present as the bowel is not in a straight line," he said during his re-examination by chief prosecutor Mohd Yusof. However, when questioned by Anwar's counsel Sankara Nair, Dr Razali said the 72-hour duration was based on his readings and not on his own medical experience as he was not trained in medical forensics.

Dr Razali was a general surgeon. On his own admission, he had limited forensic medical experience. He had simply taken the samples from the complainant's body. His opinion about how long one would expect to find traces of semen in the rectum carried little weight.

Poor handling of forensic samples

(A) INADEQUATE STORAGE OF DNA SAMPLES

A significant issue concerning the integrity of the DNA samples taken from Mohd Saiful's rectum emerged when DSP Jude Pereira testified. He was the senior police officer entrusted with the safekeeping of the samples after the medical team at HKL had obtained them on 28 June 2008.

Pereira's integrity was also questioned. Anwar's lead counsel Karpal Singh attacked Pereira's character, referring to the findings of the Human Rights Commission of Malaysia (Suhakam) in 2009, which found that Pereira had lied in his testimony given in an inquiry before it. "Jude Pereira consciously was not telling the truth or suffered from a serious problem of loss of memory," said Karpal as he read from the findings of the inquiry.[4]

Pereira testified that he took the swabs from HKL on 29 June 2008, where Dr Siew was working, and placed them in his office at Brickfields headquarters. He confirmed that Dr Siew had told him to place the samples into a freezer "so that [certain] ingredients won't be missing". He also confirmed that instead of putting the samples into a freezer, he put them into a metal filing cabinet because "there were lots of things in the freezer". He claimed that the temperature in the filing cabinet was similar to the temperature in his office, which was air-conditioned. The samples remained in the cabinet for about 43 hours.

When defence counsel Sankara Nair pointed out that Pereira had violated the Inspector-General's Standing Orders by not placing the swabs into the police station freezer despite taking a storage number, he replied, "Yes, it should be kept in a store. I broke the law, but it was my decision to do so."[5]

He also admitted that he did not inform government chemist Dr Seah Lay Hong about the conditions in which the swabs were kept.[5] He said the swabs had been lying in his cabinet for 34 hours before he sent them to the Chemistry Department. "It's actually 43 hours," countered Sankara Nair, which Pereira accepted.

Pereira admitted that degradation of the DNA samples might have occurred because the metal cabinet was not a freezer. He told the court

---

4   In an inquiry in August 2009, Suhakam concluded that the detention and arrest of five lawyers at Brickfields police headquarters in May 2009 was a violation of human rights. The lawyers were attempting to assist their clients who had earlier attended a candlelight vigil. Suhakam found that DSP Pereira had lied in his testimony about the circumstances of the arrest and detention.

5   themalaysianinsider.com, 11 March 2011

there was a freezer at the police station, but he decided to place the swabs in his office, which was air-conditioned. He said the temperature in his cabinet was similar to the temperature in his office. When asked how he knew, he said he had put his hand into the cabinet.

He also admitted that after returning to his office with the samples, he had cut open the heat-sealed plastic exhibit bag containing the containers with the swabs. He put the containers into envelopes, marked them for identification and handed them over to Dr Seah later that day. Justice Zabidin was to say, in his written reasons for acquitting Anwar, that "by cutting open the plastic bag, confidence in the integrity of the samples was gone."

(B) CHAIN OF CUSTODY OF EXHIBITS BROKEN

There were also serious questions about the 'chain of custody' of the forensic samples taken from Mohd Saiful by the doctors at HKL on the evening of his physical examination. Pereira was present at the examination and was given the samples for safekeeping and delivery to the government chemist for analysis. He was also given the task of labelling the samples so that each might be identified.

Sankara Nair pointed out to him that he had failed to notice that the date labels on some of the swabs were wrong. Pereira was asked to read out the dates of two labels, both of which said "August 26". The date written on each container should have been "June 28", which is when the forensic samples were taken by doctors at HKL as they examined Mohd Saiful. Pereira was asked why he did not notice the error. He replied that he "didn't see the mistake".[6]

The effect of breaking the chain of custody

Pereira's testimony threw up serious issues not only about the integrity of the forensic samples, but also whether there was a sufficient chain of custody from the collection of the samples until the time they were analysed.

Anwar's lawyers raised the issue of continuity because it affected the integrity of the samples that were analysed by Dr Seah. They also claimed that the prosecution's refusal to provide the notes Dr Seah made in reaching her conclusion failed to exclude the potential for contamination of the samples.

Pereira, by casually storing the samples in his office filing cabinet, confirmed that the samples were not sufficiently secured and protected from accidental or deliberate contamination. It also raised issues of whether the chain of custody was maintained or broken by his actions.

Finally, Dr Seah was unaware of the poor conditions in which the swabs were kept before she analysed them as she was not told about it.

The chain of custody can be the single most important aspect of a criminal case.[7] Ensuring the physical integrity of biological evidence throughout the forensics process is critical. It starts when a police officer takes charge of a piece of evidence. It is followed by the creation of a paper trail showing the seizure, custody, control, transfer, analysis and disposition of that evidence. Securing evidence under these standardised procedures is necessary to ensure that evidence is not substituted, contaminated, tampered with, replaced, or altered in any material way.

---

7   In every criminal case, great care is taken to record the transfer of custody
    of evidence from the moment it is collected until it is presented as an exhibit
    at court. It is especially critical in chemical sampling situations to maintain
    the integrity of the sample by documenting the control, transfer and analysis
    of the sample.

DSP Pereira may well have thought he was doing the right thing in storing the samples in his filing cabinet, but nevertheless it was an appalling lapse of proper procedure by a senior police officer. It is particularly disconcerting that he ignored the specific instructions of the forensic pathologist on preserving the samples.

It seemed to me at the time that little, if any, weight should be given to the DNA evidence in this case. That was because of the appalling lapse of police procedure in storing the samples, the significant potential for contamination and degradation of the samples because of where and how they were stored, and the obvious breach of the chain of custody.

CHAPTER 8
Judge says case to answer

In criminal trials and at the conclusion of the prosecution case, the lawyers for an accused person may conclude that the evidence presented is such that no reasonable court properly directed on the law could find the accused guilty. At this point, the defence will make a 'no case submission' in an attempt to persuade the court not to call on the accused to enter a defence.

There is no express provision in the Malaysian Criminal Procedure Code permitting defence counsel to make a submission of no case to answer at the close of the prosecution case. But the practice in Malaysia has always been to allow the defence to do so. It is the discretion of the judge to allow a submission of no case, and not a matter of right.

Having heard submissions from both parties, Justice Zabidin had to decide whether there was a case to call on the accused, Anwar Ibrahim, to enter his defence. It depended on whether the prosecution had satisfied the court there was a *prima facie* case to answer. At that stage, the judge may either order an acquittal or call upon the accused to enter a defence (section 173 (f) CPC).

Defence submits no case to answer after prosecution case closes

The defence submitted to the trial judge that there was no case to answer on the basis that the evidence before the court was not sufficient at law to convict Anwar of the offence with which he had been charged.

Justice Zabidin ordered the parties to submit written submissions no later than 18 April 2011 when he would hear further argument and make his decision whether to acquit Anwar or require him to enter a defence. After receiving submissions from the parties, he reserved his decision until 16 May 2011 when he would also close the prosecution case.

Judge presents his reasons and calls on Anwar to enter his defence

On 16 May, in a lengthy 68-page decision, Justice Zabidin reviewed all of the prosecution evidence.

The evidence included the testimony of the complainant Mohd Saiful (PW1) who described the circumstances in which he claimed to have been sexually assaulted.

It also included what the judge regarded as corroborating evidence — evidence confirming that Mohd Saiful was at the condominium complex at the time he said he went there, the medical examination by doctors soon after the alleged sexual act, and his complaint to the police and then DPM Najib Razak.

Of particular importance was the test for DNA on the samples taken from the complainant's rectum at Hospital Kuala Lumpur. DNA samples were also obtained from items at the condominium where the sexual act was alleged to have occurred and from items used by Anwar in his cell when he was first taken into custody.

In his opening remarks, Justice Zabidin correctly identified the test to be applied in evaluating the prosecution evidence. (See his reference to *Looi Kow Chai & Anor v PP* [2003] 1 CLJ 734.) He concluded that if the complainant's evidence of penile penetration was credible, then it was sufficient to satisfy him there was a case to answer without even having regard to any corroborating evidence to support his testimony.

Justice Zabidin did consider the defence submission that Mohd Saiful's failure to escape or make an early complaint to the police reflected adversely on his credibility. He characterised the complaint as suggesting that Mohd Saiful was an untruthful witness who had fabricated his claim.

The fact that a complainant may delay making a complaint of an alleged sexual assault to others reflects on that person's credit, but it does not necessarily indicate that the allegation is false. There may be good reason why the victim of such an offence might hesitate to make a complaint. Justice Zabidin identified reasons why Mohd Saiful did not complain to others immediately following the alleged assault, which he found "could not be the basis to find PW1 to be an incredible witness". Of course, an early complaint does not prove that it happened. It is always a question of credit to be judged by the circumstances surrounding the alleged commission of the offence.

Justice Zabidin correctly reasoned that it was not necessary for him to find there was evidence to corroborate Mohd Saiful's testimony, but in fact he found there *was* such evidence before the court. It included such things as the complainant's presence at the "vicinity of the crime scene" when he said the offence took place, the forensic evidence relating to the presence of semen in the high and low rectal region consistent with penile penetration, and the so-called "matching" of the DNA extracted from the rectal swabs and the results of the DNA profile obtained from the items used by "Male Y" which indicated that "the DNA identified came from the same source".

He concluded that: "These (sic) evidence, if accepted, would proved (sic) the unknown contributor of the semen 'Male Y' found in PW1's anus came from the accused."

Justice Zabidin considered the complaints made by the defence about the reliability of the scientific analysis, but concluded that it did not make the analysis "inherently incredible" and that it could be accepted as *prima facie* evidence. He was not persuaded that allegations of contamination and degradation of the samples were sufficient to cause him to take a different view of the analysis.

Justice Zabidin also was not persuaded that the lack of any injury to the anus was inconsistent with the account given by the complainant who said that lubricant was used and that there was "no undue force used by the accused".

Was the judge right to call the defence to answer?

One concern was Justice Zabidin's conclusion that the account given by Mohd Saiful to the medical doctors corroborated his claim of having been sodomised. He said: "The medical history narrated by PW1 and noted by the Medical Doctors PW2, PW3 and PW4 is corroborative evidence which lend (sic) credence to PW1's evidence."

That was a clear error of law. A person can never corroborate himself by telling others an offence happened. Mere complaint is not evidence capable of amounting to corroboration; neither does it make the allegation true. Furthermore, and as I have said earlier, the lack of injury is a neutral fact. It does not mean that penetration has not occurred, even though it is potentially inconsistent with forceful penetration.

But it was Justice Zabidin's concluding paragraph that raised some concerns as to whether he had applied the correct test at law. He said:

> "Based on all the above reasons, I find the prosecution, through the evidence of PW1 which had been corroborated in material particulars, had (sic) proved all the facts required to establish all of the ingredients of the charge. I find a *prima facie* case as defined under Section 180 of the Criminal Procedure Code had (sic) been made out against the accused. Therefore, the accused is called to enter his defence."

The first sentence of this paragraph seems to suggest that the judge had applied the higher standard of proof in concluding that the prosecution had "proved all the facts required to establish all of the ingredients of the charge". That was not an appropriate standard of proof at this intermediate stage of the proceedings. Whether that finding was saved or explained by the next sentence is questionable.

As Justice Vincent Ng said in *Public Prosecutor v Ong Cheng Heong* [1998] 4 CLJ 209 at p. 225: "While *prima facie* evidence is evidence which is sufficient to establish a fact in the absence of any evidence to the contrary, it is not conclusive."

It is arguable that Justice Zabidin may have adopted the erroneous view that the prosecution evidence conclusively proved the case. If so, that was not a conclusion open to him at the close of the prosecution case. He could only make that finding after hearing all of the evidence, not just the prosecution witnesses. It was also disconcerting to hear the judge declare that he found Mohd Saiful to be a "truthful witness" when the complainant's testimony had not been tested by all of the evidence.

Non-lawyers seem to believe that a finding by a trial judge that there is a case to answer is conclusive of the issue of guilt. That is never the case. It simply means that the judge has, after evaluating the prosecution evidence, come to the view that there is sufficient, but untested, evidence to call for an answer by the accused.

In my view, the evidence referred to by Justice Zabidin was sufficient to require Anwar to answer the prosecution case. Notwithstanding the inconsistencies and contradictions of the complainant's testimony, it alone was sufficient to do that. Some of the evidence referred to by the judge was capable, if accepted, of corroborating the complainant.

Justice Zabidin set 6 June 2011 for the defence to present its case.

CHAPTER 9
Defence case begins; prosecution applies to reopen case

When the court reconvened on 6 June 2011 to start the defence case, Anwar's lawyers once again applied to Justice Zabidin to disqualify himself on account of bias. He refused to do so and the matter went on appeal to the Court of Appeal. The case was then adjourned to 13 July 2011.

Justice Zabidin set aside three weeks for the defence case to be heard and ordered that the trial commence on 8 August 2011. Anwar's lawyers already had their own witnesses lined up and ready to call, but they also wanted access to the witnesses the prosecution had subpoenaed to testify but had not called as part of its case. Karpal Singh asked the judge to order the prosecution to make its witnesses available to them to be interviewed. The judge reserved his decision to consider the request.

Judge orders prosecution to make witnesses available to defence for interview

At the start of the hearing on Monday, 8 August, Justice Zabidin unexpectedly ordered the prosecution to make 15 witnesses available to the defence. He adjourned the proceedings for a week to allow them to conduct the interviews.

The interviews were intended to be an informal process. They were not conducted in court, and the judge and prosecution would not be present. It was simply a means by which the defence could informally speak with a proposed witness to assess whether to call them as part of the defence case. The interviews were private and what was said was not to be on the public record unless the parties to them chose to say what had been discussed.

It had been anticipated that Justice Zabidin would ask the defence to subpoena these witnesses to testify, as was the usual procedure, but in this instance, he simply ordered for them to be made available for interview. The witnesses included Prime Minister Najib Razak and his wife Datin Seri Rosmah Mansor. "The defence has the right to interview the witnesses on the condition they are willing," he told the parties. Of course, the defence was not bound to call any of the persons it interviewed to testify.

Persons served with a subpoena are not obliged to participate in any interview process, but they must attend court to testify. However, they may object and apply to the court to set it aside. Former Prime Minister Mahathir Mohamad was able to avoid testifying in one of Anwar's previous trials after successfully challenging a witness subpoena.

The prosecution took the view that the judge's ruling meant that any witnesses sought by Anwar would be made available to be interviewed by the defence, but that they were not legally bound to testify. However, they objected to Anwar being present at the interviews on the ground that he was capable of intimidating prospective witnesses. Karpal stated that the witnesses would be bound by the court's ruling and said, "Anwar has the right to be there. He's the accused."

The application was heard the following day. Justice Zabidin ordered that Anwar could be present at the interviews, but he would not be allowed to question the people being interviewed.

Defence interviews witnesses

The defence had originally told the court that it wanted the prosecution to make 15 witnesses available for interview, but ultimately Anwar's lawyers did not interview all of them.[1] Among the witnesses they interviewed were Anwar's driver, Abdullah Sani Said, and his bodyguard, Mokhtar Mustafa. Both men were apparently with Anwar on the night he went to the condominium where the sexual assault was alleged to have taken place.

Two other alibi witnesses were Haji Hasanuddin Abdul Hamid, the owner of a condominium adjoining the unit where the offence allegedly occurred, and his wife, Noor Sham Abdul Hamid. They were scheduled to be interviewed on Thursday, 11 August. As the interviews were private, we do not know exactly what was said when they attended, but it was expected they would say that Anwar was with them in their unit and not in the condominium where the offence was alleged to have occurred. In the end, they were not called to testify as witnesses on behalf of the defence. No formal reason was given, but Anwar later said in his dock statement that the police had intimidated Hasanuddin by interrogating him for over 30 hours. Anwar gave it as one of the reasons why the defence chose not to call them to testify.

Hasanuddin's two Indonesian maids were also to be interviewed. However, one of them could not be found. Karpal expressed the fear that some of the witnesses had been intimidated and may be reluctant to testify.

Four other witnesses the defence wanted to interview were former Inspector-General of Police Musa Hassan, Senior Assistant Commissioner Mohd Rodwan, Prime Minister Najib and his wife. The defence did not expect any of them to voluntarily appear to be interviewed;

---

1   We simply do not know how many or who the defence interviewed because the interviews were private. We only know whom they interviewed when their names were mentioned in court or to the media. The defence was also playing loose with the number of witnesses it wanted to interview so as to delay the process for tactical reasons. In the end, they did not interview the full number they asked for.

they took that view based on an affidavit filed at court by Deputy Prosecutor Mohd Hanafiah Zakaria. In the affidavit, he stated that the four witnesses refused to be interviewed as they considered themselves not to be material witnesses to the charge, and he reported them saying that they would only testify if they were subpoenaed to do so.

PM Najib and his wife refuse to be interviewed

On Friday 12 August, PM Najib and his wife unexpectedly appeared at the court complex. It was a brief appearance lasting a matter of minutes. According to Anwar's lawyers, Mr Najib had told them that both he and his wife were not prepared to be interviewed by the defence. As the PM left the court building, he told the media: "...as a Malaysian citizen, I must respect the decision made by the judge, regardless of [my] position." He declined to say what he had told Anwar's lawyers, but added, "I know my rights and I have conveyed them to the lawyer representing Anwar, and Anwar was also present there."

Mr Najib and his wife did not attend in answer to a witness summons, but went voluntarily to the interview obviously in response to the judge's order that the prosecution make the witnesses available. The PM's comments indicate that. However, they could not be compelled to participate in the interview and that is exactly what happened. If they were not prepared to cooperate, then the only option for the defence was to take formal steps to compel them to attend court to testify on behalf of the defence. Anwar's lawyers immediately issued and served witness summons on both of them.

...and apply to strike out witness summons

As they were entitled to do, Mr Najib and his wife applied to have the witness summons served on them by the defence set aside. The applications were ultimately heard on 3 October 2011.

Anwar said outside the court: "...these witnesses were offered to us. When they refused to cooperate Prime Minister Najib said that 'if subpoenaed, I will attend'. And now he has applied to set aside."

Recall that Mohd Saiful had testified that he had gone to see Najib (who was at that time deputy prime minister) at his house two days before the alleged offence. He said that he had met with Najib for an hour during which time he told the DPM that Anwar had sexually assaulted him. He claimed that Najib told him to report the matter to the police. Najib initially denied meeting with Mohd Saiful, but later conceded that he had met with him to discuss education scholarships. Mohd Saiful also met with Mohd Rodwan (then deputy director of the Criminal Investigation Department of the Royal Malaysian Police Force) in Room 619 at the Concorde Hotel in Kuala Lumpur.

Senior criminal lawyer Hisyam Teh Poh Teik, whom Karpal playfully dubbed 'Lord of Thunder' for his booming voice, represented PM Najib and his wife. He submitted that his clients had no material or relevant evidence to provide to the court. He said that although Najib in his affidavit admitted that he had met Mohd Saiful two days before the alleged offence, there was no connection to the charge faced by Anwar. What transpired between them during the meeting was not relevant to the case.

Teh also submitted that it was for the party that issued and served the witness summons (i.e. the defence) to establish on the balance of probabilities that the proposed witnesses could give relevant and material evidence at the trial.

He further submitted that although parties could summon witnesses to testify at a trial, it would be an abuse of process if the true purpose was *male fide* and intended to "provoke confrontation" or brought out of "spite or to annoy". He submitted that it was clear from Anwar's affidavit in support of the witness summons that the focus was on what happened at that meeting and that it was no more than a "fishing expedition".

He read from the affidavits filed in support of the applications in which Najib and his wife "stressed there was no conspiracy whatsoever against Anwar and nor did they instruct anyone to fabricate incriminating evidence against the accused". He added: "The law, as it stands, allows both the applicants to have the subpoenas set aside if the party requesting the summons to be issued cannot pass the twin tests of relevancy and materiality."

In reply, Karpal told the court that the purpose of the witness summons was to obtain clarification and explanation of Mohd Saiful's meeting with Najib, which Najib's former special officer had said lasted for an hour. He said that was a substantial amount of time and the defence wanted to know what actually transpired. He submitted that the prime minister was in a position to give relevant and material evidence as, if what he said in his affidavits were correct, this would impinge on the credibility of Mohd Saiful. He said that what was said to Najib at the meeting was directly relevant in assessing Mohd Saiful's state of mind and whether he was "frightened or whether the prime minister would have expected him to follow his advice". Karpal denied that the witness summons were motivated by *male fide*. He said that the prime minister and his wife had refused to be interviewed, which left the defence with no option other than to issue witness summons.

Again it is to be recalled that the sexual assault — which was the subject of the charge — allegedly happened two days *after* Mohd Saiful had met with Mr Najib. Karpal's point was that Mohd Saiful's mental state was relevant because on his own account, after the meeting with Najib and receiving advice to report the sexual activity to the police, he allowed himself yet again to be sodomised by Anwar.

Karpal also submitted that the PM's wife had given a witness statement to the police which had not been disclosed to the defence on the basis that it was privileged. He argued that the statement had been given pursuant to section 112 of the Criminal Procedure Code which allowed the police to "examine orally any person supposed to be acquainted with the facts and circumstances of the case". It further required the police officer to reduce any statement made by that person into writing. The witness was bound to answer all questions relating to the case and was legally bound to tell the truth. He argued that because Datin Seri Rosmah had refused to be interviewed, the only way her evidence could be disclosed to the court was by allowing her to testify. He further said: "It is obvious under s. 112 she is 'supposed to have been acquainted with the facts and circumstances of the case...' and that her evidence was relevant and material."

Justice Zabidin reserved his decision until 6 October.

When the proceedings resumed, Justice Zabidin delivered his decision in favour of the applicants and set aside the witness summons. He gave very brief reasons, stating only that "after going through the affidavits and submissions, I find that the respondents [Anwar's lawyers] have failed to show the relevancy and materiality of both Najib and Rosmah to the trial."

When speaking to the media outside the courtroom, Anwar said he was disappointed with the court's ruling. "Of course, I'm disappointed because both of them were clearly involved. We have evidence to support that ... Our position is that this was planned. Now he [Najib] should come and deny it," he said. He added that the prosecution had offered them as witnesses. "[So] if they are not relevant, why were they offered?"

Karpal said the defence would appeal against the decision at the Court of Appeal the next day. He said he was also disappointed that the judge did not give any reasons for the decision to set aside the summons. "He ought to have given the reasons," said Karpal.

Defence case begins; Anwar makes statement from the dock

At the commencement of the first day of the defence case on Monday, 22 August 2011, Justice Zabidin explained to Anwar the options that were available to him — to remain silent, to make a statement from the dock, or to testify in the witness box and be subject to cross-examination — and asked him to make his choice. Anwar elected to make a statement from the dock.

The option of making a statement from the dock is an old practice of English law still permitted in Malaysia. It has now been abolished as an option in most other countries. If an accused elects to make a statement from the dock, he or she will not be liable to be cross-examined. But it is part of the evidentiary material before the court, which the trial judge must consider in arriving at a verdict. The weight to be given to it is one for the trial judge to decide; as the statement is not made on oath or tested by cross-examination, it does not carry as much weight as testimony given and tested under oath.

In his statement from the dock, Anwar said that he had chosen not to give evidence under oath because the trial was so contrived against him both in a legal and political sense. Below is a summary of Anwar's statement:

1. The complainant's allegations were a pure fabrication.

2. The prosecution had failed to discharge its duties professionally. It had consistently refused to disclose material critical to the defence that would enable it to meet the prosecution case, including the prosecution witness list, the primary hospital examination notes written by Mohd Saiful's medical examiners at Hospital Kuala Lumpur, witness statements (including that of the complainant), and forensic samples and exhibits for independent examination and verification — all of which Anwar claimed had severely prejudiced him.

3. The forensic evidence adduced by the prosecution was either a "pure fabrication" or the product of incompetence and gross negligence. The experts called by the defence would say that the results produced by the government chemist were totally inconsistent with the known history of the samples and contrary to scientific experience.

4. The chain of custody of the samples obtained by the doctors at the examination of Mohd Saiful was broken because it was not established they were the samples analysed by Dr Seah Lay Hong of the Chemistry Department. The police accessed the tamperproof bag into which the samples had been placed, ostensibly to relabel the containers before any analysis had taken place. Dr Seah also failed to observe the protocols and guidelines of her own laboratory when dealing with the samples.

5. It was implausible that a 60-year-old man with a history of back injury could forcibly commit an act of sodomy against the will of "a man in his early 20s, a six-footer, physically fit and robust and with powerful connections in the top police brass as well as the political elite with access to the very inner sanctum of power".

6. There was no physical injury to the complainant's anus and rectum particularly as he was alleging non-consensual anal penetration and which he described as "painful and coarse". Mohd Saiful had also admitted bringing lubricant to the condominium and voluntarily applying it to his anus before being anally penetrated, which was hardly consistent with an unwilling party.

7. The behaviour of the complainant after the alleged sexual act was inconsistent with a person who has been sexually penetrated against their will. Mohd Saiful did not immediately report the assault or seek medical attention, but instead attended an

opposition party function the following day and joined a meeting of the Anwar Ibrahim Club at the house of the accused.

8. The role of the prime minister, his wife and senior police officers, and their involvement with Mohd Saiful before the alleged offence occurred was evidence of a political conspiracy against him.

9. The police had by their intimidation and harassment of the alibi witnesses "scuttled" his defence.

Anwar also stated that the trial judge had failed to ensure a fair trial as evidenced by:

1. his refusal during the course of the trial to order disclosure of material critical to Anwar's defence, most of which the judge thought was sufficiently relevant to the case and which he also thought fairness required that he should order it to be disclosed to the accused before his trial. The judge's failure to fairly and properly exercise his judicial discretion to order disclosure was contrary to Malaysian law and also violated the international standards expected of a modern state which purported to practise the rule of law.

2. his failure to respond during the course of the trial to several attempts by persons hostile to Anwar to discredit him by commenting on aspects of the trial. Examples included whether the accused should provide samples of his DNA, blaming the defence for the delay of the proceedings and reporting on matters that were the subject of a suppression order. These public comments were made in defiance of the trial judge's orders. They were made by Umno officials and politicians, including the prime minister, and orchestrated through the controlled electronic and print media, such as *Utusan Malaysia*, *Berita Harian*, the *New States Times* and

TV3. The constant comments by the prime minister and Umno officials in the media and adverse comments on the progress of the trial were calculated to discredit Anwar and influence the trial judge.

3. his failure to respond appropriately or at all to the flagrant act of leaking and publishing in the media of prosecution submissions before the matter was heard in court.

4. his failure to order that witnesses critical to Anwar's defence attend the trial to testify, in circumstances where their involvement was patently material to the issues at trial. These witnesses related, said Anwar, to the circumstances in which Mohd Saiful came to make his early complaints against him. Nothing could be more material to the credit of the complainant.

5. his finding that the complainant was a "truthful witness" at the close of the prosecution case and before hearing all of the evidence, which clearly showed pre-judgement and bias against Anwar.

6. his finding that the complainant had corroborated himself by complaining to the medical doctors of sexual assault, which was a glaring error of law and contrary to the forensic evidence.

7. his acceptance without hesitation of the prosecution forensic evidence as corroborative of the complainant's account in circumstances where there were obvious concerns about how those samples were obtained, labelled, stored and analysed.

8. his ignoring the fact that Mohd Saiful's intimate affair with a member of the prosecution team would have given him access to the statements of other prosecution witnesses and, as such, would have plainly compromised the prosecution case to the prejudice of the accused.

9. his failure to apply the proper test of assessing the strength of

the evidence at the close of the prosecution case, namely finding the case proved and the complainant's account to be truthful in circumstances where he had not even heard the defence case.

10. his refusal to exclude the evidence of his DNA obtained unlawfully from his cell after his arrest.

Defence witnesses called to testify

It was clear that Anwar's lawyers would rely heavily on expert witnesses to debunk the prosecution's claim that the forensic evidence corroborated the complainant's testimony.

Anwar after all had been charged with an act of sodomy. That meant an allegation that he had penetrated the complainant's anus with his penis. The prosecution not only relied on the testimony of the complainant but also scientific evidence which, for the most part, was the DNA analysis that claimed to link Anwar to sexual activity with the complainant.

If semen had been obtained from Mohd Saiful's rectum, then it would be significant evidence of recent penile penetration. In a practical sense that is correct, but perhaps it was put more accurately by defence expert witness Professor David Wells when he testified that it would be a finding consistent with a "penetrative event with ejaculation". However it might be expressed, if Anwar's DNA had been extracted from the sample of semen found in Mohd Saiful's rectal passage, then that may be accepted as evidence that he was the person who had committed the act of penetration.

During the prosecution case, the defence lawyers vigorously challenged the sufficiency of the medical examination and the failure of the medical staff from Hospital Kuala Lumpur (HKL) to accurately record the complainant's history and their findings. They also questioned the integrity of the samples taken from Mohd Saiful by the medical staff. In particular, they criticised the incorrect labelling and storage of the containers holding the samples before they were sent for analysis. Finally, the defence challenged the conclusions made by prosecution expert witnesses about their conclusions from the DNA analysis.

The defence called three medical witnesses: Dr Mohd Osman Abdul Hamid, who conducted the first medical examination on Mohd Saiful, forensic expert Professor David Wells, and DNA expert Dr Brian McDonald.

Defence calls Dr Mohd Osman

The first witness was Dr Osman, the doctor at Hospital Pusrawi who first examined Mohd Saiful. He testified on 23 August 2011, the day following Anwar's defiant dock statement.

For some reason, the prosecution did not call the doctor to testify, which was strange as he was obviously a material witness being the first person to see and examine Mohd Saiful after the alleged sexual assault. Dr Osman was an important witness because whatever the complainant said to him at the medical examination was relevant to the general assessment of his credibility. Anything that Mohd Saiful might have said later that was inconsistent with this first complaint was capable of impeaching his credit. Furthermore, Dr Osman was also the first medical doctor to examine the patient for any evidence of injury consistent with anal penetration. He found none. There was no evidence of rectal bleeding or any injury to the anus.

Dr Osman recorded in his report that Mohd Saiful complained to him of "pain in the anus when passing motion". He testified that he asked the patient whether he was constipated and if there had been any bleeding from the anus. Mohd Saiful said only that there was "just pain". He also recorded in his report that the complainant told him he was "assaulted by the introduction of plastic into the anus". He testified he was told about the "introduction of plastic" after he had completed the examination. He said that Mohd Saiful also told him that he had been penetrated by a "VIP" and that he was "scared to go to the police and make a report". Dr Osman said he told Mohd Saiful that he should go to a government hospital to be properly examined.

There are interesting aspects of Mohd Saiful's complaint to Dr Osman about his anus being penetrated by a plastic object. When Mohd Saiful was cross-examined by defence counsel, he denied ever having said that to Dr Osman. When challenged about this point, Dr Osman was unshaken and responded, "Saiful told me that and I recorded it [in my notes] at the same time and date".

There was no apparent reason why Dr Osman would not tell the truth. When the defence had finished questioning Dr Osman, he was then cross-examined by the prosecution. However, no motive to lie was put to him nor was anything suggested to him that would even give rise to a suspicion that was so. Dr Osman had also recorded what Mohd Saiful had told him, so to that extent his explanation was consistent with contemporaneous examination notes.

So if it is accepted that Mohd Saiful told Dr Osman that a plastic object was inserted into his anus, then what is to be made of that? Was Mohd Saiful confused or was he having difficulty getting his story right, or did he even say it? He did complain that a VIP had penetrated him, so that part was consistent with his final allegation, but the mention of the plastic object was not. Whatever view is taken, it is a pertinent point to be considered when assessing the credibility of the complainant.

Mohd Saiful was recorded by Dr Osman as saying that he was "scared to go to the police and make a report". However, that is hardly consistent with the known facts because he had already done that. He had, on his own admission, met with then DPM Najib and the senior assistant commissioner of police to complain about the sexual assaults allegedly committed against him by Anwar. As such, he could not possibly be embarrassed about making a complaint to the police or fearful of doing so. It was an explanation that lacked credibility.

Most legal systems impose upon the prosecution an obligation to call material witnesses unless, with good reason, the witness is deemed to be unreliable and untruthful. This is because it is expected that the prosecution should act as the model litigant. It should not refuse to call material witnesses because they do not advance the prosecution case. Anwar's lawyers maintain that Dr Osman was not called because his account of the medical examination of Mohd Saiful did not fit within the prosecution case theory.

Defence calls Professor David Wells

The second witness was Professor David Wells, head of forensic medicine at the Victorian Institute of Forensic Medicine and an associate professor in forensic medicine at Monash University, Australia. He has dealt with sexual assault cases over the past 25 years and is a recognised expert in his field.

He testified about a number of issues on the afternoon of 23 August 2011. These included procedures for examining victims of sexual assault, recording the history of a complaint of sexual assault and the nature of the assault, the taking and packaging of samples obtained from complainants and other matters relating to specific medical aspects of the case.

Professor Wells was critical of what he described as inadequate recording of information by the medical doctors at HKL in the hospital's proforma document, which he said was "lacking in key elements". For example, he said it failed to document an adequate history or record of physical findings; there was inadequate information about details of the

THE MEDICAL NOTES OF 28 JUNE 2008 TAKEN BY DR MOHD OSMAN OF HOSPITAL PUSRAWI, TENDERED AS AN EXHIBIT AT THE TRIAL.

(A) MOHD SAIFUL'S COMPLAINT

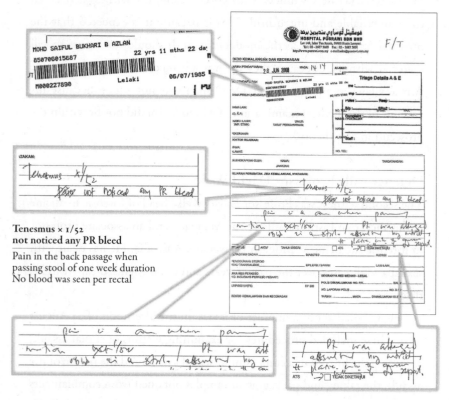

Tenesmus × 1/52
not noticed any PR bleed

Pain in the back passage when
passing stool of one week duration
No blood was seen per rectal

Pain in the anus when passing motion × 1/52
0⁰ blood in the stool

Pain in the back passage when passing stool
of one week duration
No blood in the stool when stool is passed

Pt. was alleged assaulted by introducing plastic ♯ into the anus → wanting to do report

Patient claimed that he was assaulted with a plastic item in the anus thus he wanted to do a medical report

(B) THE DOCTOR'S FINDINGS

O/E: pink ✓
On Examination:
colour is pink –
good colour,
good oxygenation.
Not blue

Conscious, alert ✓
Patient is conscious
and alert

[0] **pallor**
Not pale

Comfortable
General condition
is satisfactory

Afebrile
No fever

P/R   [0] active bleeding
      [0] ulcer or pus seen
      [0] injury shown
      [0] tear seen

Per Rectal examination:
no bleeding from rectum
no wound or evidence of infection
no injury seen
no tear of the rectal/anal area

(signed)
Dr Mohamed Osman Abdul Hamid
MBBS (Rgn)
Pegawai Perubatan
Hospital Pusrawi Sdn. Bhd.

TRO Assault (sodomise)
Advise to go to the government hospital (plan to do police report)

To rule out assault or sodomy

patient's history, physical findings and the actual circumstances of the alleged assault. What information there was in the proforma also lacked sufficient context. In addition, some of the information was not relevant.

He also said the report was "certainly ambiguous at best" when it described the physical findings. He said the doctors found no evidence of trauma or injury, yet they used words such as "conclusive" and "significant" that seemed to qualify that finding. He said he was not sure whether that ambiguity was brought about by "clumsiness, inexperience or bias".

He noted that the proforma contained at least one obvious error. The accused was charged with an act of penetration, but the sexual assault was described in the document as an "attempt". That was not something alleged by the complainant or the prosecution. He was also concerned that only a limited portion of the proforma had been completed. He expected that good practice would require that the proforma be completed in full.

Professor Wells concluded by saying he could not comment on the capacity of the doctor who examined the complainant (Dr Mohd Razali Ibrahim), but there were aspects that raised doubts about his abilities, namely in the way the case history was taken, the partial completion of the proforma document and the way in which the samples were taken. He got the impression the medical examiner was someone without experience.

When cross-examined, Deputy Prosecutor Mohd Yusof suggested to Professor Wells that any apparent omission of details in the proforma may well have been covered in the medical notes (the handwritten clinical notes) recorded by the examining doctors. Professor Wells replied that as he had never seen the notes, he was unable to verify the claim.

The so-called 'medical notes' referred to by the prosecutor had never been provided to the defence. The trial judge had also refused to order the notes to be disclosed to them. As such, Mohd Yusof's assertion that the medical notes covered the deficiency of the proforma was one that was just unknown. What he said in his question to Professor Wells was not evidence, so for the purposes of the trial the judge could not accept that such documents existed. Lack of disclosure of material, which this exchange confirmed was relevant, was one of the long-standing complaints of the defence.

Professor Wells also expressed the view that contamination was a real issue in forensic investigation. Contamination of forensic samples could come from a variety of sources: the medical instruments (for eample, the proctoscope), the medical staff examining the patient, the examination room, the crime scene, police officers and even the laboratory itself. He said it was not possible to guarantee that contamination had not occurred and that considerable caution had to be exercised to minimise the risk.

When taking samples for DNA examination, Professor Wells explained that great care is needed to limit the proliferation of bacteria which could potentially destroy any protein and render the extraction of DNA impossible. To avoid degradation, he suggested that samples should be frozen or air-dried. This was especially crucial, he said, where bacteria, moisture and heat are present as such conditions provide a perfect environment for bacteria to grow, making the samples unsuitable for testing.

In this case, he observed, the samples were stored at room temperature for 43 hours. He thought the samples would have degraded quite quickly and that he would be "exceedingly surprised if DNA could be extracted after 48 hours". He said he expected that the samples would survive for no more than 24 to 36 hours, and that after 72 hours it would be "hardly worthwhile to test for DNA".

Professor Wells was concerned that the police had opened the "tamperproof" bag to relabel the containers before they were sent for analysis. He thought that the "integrity of the sample was critical" and that

Dato' Param Cumaraswamy (standing) speaking to Anwar and Karpal.

he would be "horrified if a sample of mine arrived at the laboratory other than intact in the way it was [originally] sealed". He was also concerned that at least two of the containers apparently had the wrong date marked on them and that no checks were made by the scientist who received them to clarify the matter.

Under cross-examination, Professor Wells was asked about a scientific article by UK researchers that found evidence of spermatozoa from rectal swabs after 65 hours. The article, "Spermatozoa: Their Persistence After Sexual Intercourse", from the *Forensic Science International Journal* (1982) by G.M. Willot and J.E. Allard of the Metropolitan Police Forensic Science Laboratory, London, reported a finding of spermatozoa on a rectal swab after 65 hours and 46 hours on an anal swab. Based on the article, the prosecution suggested to him that there could have been detectable traces much longer than he thought possible.

Professor Wells responded that he was aware of the article, but that in the 30 or so years since that single result, to his knowledge no other similar case had been reported nor had he or his colleagues ever found a similar result. He stated that an aberration did not establish a scientific fact. He considered that apart from this one exception, the medical literature concluded that spermatozoa had a shelf life of about 36 hours. He said that to get an extraction after 36 and up to 48 hours was "exceedingly rare" and that "after 54 hours the chance of obtaining DNA from a living person was zero". He emphasised that those times were reduced if the sample was not kept in anything other than optimal circumstances.

When asked why semen might be found in the rectal passage other than by penile penetration, he replied there were other equally plausible explanations. For example, semen may have been introduced into the rectum when the medical examination took place; it could have been present on the patient's skin in the anal region and introduced into the rectum when the examiner inserted the proctoscope. The situation was complicated by the fact that two proctoscopes had been used to examine Mohd Saiful's rectum. Semen could also have been introduced by the insertion of any other object into the rectum or the sample may have been contaminated during the DNA extraction process.

Professor Wells was asked whether the finding of the absence of injury to the anus and rectum was inconsistent with penile penetration. He agreed it was not, saying that it may indicate either that penetration had not occurred or penetration had occurred but left no signs. He offered some reasons why there would be no findings of injury, such as insufficient force, bruises may not be apparent soon after penetration, and that the injury was minor and had faded away.

Defence calls Dr Brian McDonald

The third witness was Dr Brian McDonald, a molecular geneticist who was called to testify on 26 August 2011. He specialises in the area of DNA testing for forensic and diagnostic matters. He has over 20 years experience in testing and analysing DNA data and is a director of DNA Consultants, a company that provides forensic opinion work. He has given advice in more than 500 cases and testified in at least 100 cases in Australia, Singapore and Brunei.

Dr McDonald was critical of various aspects of the prosecution forensic evidence. Laboratory chemists Dr Seah Lay Hong and Nor Aidora Saedon had testified for the prosecution that they were able to positively match Anwar's DNA with DNA obtained from semen from the complainant's anus (identified by Dr Seah as "Male Y").

He questioned that conclusion. He said that the process of attributing a particular profile from an unknown sample to the donor of a reference sample is essentially never done. It is a matter of statistically measuring the likelihood of a match. The possibility is expressed in terms of "not excluded, but not proven ... you can never say it is that person". He was concerned that these witnesses expressed so confident an opinion without performing any statistical analysis.

During his testimony, issue was taken with the international accreditation of Dr Seah's laboratory. It was clear from documents produced by the defence that the American Society of Crime Lab Directors accredited her laboratory by reference to the Legacy standard for forensic science in 2005. However, the laboratory failed to meet ISO 17025 guidelines in 2010, and was given an extension in that year and a second extension in 2011. The extensions were granted to enable the laboratory to meet those guidelines. It must be said that whatever the status might be of the laboratory in 2010–11, at the relevant time of testing in 2008, the laboratory was certified.

Dr McDonald was critical of the reporting criteria adopted by the chemists. He considered they had failed to apply or conform to internationally recognised reporting standards and testing guidelines. He said they had failed to even comply with the guidelines and protocols of their own laboratory. In fact, he noted that they gave contradictory evidence regarding the testing of samples. In one instance, he said that Nor Aidora, when faced with evidence that clearly indicated a mixture of DNA from different persons, simply ignored her own laboratory guidelines and reported that it was from a single donor. In another instance, when referring to the interpretation of data, he thought that if they "did that at school they would fail".

Dr McDonald was also critical of the way the forensic samples were labelled and handled. He was particularly critical of Dr Seah's failure to enquire about the apparent mislabelling of two sample containers. She had testified that when she noticed the apparent error in labelling, she gave the benefit of the doubt to the person who labelled the containers. She confirmed that she did not make any checks and simply "assumed" that they were samples taken by the medical doctors at the examination. He said that it just was not acceptable for a scientist to assume anything and in his view would be a "sackable offence". It was "absolutely fundamental to laboratory practice" to check if there had been a mistake and to ignore it was "not an option open to the receiving scientist". Defence counsel Ramkarpal Singh asked him further about this aspect of the evidence.

Ramkarpal: If this was a mistake, what should have been done?
Dr McDonald: We have to first verify with the person who wrote it, and if there is a mistake, we have to make a correction and document it. This is a basic procedure.
Ramkarpal: In this case, was there any evidence that it was corrected?
Dr McDonald: No.

Furthermore, no slides were taken of the samples at the time the swabs were taken from Mohd Saiful or soon after. Dr McDonald testified that it had been standard practice for at least 30 years to microscopically examine the samples by using slides before sending them to the laboratory for analysis. He said it was the only way one would know what was on the swabs. It was absolutely essential in cases of alleged sexual assault.

He said that samples once taken should be air-dried (simply by waving the slide in the air) before being frozen at an ideal temperature of -20° Celsius to prevent the sample from degrading. He said storing samples in an airtight container only hastened the degradation because the swabs would remain moist. He would not expect to see sperm 56 hours after ejaculation if the sample was kept at room temperature because that would enhance bacterial activity.

> **Ramkarpal:** Do you agree that DNA samples are likely to degrade if they are not frozen?
>
> **Dr McDonald:** Yes, because bacteria will grow.
>
> **Ramkarpal:** What would be the state of samples taken 56 hours after the alleged incident and [if they] were later kept at room temperature for about 48 hours, before they were sent for analysis? (The Court had earlier heard that specimens from Mohd Saiful's rectum were taken 56 hours after the alleged sodomy. The samples were then handed to DSP Pereira who kept them in a filing cabinet in his office, albeit an air-conditioned room, for another 43 hours before he delivered them to the Chemistry Department.)
>
> **Dr McDonald:** I would not expect to see sperm or DNA from these samples. If I did, it would have been grossly degraded.

Dr McDonald was particularly concerned that the results of the swabs taken from Mohd Saiful were "pristine" and showed no signs of degradation even though they were delivered to Dr Seah for analysis 100 hours after the swabs were taken. When examined by Ramkarpal, he responded saying that "the DNA taken from the rectal region showed pristine results. This was inconsistent as a high level of degradation ought to have been seen."

> **Ramkarpal:** Would the DNA result for the rectal area be consistent with the history of the case?
> **Dr McDonald:** No. For samples that have been kept that long, it does not reflect the case history.

Ramkarpal then went through the results of Dr Seah's DNA analysis, focusing on the samples taken from Mohd Saiful. These had been translated into a graphic format known as an electropherogram that plots DNA fragments by size. The electropherograms were one of the materials disclosed to the defence and Dr McDonald was able to analyse them before testifying. He said he was surprised to see there was no evidence at all of any degradation and found that to be inconsistent with the history of the samples. He then explained that in sexual assault cases, a process called differential extraction had to be done to separate sperm cells and non-sperm cells to obtain DNA profiles. He said that according to Dr Seah, some of the DNA within the mixture did not come from sperm cells. He was asked about that.

> **Ramkarpal:** What if the sample shows a mixture of sperm and non-sperm cells?
> **Dr McDonald:** In this case, some of the DNA did not come from sperm. So there was no appropriate separation.

Ramkarpal: Did the chemist conduct a proper extraction process?

Dr McDonald: She did not do it properly as the complainant's DNA should not have been there. I would say her evidence is a guess.

Ramkarpal: Why is that so?

Dr McDonald: She did not test a sample for sperm cells on a slide to determine if it was totally pure.

Prostatic acid phosphatase (AP) is an enzyme that is present in semen, and if found can be used as a presumptive test for semen. It is customary to perform a spot test on stains or swabs for the presence of AP which, if positive to semen, record a change of colour on the filter paper. Dr Seah conducted the AP test, which she claimed was positive to semen. However, Dr McDonald said that based on the literature one would not expect to see much evidence of spermatozoa or AP after about eight hours from ejaculation.

He concluded: "What we have here is a serious disconnect. Whatever Dr Seah saw wasn't semen obtained 56 hours after the assault and after being kept 43 hours at room temperature. The positive AP activity [she saw] was inconsistent with the history. Bells would be ringing. It would alert a scientist that the result was inconsistent with the known history."

Dr McDonald continued his testimony the next day. His attention was directed to the numbering system adopted by Dr Seah for the samples she analysed. He said that Dr Seah did not identify any swabs as coming from the complainant's rectum. Rather than use the numbering system adopted by the examining doctors at HKL to ensure there was a proper chain of custody, she used her own numbering system. There was an assumption that she analysed samples provided by the HKL doctors, but it was no more than that because there was no record of continuity between them. There was no recorded basis to assume the samples were the same.

The proceedings were adjourned part-heard on 27 August 2011 because the time allocated for trial for the month of August had expired. Dr McDonald did not complete his testimony and testified again when the hearing resumed on 19 September when he was cross-examined by Deputy Prosecutor Mohd Yusof. At the conclusion of his testimony on 21 September, Justice Zabidin adjourned the hearing until the week commencing 3 October.

Prosecution cross-examines Dr McDonald

I was unable to be present at the prosecution's cross-examination of Dr McDonald on 19 September, but I was able to take advantage of the video recordings of the proceedings, an innovative reform implemented by the previous Chief Justice Tun Zaki bin Tun Azmi. There were several issues that arose in Dr McDonald's cross-examination.

(A) DNA FROM "MALE Y"

The prosecution claimed that its forensic analysis had proved that the DNA taken from Mohd Saiful's rectal swabs and identified by Dr Seah as "Male Y" was the DNA of Anwar Ibrahim.

Dr McDonald accepted that the DNA labelled "Male Y" was present in three samples analysed by her, but he claimed the chain of custody had been broken, which supposedly linked the samples she analysed to the samples taken by the examining doctors at HKL. Instead of adopting the description given to the samples by the examining doctors, for no apparent reason she had given each sample her own description. He said by doing that, there was no verification that she had in fact analysed the swabs taken from the complainant.

(B) LABORATORY ACCREDITATION

Mohd Yusof challenged Dr McDonald's claim that the Chemistry Department was not internationally accredited, referring to a certificate that confirmed that it was accredited when the tests were carried out in 2008.

Dr McDonald pointed out in his testimony that the Chemistry Department had operated, since 2010, on a provisional accreditation by virtue of extensions given by the American Society of Crime Lab Directors (ASCLD) by reference to the Legacy standard for forensic science. He maintained that the laboratory had not met ISO 17025 guidelines. Those points were later confirmed by Dr Lim Kong Boon, director of the forensic division of the Chemistry Department. Nevertheless, the laboratory was accredited when it conducted the tests in 2008.

(C) THE PROSTATIC ACID PHOSPHATASE (AP) TEST

When cross-examined by the defence, Dr McDonald had suggested that Dr Seah performed AP testing on the rectal swabs provided to her by HKL and said that the AP test was unsuitable for swabs.

Mohd Yusof said to Dr McDonald that he was mistaken because Dr Seah had told the court that she conducted the test only on the complainant's clothing, not the swabs. Mohd Yusof suggested that Dr McDonald was attempting to mislead the court and put Dr Seah in a bad light.

Dr McDonald replied that he had no intention of misleading the court and that "it was a mistake" on his part. He said, "It wasn't a question of honesty, but my misreading of her testimony."

(D) DR MCDONALD'S EXPERTISE AND EXPERIENCE

The prosecution challenged Dr McDonald's experience in performing DEP (differential extraction process) tests and suggested that his qualifications, which we obtained in 1992, were obsolete.

Dr McDonald conceded that he had not performed a laboratory extraction since 2004, but that did not affect his interpretation of the results. He said he was not a technician but a senior scientist and DEP tests were tasks usually left to junior technicians and robots. By way of example, he said that the senior partner in a law firm would not be answering the telephone at the firm's reception.

He said that he was a senior National Association of Testing Authorities, Australia evaluator of forensic laboratories for the ISO 17025 certification. He explained that although he had obtained his qualifications more than 20 years earlier, he had acquired expertise by working in the field for more than 25 years and by conducting tests and analyses. He explained that his expertise was in interpreting the results.

(e) THE BROPHO CASE

The prosecution confronted Dr McDonald with the Bropho case.[2] It was a decision of the Western Australian District Court in which the trial judge ruled that Dr McDonald should not be permitted to give expert evidence. Mohd Yusof quoted the trial judge as saying there was insufficient evidence before the court that Dr McDonald was an expert in DNA and molecular genetics.

Dr McDonald responded saying: "...this is the opinion of the judge. All I can do is just give my expert evidence. It is up to the court." He then explained that what was called into question was his expertise in the "evaluation of statistical data". The issue in that case was not about DNA testing, but concerned the statistical model of the aboriginal population in the State of Western Australia.

---

2 *Bropho v State of Western Australia* [2007] WADC 77

The judge thought that was an assessment that should be left to a mathematician specialising in genetics. He stated that his qualifications and expertise had been accepted in the 500 cases in which he had given advice and 100 cases in which he had testified at court.

(F) CONTRADICTORY SCIENTIFIC REPORTS

Mohd Yusof also challenged the earlier claims by Dr McDonald and Professor Wells that it was "exceedingly rare" to get a positive sperm cell extraction after more than 20 to 36 hours.

He produced material, apparently from various scientific journals, that suggested there were cases where semen was found well in excess of the time limit of 36 hours. For example, one article claimed to have found semen in the rectum 113 hours after ejaculation. He referred to a research paper published in a medical journal in 1997 by Willott and Ellard entitled "Sexual Assault and Semen Persistence" that reported sperm surviving in the rectum up to 113 hours before being extracted.

Dr McDonald said that although it was "surprising and rare", it was not impossible. He thought there was only a one in 3,000 chance of finding sperm after 56 hours, as in Mohd Saiful's case.

Mohd Yusof then pointed out that compared to the Australian practice of taking rectal swabs no more than 36 hours after sexual intercourse, the recommendation in the United Kingdom was that rectal swabs could be taken up to 72 hours and even after defecation or a shower. He showed Dr McDonald an article regarding research done at the Srinagarind Hospital in Thailand that he claimed had found semen 120 hours after ejaculation and 19 days in the vagina.

Dr McDonald pointed out that, except for a brief excerpt in English, most of the article was in the Thai language. He declined to make assumptions about the findings suggested by it. He also said he was unsure of the source of the article and how the authors came to that conclusion. He added: "Also, it does not mention anal swabs, which is what this case is about. I don't see the relevance of it. You're asking me to take this at face value, but the only face I see is that it is all written in Thai."

Of course, the authors of these articles were not called to testify and explain their findings. Unless Dr McDonald adopted the findings, they could not be accepted as evidence at the trial.

Defence calls Mohd Najwan Halimi

Mohd Najwan was the sixth defence witness. He was a contemporary of Mohd Saiful and had known him since 2003 when they were students at Universiti Tenaga Nasional. He was then an officer at the Selangor economic adviser's office, which is an office held by Anwar Ibrahim. The defence had kept his identity secret until the morning of his testimony on 4 October 2011.

Mohd Najwan told the court that he and Mohd Saiful were in the same orientation group and their rooms were next to each other at the same hostel. Both of them held positions in the university's Student Representative Council; Mohd Saiful was deputy president, while he was secretary.

He testified that he was shocked when he heard that Mohd Saiful was working for Anwar because Mohd Saiful had been pro-Barisan Nasional (BN) during his university days. He told the court: "I was surprised. As far as I knew, he hated Anwar."

He said that Mohd Saiful never idolised Anwar, as he had claimed. He told the court how, some time before March 2008, he saw that Mohd Saiful had posted a BN emblem on his 'Friendster' profile (social networking website) as well as a photo of Anwar with the caption *Anwar Ibrahim pemimpin munafik* ("Anwar Ibrahim a hypocrite leader"). He had also seen photographs of Mohd Saiful posing with BN officials on the profile. He described the complainant as being "publicity crazy and an attention seeker".

Mohd Najwan told the court that he had attended a political rally during the 2008 general election campaign and saw Mohd Saiful with members of Anwar's staff. He was told that Mohd Saiful was there to listen to the speeches. A few weeks later, he learnt that Mohd Saiful had joined Anwar. He said he then sent an email to Anwar warning him that Mohd Saiful could not be trusted. He said in his testimony that Mohd Saiful was "anti-Anwar" and campaigned for BN although he followed Anwar throughout the country.

He admitted during cross-examination by Mohd Yusof that it would not have been unusual for Mohd Saiful to be photographed with government officials as he was a student leader.

Mohd Yusof: Is it something unusual if Mohd Saiful, as a student leader, takes pictures with a leader?

Mohd Najwan: It is not a problem and not unusual.

Mohd Yusof: You said that during your conversation with Mohd Saiful, he did regard Anwar highly?

Mohd Najwan: He said he did not believe Anwar.

Mohd Yusof: The caption which referred to Anwar as "*pemimpin munafik*"— did Mohd Saiful post it?

Mohd Najwan: I believe Mohd Saiful did it.

Mohd Yusof: How do (sic) you feel when in late February 2008, Mohd Saiful was working with Anwar?

Mohd Najwan: I believe he is (sic) not eligible and not fit to work with Anwar.

Mohd Najwan was then asked about the email that he claimed to have sent Anwar.

>**Mohd Yusof:** Why did you send the email?
>
>**Mohd Najwan:** Because I thought Saiful was not fit to work with Anwar.
>
>**Mohd Yusof:** You were more suitable?
>
>**Mohd Najwan:** Many others were.

Defence calls Dr Lim Kong Boon

The defence later that same day called Dr Lim Kong Boon, the director of the forensic division of the Chemistry Department. He said the department was accredited with ASCLD under its Legacy programme for five years from 19 October 2005. When the five-year period expired on 18 October 2010, ASCLD granted three extensions. He said the last extension would expire on 18 January 2012. He explained that the extensions meant that the department was still accredited under the Legacy programme.

It was put to him that the laboratory had not obtained the ISO 17025 certification which was evaluated by ASCLD. He accepted that the Legacy programme was different to international certification under ISO 17025.

When cross-examined by Mohd Yusof, Dr Lim explained that the extension was to provide time for the transition from the Legacy programme to the international programme.

Defence calls Dr Thomas Hoogland

The final witness for the defence was Dr Thomas Hoogland from Munich, Germany. He was called to testify on 6 October 2011. Dr Hoogland's specialty is endoscopic spinal surgery and he has performed more than 14,000 spinal operations.

Dr Hoogland first examined Anwar in 2001 when the opposition leader was in prison. He described Anwar coming to his clinic soon after his release from prison in 2004.

He said that, at the time, Anwar was "in a bad way" and could hardly walk. He diagnosed "significant spinal disc herniation" at L5, damage to L4/5 facet joint on the left and nerve compression causing pain to his legs. He said Anwar's condition was not a result of degenerative change but from an injury suffered after an assault by police in 1998. He performed a laminectomy in 2004 to remove a portion of the vertebral bone called the lamina, which freed the sciatic nerve. He repaired the disc, which healed, but he could not do anything about the nerve that had been damaged by the prolapsed disc. Anwar was hospitalised for three weeks after which his movement improved.

Dr Hoogland told the court of his assessment of Anwar when he reviewed him in 2005. At that time, Anwar complained of back pains "every now and then". The surgeon found that the back muscles were "not in good shape" and thought there had been "some deterioration of his condition". He described how one of the two key back muscles had atrophied to be only half its normal size. He also found a limitation of movement in the hip joints and signs of early arthritis in the hips. He told the court that a range of normal rotation was about 30 to 35 degrees, but Anwar had only 25 degrees "pain free". Extension (leaning backwards) was no more than 10 degrees. Flexion (bending forward) was painful from about 15 degrees.

He said that on 8 September 2011, he reviewed Anwar at his Munich clinic together with other spine surgeons. Their diagnosis was as follows: multi-segmental degeneration of the lumbar spine with muscle atrophy at the L4/5 level; partial function loss of L5 nerve root on the left; nerve root compression/irritation on L4/5 left; active facet joint arthritis L4/5 on both sides with effusion on the left; spondylosis in the segments C4/5 till C6/7; and spinal stenosis C 5/6.

Dr Hoogland was asked about Anwar's capacity to engage in sexual activity, particularly about penetration that was "fast and vigorous", which was the allegation made by Mohd Saiful. He said that it was a sexual act requiring flexion and extension motion, and with Anwar's spine condition, "rigorous and frequent movement would cause significant back pain ... it is very, very unlikely that it was possible with his back."

During cross-examination by Mohd Yusof, Dr Hoogland was shown a video of Anwar entering a lift. In the footage taken on the day of the alleged incident (26 June 2008), Anwar is seen entering the lift, placing a bag he is carrying on the floor, putting on his jacket, then bending to retrieve the bag. It was suggested to him that the video showed Anwar moving and bending freely. Dr Hoogland was asked to comment.

He replied that the nature of the video was such that, while it showed a person entering and leaving the lift, the vision was at a faster speed when the lift was in motion. He said it was impossible to offer an opinion as he could not ascertain the speed with which the person moved. Also, there was no basis to measure pain by looking at the video. He added that he "never said [Anwar] was unable to bend, but there is no indication of pain during flexion or the speed with which he is bending" from the video.

The next part of the proceedings was held in camera at the request of the defence as it concerned actual details of the alleged sexual act. Justice Zabidin allowed me to be present, but it would not be appropriate to publish details of that portion of the evidence. Suffice to say that Dr Hoogland was questioned about it in the context of the alleged sexual act. His evidence on that point did not change at all.

Prosecution applies to reopen case

At the conclusion of Dr Hoogland's testimony, it was anticipated that the defence case would close and that would be the extent of the evidence to be given at trial. However, Mohd Yusof informed the judge that he would be making an application to reopen his case and to call rebuttal evidence. He did not reveal at the time what the evidence might be, but it was obvious that he wished to call expert testimony to counter Dr Hoogland's evidence that it was "very, very unlikely" for Anwar to indulge in "fast and vigorous" sex as described by Mohd Saiful.

It is unusual for the prosecution in a criminal trial to be allowed to reopen its case. The prosecution is expected not to split its case. However, a trial judge has a wide discretion to allow it, if it is thought that the defence evidence could not have been anticipated and the prosecution in that limited circumstance will be allowed to call evidence in rebuttal.

Justice Zabidin adjourned proceedings until the week commencing 17 October 2011, at which time he said he expected the parties to argue the application to call rebuttal evidence.

Prosecution applies to call four witnesses in rebuttal

The court reconvened on Monday, 17 October. The defence advised that following Justice Zabidin's ruling allowing the application of PM Najib and his wife to set aside the witness summons, it would no longer call former Inspector-General of Police Musa Hassan and former Malacca police chief Mohd Rodwan to testify.

Mohd Yusof applied to call four witnesses to rebut the testimony of Dr Hoogland. He said the surgeon had raised new issues and, in particular, had offered the opinion that based on Anwar's medical history, Anwar could not perform any vigorous pelvic activities. Mohd Yusof claimed that this had not been suggested in cross-examination during the prosecution case and "since a witness testified on the inability of Anwar to engage in the action as charged, we would like to apply for leave to call rebuttal witnesses".

Karpal Singh told Justice Zabidin that he had no objection to the prosecution's application to reopen its case. On that basis, the judge granted the application and adjourned the trial to the next day so that witnesses could be called.

Prosecution calls Dr S. Jeyaindran and DSP Jude Pereira

On 18 October, the prosecution called Dr S. Jeyaindran, then a senior consultant physician at HKL to testify. He had examined Anwar Ibrahim on 16 July 2008, the day after his arrest, at the request of the police. The examination was conducted together with senior consultant surgeon Dr Ee Boon Leong.

The reason for the medical examination after Anwar's arrest was obvious. The police did not want the embarrassment of again being accused of assaulting Anwar after he was taken into custody. That had happened in 1998 when Anwar was brought to court with facial injuries and a black eye, and it was later proved that he had been brutally assaulted by the then police chief. Photographs of Anwar were published around the world. The police were right to be cautious and the medical examination would establish that he had not been assaulted this time.

Dr Jeyaindran told the court that he had explained the purpose of the medical examination in detail to Anwar, who was present with his lawyer Sivarasa Rasiah.

Anwar had previously described the examination as "degrading", as he was asked to undress, and his private parts and pubic hair were measured. Upon legal advice, Anwar refused to have any instrument inserted into his anus or give any body samples for the purpose of DNA tests.

The next part of Dr Jeyaindran's testimony was the most important. It related to his observations of Anwar's physical condition at the time he examined him and his record of what Anwar had told him at that time. His testimony about the actual details of the medical examination were held in camera as it involved personal information about the physical examination, and his medical report was tendered as an exhibit. However, part of the report relating to Anwar's medical history obtained from him on 16 July 2008 when he explained having coitus with his wife was not subjected to the in camera order. The prosecution made much of this fact — that if Anwar was capable of having marital sex, he was equally capable of committing the act of sodomy as alleged by Mohd Saiful. Karpal Singh dismissed such a suggestion as fanciful.

Dr Ee Boon Leong was present at court but was not called to testify.

The purpose of DSP Pereira's testimony was simply to provide some continuity as to what happened after Anwar's arrest and the process by which forensic samples were taken, but effectively it did not add much because the purpose of the rebuttal evidence was to rebut the defence assertion that Anwar was incapable of physically performing the sexual act. Pereira testified that he was the one who brought Anwar to Hospital Kuala Lumpur at 8.30 pm on 16 July 2008. He had asked for a medical examination to be done and swabs taken from Anwar's body and nails, as well as blood samples. He said the examination was completed at 11.30 pm.

At the conclusion of the rebuttal evidence, Justice Zabidin adjourned proceedings to hear oral final submissions on 23 and 24 November 2011.

CHAPTER 10
Final submissions

Nothing in this trial seemed to go according to plan. When proceedings resumed on Wednesday 23 November 2011, the defence asked for more time to make submissions, which the judge allowed. As it turned out, both the defence and prosecution filed written submissions setting out their respective cases. But each supplemented these with oral submissions, which were finally made to the court on 12 and 13 December 2011.

Defence makes final submissions

Each of the lawyers in the defence team made oral submissions to the judge focusing on the areas they had been responsible for at trial.

Karpal Singh was first to address the court. He immediately focused on the credibility of the complainant. He listed a series of matters, which he said should be reason enough for the trial judge to re-appraise Mohd Saiful's credibility "since it takes the centre stage in the entire case".

He submitted that it was obvious from the evidence that Mohd Saiful was a "compulsive and consummate liar" and was "lying through his teeth" even though the court had found him to be a truthful witness at the close of the prosecution case. He submitted that this assessment was backed by Mohd Saiful's actions before, during, and after the alleged assault.

(A) MOHD SAIFUL'S CONDUCT INCONSISTENT WITH ACCOUNT GIVEN TO THE POLICE

Karpal submitted that Mohd Saiful's conduct, when he claimed Anwar anally penetrated him, was inconsistent with the account that he gave to the police.

He said it was difficult to believe that Mohd Saiful had acted "like a lamb", obeying Anwar's instructions when he had every opportunity to escape. "There was no evidence the bedroom door was locked. He could have rushed out from the bedroom and the hall. Instead he says the accused invited him to the dining hall and he accepted," said Karpal.

He submitted that there was no apparent physical resistance to Anwar's actions. He said Mohd Saiful was a young man, strong enough to have fended off the alleged unwanted overtures of the accused, but he did not do so.

Karpal submitted that after the alleged sexual assault, Mohd Saiful's behaviour was totally inconsistent with forcible non-consensual sex. He said the complainant had remained in the company of the accused for 20 minutes having coffee and some curry puffs. "He did not show any signs of distress. His credibility is substantially damaged by these revelations," submitted Karpal, adding that Mohd Saiful had every opportunity to complain to the occupants of the adjoining apartment or to the security guards on duty that night at the condominium complex. He also pointed out that the next day, Mohd Saiful attended a function at the Parti Keadilan Rakyat headquarters and a meeting at Anwar's house without any apparent signs of distress.

Karpal submitted that "these actions militate against a non-consensual sexual intercourse against the order of nature as repeatedly asserted by Saiful in court."

(B) MOHD SAIFUL DELAYED IN MAKING HIS COMPLAINT

Karpal submitted that Mohd Saiful's credibility was further eroded because he failed to lodge a police report until two days after the alleged incident. "There is no acceptable explanation for this delay," said Karpal.

(C) MOHD SAIFUL FOUND TO BE AN UNTRUTHFUL WITNESS

Anwar with Karpal Singh.

Karpal reminded the court that during his cross-examination, Mohd Saiful denied ever telling Dr Osman of Hospital Pusrawi that a piece of plastic had been inserted into his anus. He said, "Mohd Saiful clearly lied when he said he had not told Dr Mohd Osman about this." Dr Osman testified at the trial that Mohd Saiful had told him that plastic was introduced into his anus and he had recorded it in his examination notes.

(D) ANWAR'S BACK PROBLEM PRECLUDED HIM FROM COMMITTING SODOMY

Karpal reminded Justice Zabidin of the testimony of orthopaedic surgeon Dr Thomas Hoogland who had said that Anwar's mobility was limited due to the degeneration of his spine through severe arthritis and nerve damage. Dr Hoogland, he said, thought it was "very unlikely that a man of Anwar's age could have preformed the sexual act described by the complainant because of his back problem. He could not have carried out vigorous pelvic or hip activities without experiencing pain."

It is to be recalled that Mohd Saiful had described at trial the sexual act as *"laju dan rakus"* ("fast and vigorous"). Karpal went on to say that "what was stated by Saiful is rendered unworthy of belief when considered in the light of the evidence adduced by Dr Hoogland".

(E) MOHD SAIFUL'S AFFAIR WITH JUNIOR PROSECUTOR COMPROMISED HIS CREDIBILITY AS A TRUTHFUL WITNESS

Karpal asked Justice Zabidin to recall Mohd Saiful and to summon junior Deputy Prosecutor Farah Azlina Latif to "ensure a just decision in the case".

He submitted: "Until her alleged affair became public among the prosecution team, she would have been privy to the investigation papers. This, in turn, would have created the opportunity for Mohd Saiful to have access to the investigation papers and accordingly, tailor his evidence to the detriment of the defence."

(F) 'LUBRICANT' NEVER TESTED

Mohd Saiful had testified that he was asked by Anwar to bring some KY-Gel, which he said was used to facilitate the penile penetration of his anus by the accused. Karpal submitted that the evidence of the KY-Gel, which seemed to be an "afterthought by the prosecution", was not admissible evidence as it was never proven by laboratory tests that the contents were, indeed, lubricant.

(G) NO PROOF MOHD SAIFUL WAS EVER IN THE APARTMENT

Sankara Nair was the second member of the defence team to address the court. He submitted: "Saiful was never in Unit 11-5-1 or seen entering the unit."

He further said: "All the prosecution produced was a bad CCTV recording which is not even in full real-time, allegedly indicating that Saiful was in the vicinity of Desa Damansara condo. This is grossly inadequate and has no evidential value."

(H) MOHD SAIFUL HAD A MOTIVE TO MAKE FALSE ACCUSATION AGAINST ANWAR BECAUSE OF HIS PAST POLITICAL INVOLVEMENT WITH THE RULING PARTY AS HIS MEETING WITH NAJIB CONFIRMED

Sankara Nair also took up the theme of political involvement. He stated that it was the defence position that the prosecution was part of a "devious conspiracy by the powers-that-be to destroy the political career of Anwar" and prevent him from ever becoming prime minister. "It is as clear as daylight that the fingerprints of Najib Tun Razak are all over this sordid plot notwithstanding the desperate attempts by various quarters to smudge them," he said.

He also said that Mohd Saiful's meeting with then DPM Najib gave rise to a suspicion of some foul play, at the very least, and, at worst, of "some nefarious machination at work". He added that the prime minister's contradictory answers compounded the matter. "This begs the questions: Why did Najib not come clean the first time he was asked about this? What was there to hide? Why did he have to resort to lies?"

(I) NO RELIABLE OR ANY FORENSIC EVIDENCE TO CORROBORATE MOHD SAIFUL'S ACCUSATION

Ramkarpal Singh then made lengthy submissions about the prosecution DNA evidence, which he said "raised more questions than answers".

He submitted that the prosecution had failed to rebut the testimony of the forensic witnesses called by the defence, which he said raised a number of critical issues. For example, how could the court conclude beyond a reasonable doubt that the DNA from "Male Y" came from sperm cells?

"The evidence suggests that DNA was not retrieved from the anus of the victim but elsewhere," he said.

He also submitted that the local DNA experts had failed to adhere to their own guidelines, adding that the court should not ignore the very real possibility that the unidentified DNA profile could have belonged to someone who handled the items. "If the rectal samples were indeed taken from the anus of Saiful, why were they in pristine condition? No DNA would be in such condition if it has been in an anus for 56 hours," said Ramkarpal.

In their closing submissions at the High Court, Anwar's lawyers in summary argued that the complainant was not a credible witness, that the DNA evidence was flawed, and that the evidence adduced did not even prove that Anwar had committed the act of sodomy or even had the intention of committing it.

Karpal Singh concluded his remarks saying, "It is submitted that the defence has cast a reasonable doubt on the prosecution's case. The evidence adduced by the defence has demolished all semblance of truth in Mohd Saiful's evidence." He said that Anwar should be acquitted and discharged. The defence was right to focus upon the deficiencies of the forensic evidence.

Karpal said that Justice Zabidin had found there was a case to answer, relying upon the testimony of the prosecution expert witnesses to corroborate the account given by Mohd Saiful that Anwar had penetrated his anus with his penis and ejaculated. At the time, he expressed full confidence in Mohd Saiful's reliability and truthfulness as a witness. That was before the defence case was called.

He said the expert witnesses called by the defence challenged the accuracy and reliability of the DNA findings. They attacked the way in which forensic samples were taken from the complainant, and how those samples were stored by the police and analysed at the government laboratory. Their testimony raised significant doubts about the reliability of the prosecution evidence.

Prosecution makes final submissions

The prosecution made final submissions to the trial judge on 13 December 2011. Written submissions had been filed, but were supplemented by the oral submissions of Deputy Prosecutor Mohd Yusof.

(A) ANWAR'S DOCK STATEMENT NO MORE THAN A BARE DENIAL AND HIS REFUSAL TO RESPOND TO THE ALLEGATION ESSENTIALLY AMOUNTED TO A FAILURE TO ENTER A DEFENCE

Mohd Yusof first focused his attack on the dock statement made by Anwar. He reminded the judge that Anwar had not given evidence on oath and subjected himself to cross-examination. It meant, he said, that the court should give Anwar's statement limited weight. He submitted it was not evidence, but rather a bare denial without any explanation.

He pointed out that Anwar's denial did not dispute Mohd Saiful's claim to have gone to the condominium or that Anwar's chief of staff had sent him there. Furthermore, Anwar had failed to account for the finding of his semen in Saiful's rectum. Mohd Yusof said that Anwar's failure to respond to these issues amounted to "a failure to enter a defence and must amount to an admission of these facts."

Something needs to be said at this point about that submission because it raises significant issues that affect perceptions of the trial. Mohd Yusof's characterisation of Anwar's dock statement as being no more than a "bare denial" is true to an extent, but he went further than that in his submission. He said that the dock statement was akin to remaining silent when called upon to enter his defence because no material evidence was placed before the court for consideration. That submission was inappropriate because it not only reversed the onus of proof, it also misrepresented the nature of a dock statement.

Anwar elected to give a dock statement from the three options available to him at law. It was patently unfair of the prosecution to criticise him for doing no more than what he was entitled to do. No adverse inference may be drawn because of the exercise of that right. It would be inappropriate and wrong at law to do so.

The dock statement contained a categorical denial of guilt. It did not need to do anything more than that. It is not meant to be a comprehensive rebuttal of all of the prosecution evidence. A dock statement must be considered in the context of all of the evidence called by an accused. What weight to be given to it by the trial judge is a matter for him to decide. Of course, it carries less weight than testimony tested by cross-examination on oath, but it is denial of guilt nevertheless and is evidence that must be taken into account.

Mohd Yusof suggested that the prosecution evidence had not been challenged by the accused's 'bare denial'. That was not so. The accused called various witnesses to testify on his behalf. It is not for an accused to create reasonable doubt. The prosecution must overcome any doubts created by that evidence before it can prove its case.

The suggestion that a 'mere denial' amounts to an admission of the prosecution facts is wrong at law. A denial of guilt puts into contest all of the evidence called by the prosecution to prove the charge. However, if facts are unchallenged, a judge may more readily accept them as having been proved. Mohd Yusof referred to some facts that may fall within that category, for example, Anwar's presence at the condominium complex on the day that Mohd Saiful delivered an envelope and that Anwar had gone to the fifth floor. But those facts do not amount to an admission that the sexual act alleged by Mohd Saiful occurred. The sexual act was categorically denied and must be proven by the prosecution.

Mohd Yusof also submitted that Anwar's failure to explain his semen found in the complainant's rectum meant that "as a result, the conclusive finding of semen is left unchallenged by the defence". That is a logical nonsense. How can you explain something you say is not there? And who says it is conclusive? Anwar's denial rejects the allegation of anal penile penetration. The defence also called expert testimony to debunk the so-called "conclusive finding" that semen was present in the rectum. If the defence evidence had raised a reasonable doubt, then the trial judge cannot rely upon it to corroborate Mohd Saiful's complaint.

A plea of not guilty puts the burden on the prosecution to prove the charge. The onus of proof never shifts to an accused, who may remain silent and not testify. If he does not testify or if he gives a statement from the dock, the judge cannot draw any inference of guilt from that fact. An accused need not call any evidence on his behalf and merely test the sufficiency of the prosecution case against him. Yet again, no adverse inference may be drawn, for to do so would reverse the onus of proof.

The threshold question for a judge at the conclusion of a trial is whether he is satisfied on the whole of the evidence that the prosecution has proved the guilt of an accused beyond a reasonable doubt. It is not for the accused to raise a reasonable doubt — as Mohd Yusof had suggested — but for the prosecution to prove the charge and each part of the charge to that standard of proof. An accused is presumed to be innocent and does not have to prove anything, let alone his innocence.

A judge's task is not to choose between opposing stories, but to determine the question of whether the State has proved its case beyond reasonable doubt.

(B) NO EVIDENCE OF POLITICAL CONSPIRACY

Mohd Yusof submitted there was no evidence at all of any political conspiracy against Anwar, and even if there was some political involvement it simply was not relevant to the charged offence. The meeting with Mr Najib, the then deputy prime minister, occurred before the offence was committed (which was the reason why the judge set aside the defence witness summons served on the prime minister to testify).

Justice Zabidin was also asked to reject Mohd Najwan Halimi's testimony. Mohd Najwan was the surprise witness called by the defence and had known Mohd Saiful since their student days in 2003. He told the court that Mohd Saiful was not an Anwar supporter, but had always been a Barisan sympathiser. He claimed to have warned Anwar that Mohd Saiful was "not to be trusted". Mohd Yusof suggested that Mohd Najwan was not a credible witness and was someone who was connected with Anwar and, in any event, his testimony did not change the impact of the forensic evidence.

(C) DR OSMAN WAS UNTRUTHFUL WHEN HE SAID THAT MOHD SAIFUL HAD TOLD HIM THAT A PLASTIC IMPLEMENT HAD BEEN INSERTED INTO HIS ANUS

Dr Osman was the first medical doctor to physically examine Mohd Saiful when he presented himself at the private Hospital Pusrawi on 28 June 2008. He recalled that during the examination, Mohd Saiful told him that for the previous few days his anus was painful and that a "plastic" item had been inserted into it. Mohd Saiful denied saying this when he testified, but Dr Osman maintained it was said to him.

If what Dr Osman recorded in his notes was true, then it potentially affected Mohd Saiful's credit. It was a curious thing for Mohd Saiful to say to the doctor, but his outright denial of having said it at all suggested that he was not being truthful in his testimony. The deputy prosecutor had challenged Dr Osman when he cross-examined him, suggesting to him that it was not said and that he was being untruthful. The doctor held firm in his recollection.

Mohd Yusof submitted that Dr Osman's report was consistent with the examination at HKL a few hours later. But when it came to his claim that Mohd Saiful had mentioned the insertion of a plastic object into his anus, he suggested to the judge that there was an apparent inconsistency in his testimony as to when that comment was recorded in his medical notes. He stated at one point that the notes were written in front of Mohd Saiful, then a little later said he had written the notes immediately after seeing the patient.

He said that Dr Osman had later provided a copy of his report to the defence lawyers. "What kind of doctor does this?" he asked. Mohd Yusof concluded that because of that, the judge should not accept Dr Osman as a credible and truthful witness.

(D) DR HOOGLAND COULD NOT RELIABLY DESCRIBE THE CONDITION OF ANWAR'S BACK IN 2008 BECAUSE HE HAD NOT SEEN HIM DURING THAT PERIOD

The orthopaedic surgeon testified how he had treated Anwar for a bad back condition caused by assaults made against him when he was first taken into police custody in 1998. In 2004, after Anwar's release from prison following a successful appeal against his conviction, he performed surgery on Anwar's back at his clinic in Germany.

The effect of Dr Hoogland's testimony was that Anwar was incapable of performing the sexual act described by Mohd Saiful because of the disability brought about by a degenerative condition in his spine and nerve damage. This was significant evidence for the defence.

However, Mohd Yusof submitted that Dr Hoogland had seen Anwar in 2005 after successfully performing the operation, which he accepted had improved his condition. But he did not see Anwar again until 2011, when he was asked to reassess his patient. Mohd Yusof claimed that the surgeon was merely speculating as to the status of Anwar's spinal condition in 2008 when the offence occurred and what limitations he might have, if any, at that time.

The prosecutor relied upon the security video recorded at the condominium on 26 June 2008, which showed Anwar moving freely and apparently not troubled by any back pain. The doctor who examined Anwar at the lock-up immediately after his arrest a month after the incident saw no evidence of pain as he removed his clothing and shoes. Mohd Yusof urged the judge to reject the testimony of Dr Hoogland as being no more than speculation that went beyond his expertise.

"At no time," submitted Mohd Yusof, "did Anwar call any evidence, medical or otherwise, that in 2008 he was troubled by back pain or restricted in his movements." He concluded by saying that the court did not have the benefit of a current medical report relating to 2008 and so should accept the video evidence and testimony of the doctor who examined Anwar in the lock-up.

(E) PROFESSOR DAVID WELLS' TESTIMONY WAS NEUTRAL

Mohd Yusof submitted to the judge that the testimony of Professor Wells was effectively "neutral". While his explanation of the shelf life of DNA and the methodology of collecting and preserving samples for analysis was informative, he did not directly contradict the medical literature Mohd Yusof had produced to the court. The literature had documented instances of DNA samples surviving well in excess of the time periods suggested by Professor Wells. He also submitted that although the investigating police officer had opened the exhibit bags, "there was no evidence that the samples were tampered with by any person."

(F) DR BRIAN MCDONALD LACKED SUFFICIENT EXPERTISE WITH DNA ANALYSIS AND, AT TIMES, WAS UNRELIABLE

Mohd Yusof's most trenchant criticism was levelled against DNA specialist Dr McDonald. The forensic expert had criticised most aspects of the collection, storage and analysis of the forensic samples when he testified. These included the manner in which the samples were taken from the complainant, the chain of custody of the samples, the opening of the secure exhibit bags by the police, the police failure to store the samples in a freezer to avoid degradation, the lack of international certification of the government laboratory and the high risk of contamination. He was also surprised by what he described as the "pristine" DNA results produced by the government chemist, which he thought was completely inconsistent with the history of the samples.

Mohd Yusof submitted that even though the laboratory was not accredited with ISO 17025, it was nevertheless accredited to a different, Legacy, programme. He also submitted that the scientists who performed the tests were properly skilled and competent. In fact, he suggested that Dr Seah Lay Hong was more competent to conduct DNA testing than Dr McDonald, given that he had not performed a test since 2004 and that she had specific qualifications in forensic DNA.

Dr McDonald had been critical of the failure of the doctors who took forensic samples from the complainant to make slides to identify and preserve the alleged spermatozoa in those samples. He said that the reason for immediately making slides was to stop bacterial growth that would destroy the cells and DNA. He added that the history of the samples and their poor storage for 43 hours would have caused the samples to degrade.

However, that was something not seen by Dr Seah when she later made slides and examined them under the microscope.

Mohd Yusof submitted that the taking of slides was not essential and it was enough that Dr Seah had actually seen sperm cells when she examined the samples.

Dr McDonald had suggested that the DNA labelled "Male Y" could have come from epithelial cells, not semen as claimed by the government scientists. He took that view because he was not satisfied that the first extraction was sufficient and had removed all of the epithelial cells within the liquid.

Mohd Yusof submitted there was no evidence to conclude this was so because Dr Seah had properly washed out the epithelial cells in the first extraction, leaving only sperm cells.

He also rejected the claim that Anwar's semen may have been "planted" in the complainant's rectum. He said there was no evidence to prove that. How was that possible, he asked, without obtaining a sample of Anwar's semen?

Having heard from both the prosecution and the defence, and having also received substantial written submissions, Justice Zabidin announced that he would need time to consider the evidence and return a verdict. He said that he would adjourn proceedings until 9 January 2012 when he would deliver his verdict.

CHAPTER 11
The acquittal

On the morning of 9 January 2012, Justice Zabidin delivered his verdict in a trial that had lasted almost two years. The weeks before had been full of expectation and speculation. Most observers, including Anwar himself, were convinced that he was going to be found guilty of sodomy.

Police agree to a rally at court building with conditions

The opposition alliance Pakatan Rakyat (PR) had promised to gather a 100,000-strong crowd outside the court building on Jalan Duta as a show of support for Anwar. At first the police were firmly of the view that no demonstration would be allowed to take place. Rally organisers then met with senior police, including Kuala Lumpur police chief Datuk Mohmad Salleh. It was agreed that a rally could take place at the court complex, but that the crowd would be confined to a car park and limited to no more than 5,000 supporters.

The police later claimed that representatives of Parti Keadilan Rakyat (PKR), the political party of which Anwar is de facto head — including PKR Youth chief Shamsul Iskandar Mohd Akin, PKR strategic director Rafizi Ramli, Wanita chief Zuraida Kamaruddin and vice-president N. Surendran — had signed an agreement to abide by ten conditions in holding the rally. The representatives, however, disputed that there had been such an agreement, even though the police were able to produce a document that apparently had been signed by them.

The rally was authorised under section 27 of the Police Act. The conditions, which the police claimed were agreed to by PKR representatives, included that brochures/banners with the tagline "*Bebaskan Anwar*" (Free Anwar) were not allowed in any circumstances during the rally; no loudhailers allowed; no public speaking allowed; and that protesters were to gather only in the area marked by the police line.

The rally did not fall under the provisions of the Peaceful Assembly Act which was not assented to until 30 January 2012.

LAWASIA concerned with Peaceful Assembly Law

LAWASIA and the Malaysian Bar Council had severely criticised the new peaceful assembly legislation when it was tabled in the Malaysian parliament on 22 November 2011. LAWASIA complained that aspects of the proposed Act appeared to be in direct or indirect contravention of human rights norms, established through the Universal Declaration of Human Rights, which at Article 20(1) declares that: "*Everyone has the right to freedom of peaceful assembly* [author's emphasis] and association and which principle is entrenched in other international and regional instruments."

President of LAWASIA Ms Malathi Das, in a joint press release with the Malaysian Bar dated 30 November 2011, explained the basis of the objections:

> "LAWASIA finds particularly objectionable the constraints and severe restrictions that the Peaceful Assembly Bill places on activities and aspects that were otherwise acceptable in civilised countries. Among others, these include the prohibition of street protests, the age restrictions on who may organise and attend an assembly, and the onerous procedures required to seek permission to hold an assembly.

Further, the powers that are provided to the police to determine practical aspects of an assembly and to exercise force in dispersing an illegal assembly not only constrain considerably a universally-accepted civil liberty but also lack the definition that would safeguard members of the public from the excessive misuse of such powers."[1]

Anwar arrives at court

When I arrived at the High Court Complex, the police were strictly controlling crowd access to the area. Supporters were being held back by police officers stationed at nearby road junctions. At about 8.30 am, a crowd of about 5,000 or so had been admitted to the large car park designated for the gathering of supporters. Despite the prohibition of banners and placards, many of the supporters held them with slogans of "Free Anwar" and "Free Anwar 901". The police did nothing to remove them. The crowd was noisy, but orderly. The police presence was obvious, but they simply surrounded the court and kept the crowd in check.

At about 8.45 am, Anwar arrived at the court complex and with his family walked the 200 metres or so up the main driveway surrounded by chanting supporters. After passing through the main security gates at the end of the main driveway, he then made his way through the assembled media to enter the building. Once through the main doors, Anwar walked past a cordon of police and took the lift to Justice Zabidin's courtroom on the fifth floor.

The courtroom in which the trial took place is relatively small. The public gallery consists of five rows of bench-seats that can accommodate about 50 people. The courtroom was full of family members, supporters, foreign

---

1   www.malaysianbar.org.my, 30 November 2011

embassy representatives and local and international media. Also present was Senator Nick Xenophon, one of several Australian politicians who lodged a formal protest against the sodomy charge. Seating was at a premium that morning — all seats were taken and many had to stand. The benches set aside for lawyers were full with counsel from the defence and prosecution.

With Justice Zabidin's permission, I had throughout the trial been seated in a side-bench usually reserved for the media. On that morning, there were others sitting beside me. They included the investigating police officer Jude Pereira who had played a prominent and controversial role in the investigation. Also seated at the bench was a lawyer holding a watching brief for Mohd Saiful and who had been present during most of the trial. I have no idea why the lawyer was there or what he was expected to do on the complainant's behalf.

The judge's verdict

Court was due to start at 9 am, but as usual there were delays. It took time for the public gallery to settle. The lawyers entered the court at different times. Karpal Singh arrived late. Minutes later, the buzzer sounded to announce the judge's entry and the police usher called out "all rise" announcing the arrival of the judge and declaring that the court was in session. Justice Zabidin quickly slipped into his seat not looking at anyone and immediately began to read his decision. It took no more than a matter of minutes. He said:

> "After going through the evidence, the court could not with 100 per cent certainty exclude the possibility that the [DNA] sample is not compromised, and finds that it is not safe to rely on the sample. As such, the court is left only with Saiful's testimony. As this is a sexual crime, the court is always reluctant to convict

based entirely on Saiful's testimony, which is uncorroborated. The accused is thus acquitted and discharged."[2]

Justice Zabidin's decision was greeted with sighs of relief and cheers from the gallery, and with that he got up and quickly left the courtroom. Understandably, Anwar's family was delighted if not a little shocked by the verdict of acquittal. It was a very emotional and tearful moment for them as they hugged each other and their supporters. Anwar's wife, Wan Azizah Wan Ismail, was tearful and exhausted as she threw her arms around her husband.

Anwar, with his family and supporters, left the courtroom and walked out through the main doors of the building to be confronted by a swarm of television cameras. News of his acquittal had spread quickly to the crowd gathered outside and he was greeted with cheers and the chant of "*Reformasi, Reformasi*" ("democratic reform") from the crowd behind the main gates 50 metres away.

Anwar declared to the media that he was surprised and vindicated by the decision. He then walked to the crowd of supporters and, with his wife and daughters by his side, addressed them using a loudhailer.

Shortly after, Melissa Goh of Channel News Asia interviewed Anwar. When asked about the trial he replied: "This was a farcical trial, a travesty of justice. So a decision to the contrary would have put Malaysia in a disastrous light. That I know for a fact. Umno had made a decision that Anwar is guilty."

"Why the sudden change of mind then?" asked Ms Goh.

"Because", Anwar replied, "they [the government] also understand the anger, the public outrage here, and international repercussions."

---

2   Author's notes and as reported in major news publications

A jubilant Anwar with his wife and family after the verdict of acquittal;
Sankara Nair (second from left) with colleagues after the acquittal.

Loud explosions suddenly interrupted the interview. Anwar's
daughters, who were standing behind him, urged him to leave and he
quickly left the area. Police dispersed the crowd and declared the area to
be unsafe. They found explosive devices under police traffic cones. On
that day, five people were injured and several cars damaged. Kuala Lumpur
police chief Datuk Mohmad Salleh later said that homemade explosives
were used. Investigators said they found battery remnants, pieces of wire,
ball bearings and timers.

PM Najib's response to the acquittal

Prime Minister Najib said that the verdict showed "once again that, despite
what many have claimed, the Malaysian judiciary is independent".

He said it was an institution where neither politics nor politicians had
any influence over the dispensation of justice. This, he said, strengthened
the clear separation of powers of each branch of the government with
neither of the branches interfering with the workings of the other. He
further said that:

"As head of the executive branch, I respect the decisions of the other branch of government — the judiciary. This case was brought by a private individual and it was important that he had his accusations heard in court. Far from being a politically motivated prosecution, it has been an unwelcome distraction from the serious business of running our country in the interests of the Malaysian people."[3]

He added that the ruling meant the government had been cleared once and for all of the many baseless accusations of political interference and conspiracy against the opposition leader.

The Malaysian Bar Council's view of the acquittal

Significantly, the Malaysian Bar Council, through its President Lim Chee Wee, issued a press release on the same day saying that while they welcomed Anwar's acquittal, they had concerns about the trial process. He said:

"The Malaysian Bar welcomes the decision of the High Court in acquitting Datuk Seri Anwar Ibrahim. The principles of natural justice call for nothing less, in light of the grave concerns over whether the accused's right to a fair trial was preserved.

Based on news reports of the trial, it is clear that the High Court decision is in accord with the evidence for, amongst others, the following reasons:

1. The lack of full disclosure: Both prior to and during the trial itself, the legal team for the defence was denied access to certain

documents and physical evidence in the possession of the prosecution, which disadvantaged the accused in the preparation of his defence.

2. Unreliable DNA evidence: There were obvious concerns that the DNA sample submitted as evidence was unreliable or may have been compromised.

3. Certain unusual findings during the trial proceedings:
(a) The trial judge made an unprecedented finding at the end of the prosecution case that the complainant was a truthful and credible witness, without the benefit of having heard the defence.
(b) While the court allowed the Prime Minister and his wife to be interviewed by the defence legal team, the subpoena issued by the defence compelling the attendance of the Prime Minister and his wife was set aside by the High Court upon the application of the prosecution. The absence of curiosity in this regard casts grave concerns on the credibility of the complaint in the first place.

4. The unrefuted relationship between the complainant and a member of the prosecution team, which raised serious questions whether the complainant had access to investigation papers, which would have enabled him to tailor his evidence at trial.

The charge against Datuk Seri Anwar Ibrahim, which is based on an archaic provision of the Penal Code that criminalises consensual sexual relations between adults, should never have been brought. The case has unnecessarily taken up judicial time and public funds.

The Malaysian Bar hopes that the Attorney-General would not pursue any appeal, and will instead focus the valuable resources of the Attorney-General's Chambers on more serious crimes."[4]

Was the acquittal a surprise?

Malaysian lawyer Tommy Thomas, writing on the website The Malaysian Insider on 19 January 2012, said that the view of many observers, including the vast majority of the 13,000 lawyers of the Malaysian Bar, was that a guilty verdict was a forgone conclusion:

> "The only sure way for any lawyer to predict an outcome in a lengthy trial like Anwar's is to review the trial judge's overall conduct of that trial and then make a projection. In every criminal prosecution in Malaysia, elementary principles established over centuries forming the bedrock of our criminal jurisprudence have to be applied by every judge (juries having been abolished).
>
> In the course of a trial a judge would have to make numerous rulings on procedural and evidential matters that would have a great bearing on his final decision. He also has to make a fundamental decision when the prosecution closes its case, viz, whether the defence has a case to meet. Only if he is satisfied that these elements have been proven by the prosecution, on whom the burden solely rests, and which never shifts to the accused, should the judge call the defence.
>
> Accordingly, applying the only rational basis available to those legally trained, the conduct of the judge during Anwar's

4   www.malaysianbar.org.my, Lim Chee Wee, Press Release: 'Acquittal on charge of consensual sex between adults is in accord with evidence', 9 January 2012

trial was consistently in one direction: totally in support of the prosecution case, and wholly unsympathetic to the accused. Hence, a conviction was inevitable. In consequence, the judge's acquittal was a U-turn of massive proportions."

I share his opinion. Having observed most of the trial, it seemed to me that the judge had made up his mind and that a conviction was inevitable. My view was based not only on the several key rulings made during the trial, all of which were against the accused, but importantly from the judge's ruling on the no case submission. It was not because he ruled there was a case to answer, as I agreed with him that there was sufficient evidence to come to that view. However, the absolute terms in which he made his ruling and his observations concerning his assessment of the complainant and the forensic evidence led me to that belief. I was absolutely wrong. Like many others, I was completely surprised by the acquittal.

When asked whether the acquittal demonstrated judicial independence, some observers invoked the old adage, "one swallow does not make a summer". Some even suggested that if it was not the judge's decision to acquit Anwar, it must follow that it was a political decision. Thomas said:

"It is against a background of a very close general election that Putrajaya made a political calculation: an acquitted Anwar would cause less electoral damage to Umno than a convicted Anwar. The martyr status must be denied to Anwar."

The opposition parties and members of the international community welcomed the decision.

Was there a sound basis to acquit Anwar?

Justice Zabidin took immediate leave after delivering his verdict. It was only six months later, on 8 July 2012, that he delivered written reasons for acquitting Anwar.

In his written reasons, Justice Zabidin said that one critical ingredient of the charge which needed to be proved was the fact of anal penetration.[5] The three medical doctors who examined Mohd Saiful at Hospital Kuala Lumpur (HKL) believed that penetration had occurred because government chemist Dr Siew Sheue Feng said he had found semen, which he called "Male Y", from which he extracted DNA that matched Anwar's profile. The judge accepted that corroboration on the fact of penetration from these witnesses "hinged" on Dr Siew's analysis.

However, he was faced with conflicting expert testimony as to whether the DNA actually belonged to Anwar. The government chemist said it was Anwar's DNA, while Anwar's experts said that it would have been impossible to extract any identifiable DNA from the forensic samples.

Justice Zabidin said that to resolve that conflict in the evidence, he needed "to re-evaluate the entire evidence relating to collecting, handling and analysing the samples taken from the complainant, in the light of the defence evidence to see whether the prosecution had proven its case beyond reasonable doubt."

Ultimately, he found he could not exclude the possibility that the integrity of the samples had been compromised before they reached the laboratory for DNA analysis. As such, he could not be satisfied this evidence was capable of corroborating the fact of penetration.

That left him only with the evidence of the complainant who he had, when considering the case to answer submission, found to be a truthful and

5   "Judge's Reasons for Decision", published 8 July 2012

reliable witness. He said that although it was open to him to convict on that evidence alone, he was not prepared to do so in the circumstances. The judge expressed it in these terms at paragraphs 205, 206 and 207:

> "It was the prosecution stance that the tampering with P27 [plastic exhibit bags containing forensic samples] did not in any way compromise the integrity of the samples in the receptacles since the receptacles were individually sealed with Hospital Kuala Lumpur seal. DW3 [David Wells] when examined on this subject said that the receptacles were not tamperproof [meaning the seal could be removed and resealed] from the manner in which they were sealed and the type of material used as seals. By cutting open P27, the confidence in the integrity of the samples was gone.
>
> After going through the defence's evidence particularly those stated above, this court could not, at this stage, with 100 per cent certainty, exclude the possibility the integrity of the samples taken from the complainant had been compromised before they reached PW5 [Dr Siew Sheue Feng] for analysis. As such, it was not safe to rely on the DNA result obtained by PW5 from the analysis conducted on those samples. That being the case, there was no evidence to corroborate the evidence of PW1 [Mohd Saiful] on factum of penetration."

Justice Zabidin was left to conclude as follows:

> "This court was left only with the evidence of PW1 to prove penetration. This being a sexual offence, it is trite law that the court is always reluctant to convict an accused person based solely

on the uncorroborated evidence of the complainant. Therefore the accused is acquitted and discharged from the charge."

(A) DNA EVIDENCE

Justice Zabidin, in his reasons for acquittal, relied on the observation of defence expert witness Professor David Wells that the plastic exhibit bags, which contained the forensic samples, were not tamperproof. He said he could not be satisfied the integrity of the forensic samples had not been compromised before they reached Dr Siew Sheue Feng for analysis because the plastic bags had been opened by the police.

The defence expert witnesses had been highly critical of DSP Jude Pereira's management of the forensic samples that were obtained by the HKL doctors from their medical examination of the complainant. The samples had been placed into airtight containers and then sealed in plastic exhibit bags. The exhibit bags were then labelled and given to Pereira to deliver them to the government chemist for analysis. Pereira admitted during his testimony that he had opened the exhibit bags before delivering them to the laboratory for analysis and then, contrary to explicit instructions, had stored them in a filing cabinet in his office for 43 hours instead of in a freezer.

The defence expert witnesses were also critical of what happened to the samples when they arrived at the government laboratory. Dr Seah Lay Hong, who received the samples for analysis, also broke the essential chain of custody by ignoring the labelling given to each of them by the examining doctors and relabelling each with her own description. It meant that there was no proven continuity between the samples taken by the doctors and the samples analysed by her.

Chain of custody is critical when forensic evidence is involved. The integrity of forensic samples must be maintained by providing documentation and evidence of the control, transfer and analysis of the samples. If forensic evidence is to be used in court to convict persons of crimes, it is essential that it must be handled in a scrupulously careful manner to avoid allegations of tampering or misconduct, which can compromise the prosecution case. It requires that evidence be identified as being in substantially the same condition as it was at the time it was seized, and that it has remained in that condition through an unbroken chain of custody.

Justice Zabidin did not need to go any further than he did in concluding that he could not rely on the integrity of the samples after the chief police investigator had compromised them in the way he did, but arguably the integrity of the samples was further compromised at the laboratory.

(B) UNCORROBORATED TESTIMONY OF COMPLAINANT

Justice Zabidin, in his reasons for acquittal, concluded that he could not exclude the possibility that the integrity of the forensic samples had been compromised. That conclusion meant that he could not rely on that evidence to corroborate the complainant's allegation of sexual assault. It left him only with the uncorroborated evidence of Mohd Saiful to prove penetration. Something needs to be said about that.

The need for corroboration of a complainant's evidence in a sexual offence case is well settled at law. Whilst there is no rule of law in Malaysia (as in many other countries) that a complainant's evidence must be corroborated, it is accepted that it would be unsafe to convict in cases of this kind unless the complainant's evidence is unusually convincing or there is some corroboration of the complainant's story.

It is accepted by Malaysian courts that allegations of sodomy can easily be made and be very difficult to refute, and that the evidence in support of such a charge has to be very convincing in order to convict the accused. A trial judge hearing such a case must warn himself or herself that is dangerous to convict without corroboration. For a discussion of this principle, see the judgement of the Court of Appeal in *Datuk Seri Anwar bin Ibrahim v Pendakwa Raya* (2004) 1 MLJ 177 where the court at Anwar's first appeal dealt with a claim that there was no corroboration of the complainant's allegation. Without any DNA evidence, there was no independent evidence to support the complainant's allegation of sodomy.

Mohd Saiful's complaint of sexual assault to the medical doctors who examined him on the night of 26 June 2008 was not corroborative evidence. The fact that he said he had been sodomised could not prove that his claim was true. In his reasons for refusing the no case submission at the close of the prosecution case, the trial judge incorrectly said it did. When he delivered his verdict, he properly took a different view.

There was no medical evidence of injury of the complainant's anus or rectum consistent with penile penetration that might have corroborated his allegation.

In these circumstances, Justice Zabidin was not prepared to convict based solely on Mohd Saiful's uncorroborated testimony. No complaint can be made of that decision as it was consistent with the facts and in accordance with established legal principles.

Prosecution appeals verdict of acquittal

Section 50(3) of the Courts of Judicature Act 1964 provides that a criminal appeal to the Court of Appeal from a trial in the High Court "may lie on a question of fact or a question of law or on a question of mixed fact and law".

The court may review all of the evidence to determine whether the judge has correctly acquitted the accused at the close of the defence case. The prescribed time for parties to lodge an appeal in Malaysia is 14 days from the date of the verdict. Malaysian law allows parties to file only a notice of intention to appeal without providing grounds, which is what the prosecution did in this case. Grounds of appeal can be filed later.

On the afternoon of Friday, 20 January 2012, the Attorney-General's Chambers (AGC) filed a notice of appeal against the trial judge's verdict of acquittal. The decision was consistent with the uncompromising approach taken by the Attorney-General in prosecuting this case, and was not unexpected by some observers, particularly when it was reported that Deputy Prosecutor Mohd Yusof had recommended it.

The AGC issued a statement saying:

> "The victim's family has urged for an appeal to be filed against the said decision whilst the Malaysian Bar Council has given an opposing view. In this regard, to be fair to the parties concerned, especially the victim and Anwar Ibrahim, the Attorney-General's Chambers wishes to emphasise that in making any decision, the department acts solely on the evidence and in accordance with the law, not influenced by any emotion or parties."[6]

The prosecution was obviously keen to point out that its decision was not influenced by the views of interested parties, but was based "solely on the evidence and in accordance with the law". Nevertheless, it is interesting to note that the prosecution was still referring to Mohd Saiful as the "victim" for that was plainly inconsistent with the judge's verdict.

---

6   Reuters, 20 January 2012

Anwar's lawyer, Sankara Nair, had not formally received the notice of appeal when the media told him that it had been filed. His immediate response was:

> "However, if it is true, then it is most regrettable and atrocious given that the trial judge has stated succinctly, in his verdict, that the crucial evidence was tampered with. Hence the substratum of the prosecution case is fatally demolished, rendering any appeal, no matter how many times, a desperate act of futility. It appears to be a case of political persecution of Anwar and not prosecution."[7]

The prosecution undoubtedly filed the notice of appeal to comply with the 14-day time limit imposed by legislation and to enable the AGC to obtain a copy of the trial judge's written reasons for decision, without which it would be difficult to frame the grounds of appeal. It may also be that the prosecution had already decided, even without those reasons, to appeal because of the view it took of the evidence at the trial.

Six months later, on 8 July 2012, Justice Zabidin delivered his written reasons. The prosecution then proceeded to file its grounds of appeal on 10 July. More on the prosecution grounds of appeal is covered on pages 221–224.

CHAPTER 12

The saga continues

Anwar Ibrahim came into the news again barely five months after he was acquitted of the charge of sodomy on 9 January 2012.

On 22 May 2012, together with members of the opposition party Parti Keadilan Rakyat (PKR), deputy president Azmin Ali and party member Badrul Hisham Shaharin, Anwar was charged at the Kuala Lumpur Sessions Court under Section 4(2)(c) of the Peaceful Assembly Act 2012 for breaching a court order by taking part in a street protest. The three defendants were the first persons to be charged under the new legislation introduced on 23 April 2012.

The prosecution against Anwar and the others charged with him under the assembly law led to a surprising twist in events — the appearance of former Solicitor-General II Datuk Mohd Yusof Zainal Abiden as part of Anwar's defence team, along with Karpal Singh, Sankara Nair and Ramkarpal Singh. Mohd Yusof was not only lead prosecutor at Anwar's second sodomy trial, but was also junior counsel to the Attorney-General Abdul Gani Patail at Anwar's Federal Court appeal in 2004. He retired from the Attorney-General's Chambers shortly after Anwar's acquittal on 9 January 2012.

Bersih 3.0 rally

On Saturday, 28 April 2012, Malaysians took to the streets demanding electoral transparency ahead of a national election that was expected to be called no later than March 2013. This demonstration, dubbed 'Bersih 3.0' after the Malay word for 'clean', was a follow-up to rallies for electoral reform in 2007 and 2011. (The 2011 rally ended in violence.)

The rallies were organised by Gabungan Pilihanraya Bersih dan Adil, or the Coalition for Clean and Fair Elections. Bersih co-chairman Dato' Ambiga Sreenevasan was quoted as saying that more than 250,000 people participated in Bersih 3.0, dismissing police estimates of 25,000 as too low.

Whatever the estimate, tens of thousands marched in the streets of Kuala Lumpur on 28 April. The police had set up roadblocks to contain the rally, which included about 58 arterial roads leading into Dataran Merdeka, or Merdeka Square, in the city centre. Merdeka Square itself was declared off-limits by court order and was sealed off by metal barricades. Protesters gathered at several locations and converged on Merdeka Square. When some protesters breached the barricades, police fired tear gas and directed water cannons into the crowd in an attempt to disperse the people.

The rally ended in mayhem and more than 500 people were arrested. Prime Minister Najib Razak and other officials accused the opposition of hijacking the rally and trying to create chaos and confrontation with the police.

Malaysian Bar condemns police conduct at rally

The Malaysian Bar deployed a team of 78 observers to monitor the rally and to assist any persons arrested by the police. The president of the Bar Council Lim Chee Wee had made it clear that the Bar was not a member of the coalition of NGOs and individuals making up Bersih 3.0.[1]

An interim report prepared by the Bar Council found that the rally was peaceful until around 3 pm when the police unleashed chemical-

---

1   themalaysianinsider.com, Clara Chooi, 13 April 2012

laced water and tear gas on the crowd. It found there were reports of widespread police brutality against civilians as well as the arbitrary use of tear gas and water cannon. The police had fired tear gas directly at the crowd and their firing pattern was to box in demonstrators rather than allow them to disperse quickly. It also found that while the demonstrators had provoked police officers with jeers and insults, the police response was indiscriminate, disproportionate and excessive. The report also found there was a concerted effort by police to prevent the video recording of their actions and conduct — several journalists were assaulted and their cameras destroyed or confiscated. The Bar Council concluded that the actions of the police disregarded various international codes of conduct for law enforcement officials and the use of force and firearms.

At an extraordinary general meeting held on 11 May 2012, the Malaysian Bar approved a resolution condemning the police for using "excessive and indiscriminate" force to disperse the protesters. The motion was passed by the majority of lawyers present, with only 16 of the 1,270 members in attendance opposing the resolution. Christopher Leong, then vice president of the Malaysian Bar, said:

> "The reported breach of police barricades in some areas does not justify the police unleashing the full force of their arsenal upon crowds that were peaceful. The police have shown in this incident that they do not have the maturity, discipline and restraint required of a professional force...
>
> The promise by the government to respect democracy and human rights, and implement reforms, was tested yesterday. The government's response and actions during the Bersih 3.0 rally provided an indication of whether the new reform legislation will be perverted and abused in its use and implementation,

where the wise powers vested in the authorities call for measured,
proportionate and mature exercise. The events of 28 April 2012
do not bode well in this regard."[2]

Government attacks Bar Council

The government was obviously irritated by the Bar Council's strong
criticism of police conduct at the rally. Some ministers accused the
Malaysian Bar of being biased and pro-opposition. Some also claimed
it was being too political and suggested that perhaps Malaysian lawyers
needed to establish a second Malaysian Bar, one that would oppose the
current Council and look after the professional interests of members.
Prominent politicians like former PM Tun Dr Mahathir Mohamad and
Umno minister Datuk Seri Mohamed Nazri Aziz were most critical.[3]

Dr Mahathir was quick to respond to the demonstration, declaring
it was intended to overthrow the government. The protest, he said with
his characteristic bluster, was to destabilise the country to establish the
need for regime change with the help of foreign forces. He said: "[t]he
disturbance is because they want to establish that the country is run by
dictators ... They will be happy if foreigners bring planes and bomb Kuala
Lumpur. They would say 'I have done a good thing for this country' — that
is what the opposition and the Bersih movement is about."[4]

Government targets rally leaders for damages

As part of a multi-pronged attack on those involved in the rally, the
government initiated a civil action for damages against Ambiga Sreenevasan

---

2   www.malaysianbar.org.my, 29 April 2012

3   themalaysianinsider.com, Clara Chooi, 26 May 2012

4   Free Malaysia Today, 'Dr M doing BN more harm than good', 30 April 2012

and nine other Bersih steering committee members for damage to property allegedly caused during the rally. The action was filed on 15 May 2012.

According to the writ of summons, the members are accused of bringing "too many" protesters to the rally and failed to appoint sufficient personnel to ensure the protest was peaceful. Section 6(2)(g) of the Peaceful Assembly Act 2012 (Act 736) makes persons responsible to ensure that any rally held will not cause damage to property. The claim also states special damages of RM122,000 (USD38,500) for 15 police vehicles damaged during the protest, including two water cannon trucks. These proceedings are continuing.

Anwar charged with civil disobedience at rally

Anwar was one of those who attended the Bersih 3.0 street protest.

On 22 May, he was charged for breaching a court order by taking part in the rally. The court order, made by Magistrate Zaki Asyraf Zubir on 26 April 2012, prohibited individuals from entering Merdeka Square or participating in an assembly at that location from 28 April to 1 May. The police alleged that Anwar committed the offence between 2.30 pm and 3 pm along Jalan Tun Perak, a main thoroughfare near Merdeka Square on 28 April.

Together with two other PKR members, Azmin Ali and Badrul Hisham, Anwar was also charged with committing an offence under section 188 of the Penal Code, read together with sections 109 and 34 of the Code. The essence of this charge is disobeying an official direction, an act of disobedience which causes or tends to cause danger to human life, health or safety, or which causes or tends to cause riot or affray. It is alleged that they conspired with others to disobey the magistrate's prohibition order to enter Merdeka Square by opening the barricades at about 3 pm, which allowed protesters to enter the prohibited area resulting in clashes with police. The penalty on conviction is a jail sentence of six years, a fine not exceeding RM2,000, or both.

Prosecutors are likely to use a video recording of the rally — uploaded on YouTube — that shows Anwar gesturing to others immediately before demonstrators entered the prohibited area. The government was quick to seize on the video, suggesting that Anwar was in fact signalling Azmin Ali to encourage the crowds to breach the barricades. Anwar denied this, saying they were exchanging hand signals about negotiating with the police.[5]

Anwar characterises these charges as another attempt to remove him from the political scene. He told the media as he left court that the charges were "clearly vindictive" and meant to stop the opposition from campaigning effectively. "It is clearly a politically motivated charge. Elections are around the corner," he said.[6]

Anwar later told Radio Australia's Connect Asia programme that the charges were designed to deflect public attention from electoral corruption. He said the charges were "baseless political intimidation". Anwar went on to say that "the intention of Prime Minister Najib Razak is to deflect attention from the central issue about fraud. The whole issue is about fraud or electoral fraud. Now, he wants to go to the elections with the same system, deflect from the central issue of fraud and corruption."[7]

The prime minister's office rejected Anwar's claims of a political plot, saying in a statement that the charges were based on police investigations. It noted that two police officers were also charged in connection with violence during the rally.[8]

---

5   Today Online, 23 May 2012

6   *The Guardian*, 22 May 2012

7   ABC, 22 May 2012 (from AP report)

8   *Herald Sun*, 23 May 2012

The implication for Anwar is that if convicted of these new charges, he would be ineligible to stand as a candidate in national parliamentary elections that must be called no later than March 2013. That is because a person cannot be a member of parliament if convicted of a crime where the punishment is imprisonment of one year or more, or a fine of RM2,000 or more. Anwar would be disqualified from being nominated as a candidate as soon as parliament is dissolved. A conviction would effectively take Anwar out of the political scene.[9]

Anwar applies to strike out charges as unconstitutional

The prosecution against Anwar under the assembly law took another turn, when on 28 May 2012 Anwar's lawyers filed applications in the Sessions Court to strike out the charges on the basis that the legislation was unconstitutional because it violated the guarantees of freedom of assembly. The Public Prosecutor was named as the respondent.

The charge alleging that Anwar and others had breached an official order banning demonstrators from entering into a designated area was challenged because the 'central square' described in the charge was not specifically identified. There seems to be some support for that argument. Malaysian Bar vice president Christopher Leong offered the opinion: "The court order excluding members of the public from Dataran Merdeka is arguably defective in law due to a lack of specificity."[10]

The challenge brought by Anwar's lawyers relies on Article 10 of the Malaysian Constitution, which guarantees citizens freedom of speech, the right to peaceful assembly and the right to form associations. It is a key provision that has been regarded as being of "paramount importance"

---

9   The Malaysian Constitution, Articles 47, 48

10   www.malaysianbar.org.my, 29 April 2012

by the judiciary, but it is not considered to be absolute, as Article 10 also expressly permits parliament by law to impose restrictions in the interests of security of the Federation, to maintain public order or prevent incitement to any offence.

Prosecutor changes sides

There was a definite buzz around the Sessions Court at Jalan Duta on the morning of 22 May 2012, when Anwar appeared to answer the civil disobedience charges.

Anwar walked into the court with a throng of supporters and media at 9.15 am. The other defendants followed a few minutes later. Shortly before the court was called into session, the lawyers came into the courtroom and moved into position at the bar table. Karpal Singh was expected to appear for Anwar but, surprisingly, Mohd Yusof, who had prosecuted Anwar at his trial, accompanied him. When lead prosecutor Abdul Wahab Mohamad introduced counsel to the presiding judge (which is the custom in Malaysia), Anwar's supporters cheered and clapped. The proceedings were brief and the defendants were each granted bail.

As he left the court, Mohd Yusof was asked by reporters why he was with Anwar's team. He replied, "I am a free agent." He said that he had no hesitation after Anwar called him the previous night (21 May). He said he was a professional with no political affiliation and he did not have anything personal against either the Attorney-General or the government. He said, "I have no problems taking the case. I am willing and able. Everyone is entitled to legal representation."[11]

When Anwar was asked by reporters about Mohd Yusof joining the legal team, he said about the telephone call: "There must be an indication of preparedness. I don't simply call people." He did not elaborate. He went on to say: "Mohd Yusof came with full commitment that I get my justice." Karpal welcomed the addition of Mohd Yusof to the defence team saying it was his first case as a defence lawyer.[12]

The reaction to Mohd Yusof joining Anwar's legal team was mixed. There is little doubt his decision was a boost for Anwar, who immediately sought to capitalise on the move, describing it as showing "that those within the government know about the dirtiness that happens and are not prepared to defend all of it. If he really thinks I'm guilty, he would not be with us."[13]

Mohd Yusof certainly did not go that far in describing his reasons for joining the defence team. He refused to be drawn on any criticism of the Attorney-General or the prosecution service. He said that having retired from his position of Solicitor-General II, he was now a free agent to represent any person in court. He added that he was still bound by his prosecutor's oath of secrecy.[14]

Some government members criticised Mohd Yusof's decision as "unprofessional" as it happened so soon after prosecuting Anwar and damaged the public perception of the trial. Umno's Pulai MP Datuk Nur Jazlan Mohamad said that Mohd Yusof "should not have joined Anwar as it creates doubt in people's minds that he purposely made the [sodomy] case fail." Fellow backbencher Barisan Nasional MP from Pasir Salak, Datuk Tajuddin Abdul Rahman, questioned Mohd Yusof's integrity, saying that some people may think he was a Trojan horse and colluded with Anwar in the sodomy trial and was not serious about obtaining a conviction.[15]

12　The Star Online, Wednesday, 23 May 2012

13　Free Malaysia Today, 22 May 2012

14　*The Sun Daily*, 22 May 2012

15　themalaysianinsider.com, 26 May 2012

The de facto law minister Datuk Seri Mohamed Nazri Abdul Aziz was more restrained in his comments, saying he did not see what Anwar stood to gain from hiring Mohd Yusof as his lawyer because "Yusof is not a renowned lawyer, no one knows him."[16] The minister's remark was a bit dismissive of someone who had been the third most senior lawyer in the prosecution service and widely known as the lawyer who had prosecuted Anwar at his trial for more than two years and which had attracted international publicity.

Was it right for Mohd Yusof to join Anwar's defence team?

There was no ethical or professional barrier that would have prevented Mohd Yusof joining Anwar's legal team. Under Malaysia's Legal Profession (Practice and Etiquette) Rules 1978, a lawyer must give advice or accept any brief in the Courts except in special circumstances that may justify a refusal (Rule 2).

The professional obligation to accept any instructions — known in the English law tradition as the 'cab-rank rule' — would justify Mohd Yusof acting for Anwar. Some critics may argue that it may have been wiser for Mohd Yusof to refuse the instructions on the basis that he would be embarrassed acting for Anwar so soon after prosecuting him or that his professional conduct may be impugned for doing so (Rules 3 and 4).

Finally, although Mohd Yusof may be able to join Anwar's legal team to defend the civil disobedience charges, it would not be possible for him to act on his behalf in opposing the appeal against his sodomy acquittal because of the obvious conflict.

Some critics suggested that even though Malaysians may have a divided opinion of Anwar, they were relieved at his acquittal because it offered the chance to move away from the sleazy politics that had long dominated daily life. Prime Minister Najib Razak was quick to seize upon the verdict as proof of his 'reformist' agenda.

However, says Barry Wain of the Institute of Southeast Asian Studies, "Their groan of dismay over the prosecution's subsequent decision to appeal was equally palpable." He argues that the trial has become a liability for the prime minister and that "the value in distracting Anwar and trying to knock him out politically has been offset by the damage to Najib's reputation as a putative reformer".[17]

The prime minister's reformist reputation, which he was keen to cultivate at that time, would inevitably vanish by his abandonment of his promise to repeal the sedition law. The conservatives within his own party were dismayed with his repeal of the draconic ISA legislation, but after the ruling coalition almost lost the 2013 national election he was under considerable pressure to keep the sedition law firmly in place. For Mr Najib, it became a matter of his survival as leader. Not only did he not repeal the sedition law, but also the government used it as a means to stifle dissent by arresting and charging opposition MPs, academics, journalists and students.

For Anwar, the prosecution appeal meant that his political fortunes were still bound up in the legal process. Once more the independence of the judiciary and its capacity to apply the law impartially in politically sensitive cases would become an issue as the appeal process played out in the superior courts.

---

17   Barry Wain, East Asia Forum, 10 February 2012

Prosecution files grounds of appeal

The prosecution filed its grounds of appeal on 10 July 2012, having received Justice Zabidin's written judgement together with the appeal record two days before. The document[18] set out nine grounds of appeal, which, in summary, claimed that:

1. [Ground 1] The trial judge's decision is against the weight of the evidence at trial.

2. [Grounds 2, 3] The trial judge's finding that he could not be satisfied that the integrity of the forensic samples had not been compromised was inconsistent with his earlier findings at the close of the prosecution case, when he had called upon Anwar to enter his defence, because:

   i.   there was no evidence of tampering with the forensic samples;

   ii. the DNA extract "Male Y" matched Anwar's DNA obtained from items taken by DSP Jude Pereira from his cell after his arrest; and

   iii. there was no way Pereira could have tampered with the forensic samples to produce that result.

3. [Grounds 4, 6, 7] The trial judge relied on the testimony of the defence expert witnesses, Professor David Wells and Dr Brian McDonald, whose opinions were based on "incomplete and incomprehensive theories", without taking account of the testimony of the prosecution experts, whose opinion was based on their own examination and analysis.

---

18 "Petition of Appeal to the Learned Judges of the Court of Appeal", dated 9 July 2012

4. [Ground 5] The trial judge failed to assess Dr McDonald's expertise and experience, which the prosecution disputed.

5. [Ground 8] The trial judge failed to take account of "other evidence" that supported the complainant's allegation, which he relied upon at the close of the prosecution case to require the accused to enter a defence.

6. [Ground 9] The trial judge imposed a higher standard of proof upon the prosecution to prove its case than required of it at law.

The Attorney-General's Chambers in the Petition of Appeal to the Court of Appeal sought to set aside the trial judge's verdict of acquittal and asked the court to convict Anwar of an offence under section 377B of the Penal Code.

The legal teams would, in due course, lodge comprehensive written submissions in support of their respective submissions. However, at this point in the narration it would be unfair to the reader not to at least offer some general observations about the key assertions on which the prosecution grounds relied.

First, the prosecution asserted that the trial judge in effect disregarded the testimony of its own expert witnesses in preference to the expert witnesses called by the defence. Justice Zabidin was entitled to prefer one body of expert opinion as opposed to another, but I do not think it gets that far. If he could not exclude the possibility that the forensic samples obtained by the doctors from Hospital Kuala Lumpur had been compromised before they were delivered to chief government chemist Dr Siew Sheue Feng for analysis, then there was no need to consider the expert evidence relating to DNA — and he did not.

Secondly, the prosecution asserted that Justice Zabidin's final conclusions were not consistent with the findings he made at the close of the prosecution case, when he had to decide whether or not to require the accused to enter a defence. His findings, at that point of the trial, were made after hearing only the prosecution case and applying a lesser standard of proof. He was not bound by those findings and it is hardly surprising that he may have taken a different view after hearing all of the evidence.

Thirdly, the prosecution asserted that Justice Zabidin imposed a "burden of proof higher than that of beyond a reasonable doubt" in proving its case. I am sure the author meant to say "standard of proof" rather than "burden of proof". They are different things. The prosecution always has the burden of proving its case, but the appropriate standard of proof in a criminal trial is "beyond a reasonable doubt".

I am sure the prosecution relied on the part of the trial judge's decision where, at paragraph 206, he said:

> "After going through the defence's evidence particularly those stated above, this court could not, at this stage, with 100 per cent certainty, exclude the possibility the integrity of the samples taken from the complainant had been compromised before they reached PW5 [Dr Siew] for analysis."

It seems to me on reading this extract that Justice Zabidin was not referring to the ultimate standard of proof he must apply before he could be satisfied the prosecution had proved its case. He is saying that before he could be satisfied the DNA extracted from the complainant's rectal samples matched Anwar's profile, he had to exclude the possibility that the integrity of the samples had been compromised. He did not need to add the phrase "with 100 per cent certainty", for his meaning was clear without it.

Finally, the prosecution asserted that the trial judge did not take account of "other evidence" that he said corroborated the complainant's allegation, and which he relied upon at the close of the prosecution case to require Anwar to enter his case.

The so-called "other evidence" included the fact that the DNA extraction by Dr Seah Lay Hong matched "Male Y" to Anwar's profile, that the complainant had made an allegation of sexual assault to the medical doctors who examined him on 28 June 2008, and that both the complainant and the accused were in the vicinity of the alleged crime scene on the day of the alleged offence.

The DNA evidence was obviously excluded, given Justice Zabidin's finding that the integrity of the forensic samples could have been compromised by DSP Jude Pereira's conduct in opening the exhibit bags and failure to properly store the samples.

As I have observed elsewhere, the fact that Mohd Saiful complained to the doctors that he had been sexually assaulted could never at law prove his allegation was true. Justice Zabidin had thought it was corroborative evidence when he considered the case to answer submission, but he obviously changed his mind when he came to consider the ultimate question of guilt. He was right to do so.

That only left the evidence that both the alleged victim and the accused had been in the vicinity of each other on the date of the alleged crime. Mohd Saiful testified that he went to the condominium upon the instructions of Anwar's chief of staff, who had told him to take various documents to Anwar where he was attending a meeting with others.

It is doubtful this evidence alone was capable of corroborating the allegation of sodomy. Mere opportunity alone does not amount to corroboration. There was nothing about the character of the opportunity as to bring in the element of suspicion. It would be difficult to say that the circumstances and the locality of the opportunity was such as in themselves to amount to corroboration.

THE FINAL PLAY
March 2014 – February 2015

The courtroom at the Palace of Justice in which the final verdict was delivered on 10 February 2015.

CHAPTER 13
Government wins
13th General Election

Opposition parties defeated

Malaysia's 13th General Election was held on Sunday, 5 May 2013. The opposition expected to win the election as Anwar Ibrahim's popularity had never been higher and there was every indication that the electorate was disillusioned with the ruling coalition.

But Barisan Nasional came back into power taking 60 per cent of parliamentary seats even though it won only 47.38 per cent of the popular vote, while the Pakatan Rakyat coalition led by Anwar Ibrahim won 50.87 per cent.

The discrepancy was due to widespread gerrymandering. The factor of difference between some seats in the Malaysian Parliament was as much as twentyfold, where some seats may have 5,000 voters and others over 100,000. The government won nine out of 12 states, including Kedah and Perak, which were won by the opposition at the previous election in 2008.

Nevertheless, it was Barisan Nasional's worst ever showing. There had been a swing against the government of 2.89 per cent resulting in a loss of seven seats. The opposition picked up seven seats with a swing to it of 4.12 per cent, but it was not enough to take government.

Allegations of electoral fraud

The election was marred by a number of incidents, which the opposition claimed were deliberate acts by the ruling coalition to rig the vote.

For instance early voters had been required to mark their finger with indelible ink to prevent multiple voting, but there were many reports that the ink could easily be washed off using general cleaning fluids. Another claim made was that foreign workers had been bused with police escorts to polling stations to vote. Other claims included foreigners using false ID cards, vote buying at polling stations, identity theft and irregular electoral rolls.

There were reports of scuffles on the night of 5 May at the Bangsar polling station (the hotly-contested Lembah Pantai seat held by Anwar's daughter Nurul Izzah) when opposition scrutineers managed to prevent vehicles attempting to bring suspect ballot boxes, which were marked with another electorate's ID code, into the polling station.

Furthermore, in electorates with opposition victories, it was alleged that extra votes had been smuggled into polling stations when votes were being recounted. Blackouts had occurred during the recounts, following which vote recounts revealed that government candidates had in fact won the seats.

Anwar: "The worst electoral fraud in our history"

Anwar reacted angrily, claiming the election had been fraudulently stolen and the win the result of the "worst electoral fraud in our history". He singled out the Election Commission, a body responsible for the running of the election, which he said was "complicit to the crime".[1]

---

1   World News Australia, 7 May 2013

He called for two days of protests and led a rally on 8 May. Some 110,000 black-clad protesters participated at the rally held at a Kuala Lumpur football stadium. Anwar was to hold many more protest rallies around the country in the months following the election.

Najib: "Chinese tsunami"

Predictably, the governing coalition won most of its seats in the rural states populated by *Bumiputera* (Malays). The opposition picked up seats in the largely urban regions with a great proportion of ethnic Chinese, who make up about a quarter of the population, leading the swing away from the government.

It was hardly surprising, accelerating a trend seen in the 2008 election. The Chinese community had increasingly become disaffected by years of discrimination in education, employment and business. It led to a near-total rejection of Umno's two Chinese-based parties, MCA and Gerakan, and a swing to the secular and largely Chinese opposition Democratic Action Party.[2]

Prime Minister Najib Razak blamed a "Chinese tsunami" for the poor showing of his party, saying that the Chinese community "had been deceived and manipulated" by the opposition parties.[3] His comments had all the hallmarks of race politics, putting a racial interpretation on the election result that would have appealed to Umno traditionalists and encouraging anti-Chinese headlines in the Malay-language press.

---

2 "Ruling Barisan wins Malaysian elections, but opposition score bigger wins", Channel News Asia, 6 May 2013; Rudra Gobind, "Racial fearmongering poll's unintended result", *The Canberra Times*, 8 May 2013

3 "Malaysia election: Opposition manipulated Chinese community, says PM Najib", Asia One, 7 May 2013

Utusan Malaysia, a newspaper controlled by Umno, sought to portray Sunday's election result in racial terms with one headline saying: "What more do the Chinese want?"[4] The implication being the Chinese had betrayed the government.

This reaction was picked up by more than 20 non-governmental organisations and the Muslim Consumers Association of Malaysia (PPIM) calling upon the country's Malays to boycott Chinese firms to teach them "a lesson" for backing opposition candidates.[5]

Former Prime Minister Mahathir Mohamad, still a powerful figure in Umno, was quoted by local media as saying "ungrateful Chinese" and "greedy Malays" were to blame for the result.[6]

While Mr Najib urged national reconciliation and called ethnic-based campaign politics "unhealthy", some commentators said his "tsunami" comment only magnified the ethnic debate in Malaysia and exacerbated post-election tensions. Malaysian newspaper columnist and political observer Karim Raslan said at the time "the political divide in Malaysia is poisonous".[7]

There is no doubt that the election result shocked Umno. It was its worst result ever for the ruling party. For the first time, it looked in real danger of losing control of the government it had held since independence in 1957.

Anwar had said before the election he was "willing to forgive but not necessarily forget" his dismissal and imprisonment. Still, Lim Teck Ghee,

4   Jerrenn Lam, Global Voices, 12 May 2013

5   *South China Morning Post*, 25 May 2013

6   Reuters US Edition, 8 May 2013

7   *New York Times*, 10 May 2013

head of the Centre for Policy Initiatives in Kuala Lumpur, said there remained widespread concern within Umno that Anwar would open legal inquiries against Dr Mahathir, Mr Najib and other senior party officials should he ever become prime minister.

"It's not simply concern about who is the next prime minister," Mr Lim said. "Mahathir's very afraid that if Anwar and the opposition come to power, Mahathir's place in history is going to be smeared, and I think he is fighting that very, very strongly, and this feeds into the politics of hate in the country."[8]

8 *New York Times*, Asian Edition, 11 May 2013

CHAPTER 14
Attempts to disqualify prosecutor

Anwar's acquittal at the High Court on 9 January 2012 was a welcome surprise. It was also the correct decision based on the evidence. The trial had lasted almost two years during which time there were many highs and lows for the beleaguered opposition leader, but in the end the trial judge Justice Mohamad Zabidin Mohd Diah was not convinced the evidence was sufficient to prove Anwar's guilt.

Shortly after Anwar's acquittal, the trial prosecutor Mohamed Yusof Zainal Abiden announced that the Attorney-General's Chambers would be appealing the decision. The appeal petition was filed at the Court of Appeal on 10 July 2012. The prosecution attacked the trial judge's finding that he wasn't satisfied that the integrity of the forensic samples had not been compromised. The prosecution also challenged the expertise and testimony of the defence experts, which the trial judge relied upon in preference to the local DNA experts.

The appeal against the acquittal was ultimately listed for hearing 14 months later, on 17 September 2013. The prosecution team would be led by Tan Sri Muhammad Shafee Abdullah. His appointment would prove to be controversial.

Court of Appeal hearing: 17 Sept 2013

The appeal did not get very far because at the hearing on 17 September, Anwar's lawyers sought to disqualify two key participants: Justice Tengku Maimun Tuan Mat, one of the judges scheduled to hear the appeal, and Shafee Abdullah, the leader of the prosecution team. (The other two judges in the panel were Datuk Mohd Zawawi Salleh and Datuk Ramly Ali.)

Judge disqualified from hearing case

The application to disqualify Justice Maimun on account of perceived bias came about when the defence discovered that she had previously sat as the judge on an application to strike out a defamation case brought by Anwar against former Prime Minister Mahathir Mohamad in 2007.

In dismissing Anwar's defamation claim as an abuse of process, she cited with approval the remarks made by judges of the Federal Court at Anwar's appeal against his conviction in 2004, which included the observation that homosexual activity had taken place even though it could not be proved in this specific instance.

Karpal Singh submitted to the Court of Appeal that in adopting the finding of the Federal Court, Justice Maimun gave the perception that she was biased against Anwar. He said, "The court would also have to deal with the public perception that if she sits on the panel, she would be biased and public perception will be against her sitting on the panel."

The Court adjourned briefly. When the judges returned, Justice Ramly Ali, who was leading the panel, announced that Justice Maimun had agreed to withdraw from the case.

The hearing was adjourned to the next morning so that a replacement judge could be appointed to hear the application to disqualify Shafee Abdullah.

First application to disqualify prosecutor: 18 Sept 2013

Proceedings resumed the next morning with Justice Maimun's replacement Datuk Rohana Yusof joining the bench. Anwar's lawyers submitted to the Court that Shafee Abdullah should be disqualified from prosecuting the appeal on behalf of the Attorney-General Tan Sri Abdul Gani Patail. They complained that his background made him an unsuitable person to prosecute the appeal. They also challenged the validity of his appointment, submitting that he had a conflict of interest having been a potential material witness at Anwar's recent trial.

The A-G's appointment of Shafee Abdullah was controversial not only because he wasn't a member of the government prosecution service, but also because of his reputation as a prominent Umno lawyer. He had been a confidant and personal lawyer not only to PM Najib Razak, but also to many of Umno's senior politicians and major supporters.

Furthermore, Shafee Abdullah had a direct connection to the Anwar trial. He was at Prime Minister Najib Razak's house at Taman Duta on the night that Mohd Saiful came calling, supposedly to ask about his prospects of obtaining a scholarship for tertiary studies. As far-fetched as that explanation might seem, the discussion that night between Mr Najib and Mohd Saiful turned to his allegation that Anwar had sexually assaulted him. This was a critical point in time because it was only three days before the alleged sexual assault, which was the basis of the charge brought against Anwar.

After meeting with Mr Najib at his home, Mohd Saiful later that night met with Senior Assistant Commissioner of Police Mohd Rodwan Mohd Yusof at a room in the Melia Hotel, and again the next day at another room at the Concorde Hotel in Kuala Lumpur.

Shafee Abdullah admits being in Mr Najib's house while the discussion with Mohd Saiful was taking place, but he says he was not part of it and remained in another part of the house. He told me during the appeal hearing that he was coincidentally at the house only to advise Mr Najib's wife on difficulties she was having with the blogger Raja Petra.

Anwar's supporters say it is inconceivable that given the seriousness of the allegation made by Mohd Saiful against the opposition leader, and the obvious political implications for the opposition, that Shafee Abdullah's advice would not have been sought or indeed that he would not have been part of the conversation. Whatever their suspicions, there is no evidence to the contrary.

The court unanimously dismissed the application and listed the main appeal to be heard by the Court of Appeal on 11–12 December 2013.

Anwar's lawyers announced to the media outside the courtroom that they would immediately appeal the decision. The appeal was later heard by the Federal Court, which is the highest court of appeal in Malaysia and which delivered its decision on 21 November 2013.

Federal Court dismisses appeal to disqualify prosecutor: 21 November 2013

The Federal Court unanimously dismissed Anwar's appeal to disqualify the prosecutor. First, it ruled that Shafee Abdullah's appointment as deputy prosecutor was valid. Justice Tan Sri Raus Sharif, who led a five-judge bench, read out the court's decision saying:

> "We are of the same view of the Court of Appeal that section 378 of the Criminal Procedure Code (CPC) must not be read in isolation and that it must be read with section 376 (3) and section 379 of CPC. Hence, we see no merit for the first issue raised."

Secondly, the court rejected the submission that Shafee Abdullah was conflicted because he was a potential witness during Anwar's sodomy case, saying it was a "non-issue". That ground of appeal was also dismissed.

The mere fact that Shafee Abdullah had formerly acted against Anwar on behalf of his political opponents, which included the ruling political party and its leaders, by no means was sufficient to disqualify him from prosecuting the appeal. Lawyers are entitled and, indeed, are expected to act for anyone subject only to the restriction that there must be no conflict of interest in doing so. A conflict of interest would definitely arise in circumstances where a lawyer was acting against a former client.

A conflict arises because the lawyer may have learnt information about the former client that should remain confidential and that may directly or indirectly be used against that person. Shafee Abdullah had never acted for Anwar, so there could be no conflict that would disqualify him from prosecuting the appeal.

In any event, both the Court of Appeal and the Federal Court ruled that Shafee Abdullah was validly appointed and it seemed that the appeal would proceed with him leading the prosecution team.

The Zain Statutory Declaration and the second application to disqualify prosecutor: 6 December 2013

On 6 December 2013, Anwar's lawyers filed a second application to disqualify Shafee Abdullah from leading the prosecution team.

Leading the legal team this time was prominent constitutional lawyer Tommy Thomas. The application asserted new grounds of appeal based upon information contained in a statutory declaration made by Datuk Mat Zain Ibrahim, the former chief of the Kuala Lumpur Criminal Investigation Department (CID). Mat Zain was the senior police officer investigating what became known as the "black eye" incident when Anwar was assaulted by then Inspector-General of Police (IGP) Abdul Rahim Noor while in custody on 20 September 1998. Noor subsequently pleaded guilty to the assault.

In 2008, Anwar lodged a police report against Mat Zain, Abdul Gani Patail (the senior deputy public prosecutor at Anwar's first sodomy trial in 1998, but now Attorney-General), Musa Hassan (the then Inspector-General of police) and Dr Abdul Rahman Yusof (pathologist at Hospital Kuala Lumpur), alleging fabrication of evidence in the "black eye" incident.

The complaint was referred to the Malaysian Anti-Corruption Commission (MACC), and in a majority decision it cleared Musa Hassan and Gani Patail of the allegation of fabricating evidence. Mat Zain has since then been lobbying for the case to be re-opened in a series of open letters penned to the Malaysian Police and the government, continuing to insist that Gani Patail was complicit in the alleged fabrication of evidence in the case.

Anwar's application to disqualify Shafee Abdullah from leading the prosecution team was listed to be heard on 6 December 2013. Four days before that, Mat Zain distributed his statutory declaration to news outlets and selected members of parliament. The contents of the document alleged that Shafee Abdullah had made statements that implicated A-G Gani Patail in criminal misconduct and corruption.

Citing Mat Zain's statutory declaration, Anwar in his affidavit in support of his application said that Shafee Abdullah claimed that Gani Patail had fabricated evidence against him when he was taken into custody before his original trial in 1998. (See Anwar's Affidavit, paragraph 9)

Mat Zain was further quoted as alleging that more recently Gani Patail had corruptly taken bribes over the Pulau Batu Puteh (the Pedra Branca islands) territorial dispute between Malaysia and Singapore. According to Mat Zain, bribes were paid to Gani Patail for suppressing evidence at the hearing at the International Court of Justice in 2007. That hearing resulted in Malaysia losing the island to Singapore.

Quoting again from the statutory declaration, Anwar said that Shafee Abdullah allegedly told Mat Zain that "you will not believe your eyes if you were to see the amount of cash that was transferred into Gani's account in Hong Kong". (See Anwar's Affidavit, paragraph 9(ii))

Anwar said in his affidavit: "Shafee agreed with Mat Zain that Gani had fabricated evidence against myself during the 'black eye' investigation. Shafee agreed it was indeed true that Dr Abdul Rahman bin Yusof, a forensic consultant at Kuala Lumpur Hospital had fabricated evidence in my 'black eye' investigation." (See Anwar's Affidavit, paragraph 22)

Anwar further noted that Mat Zain also claimed that Shafee Abdullah was of the view that the three-member MACC panel, which cleared Abdul Gani and former IGP Musa Hassan of allegations of tampering with his blood sample, had been an "unconstitutional sitting". (See Anwar's Affidavit, paragraph 9(v))

These statements were apparently made in conversations between Mat Zain and Shafee Abdullah at his office and later with former Prime Minister Mahathir at his home at Seri Kembangan.

Anwar submitted in his application that because of this conduct, Shafee Abdullah had shown himself not to be a fit and proper person to act as a deputy public prosecutor and should be disqualified from prosecuting the appeal. "It is plain and obvious that Shafee's professional conduct is gravely challenged and there would be abuse of court process and oppression if he acts in the appeal," Anwar said. (See Anwar's Affidavit, paragraph 11)

He added that Shafee Abdullah would not be able to comply with the requirement of the Legal Profession (Practice and Etiquette) Rules 1978 to conduct the appeal. Anwar said he would not receive a fair hearing if Shafee

Abdullah led the prosecution team. (See Anwar's Affidavit, paragraph 26)

Finally, Anwar submitted in his affidavit that Shafee Abdullah was also further motivated to ensure that a conviction of the sodomy charge was secured against him because he acted as the solicitor for a few high-profile personalities who had been sued for defamation and rely on the defence of justification that Anwar is a homosexual. He referred to defamation suits he had brought against Khairy Jamaluddin (in Civil Suit No: S7-23-44-2008) and Datuk S. Nallakaruppan (in Civil Suit No: 23-NCVC-42-03/2012). (See Anwar's Affidavit, paragraph 15)

Shafee Abdullah's response

Responding to the application, Shafee Abdullah said Anwar's application was "frivolous, vexatious and an abuse of court process", adding that Anwar had a history of attempting to disqualify judges and prosecutors. He said the current grounds raised by Anwar to disqualify him also had no bearing on his appointment and Anwar's fear of not getting a fair trial was baseless. (See Shafee Abdullah's Affidavit, paragraph 4)

He said Mat Zain's statutory declaration, which Anwar was now relying on, merely showed that the former police officer was an "angry man" over the way the authorities dealt with him over the 1998 "black eye" incident. (See Shafee Abdullah's Affidavit, paragraph 7(a))

In his affidavit in reply, Shafee Abdullah said it wasn't him, but rather former Commercial Crime Investigation Department Director Datuk Ramli Yusof who brought Mat Zain to his office at Bukit Tunku to determine certain facts and documents relating to a civil case on which he had yet to decide whether to represent Ramli.([See Shafee Abdullah's Affidavit, paragraph 7(q)(i))

"The conversation in my office was only in relation to Mat Zain's many investigations, including the 'black eye' incident," Shafee Abdullah said. He said the idea of Mat Zain going to Dr Mahathir's house was an impromptu decision made in his office and there was no agenda except to pay respect to Dr Mahathir for the festive season. (See Shafee Abdullah's Affidavit, paragraph 7(q)(ii)-(v))

Shafee Abdullah also denied being involved in any meeting to discuss Gani Patail's conduct or the Pulau Batu Puteh issue; nor did he insinuate or mention anything about funds being transferred into a bank account in Hong Kong after the Pulau Batu Puteh case was decided by the international court. (See Shafee Abdullah's Affidavit, paragraph 8, 10)

Shafee Abdullah denied being involved in any conspiracy against the Attorney-General saying, "I wish to state there was never a plot to unseat Gani from his office." He further denied that he had commented on Anwar's "black eye" investigation. (See Shafee Abdullah's Affidavit, paragraph 5, 9)

Parties release their affidavits to media

The fitness of Shafee Abdullah to act as prosecutor continued to be played out in the media as the parties released their affidavits dealing with these allegations. The pressure on him also increased when it was reported by the media that Mat Zain had lodged a police report against him alleging he had lied in his affidavit-in-reply.

In his police report, Mat Zain claimed Shafee Abdullah had committed at least two offences under the *Penal Code*, the first for making false statements in the affidavit. He alleged that Shafee Abdullah had also suppressed material evidence with the intention of deceiving the court and that his reply was "a load of rubbish".[1]

---

1   "Matt Zain Files Police Report against Shafee, says lawyer lying", by V. Anbalagan, Assistant News Editor, *The Malaysian Insider*, 15 December 2013

Mat Zain then went one step further by calling on the Attorney-General to explain why he had allowed the prosecution to file Shafee Abdullah's affidavits at court when they were obviously false.

He called on Gani Patail to immediately remove Shafee Abdullah as lead prosecutor in the appeal. He said that "...now that Abdul Gani has discovered Shafee's affidavit to be false, or at the very least that there are strong grounds to suspect that the senior lawyer's affidavit to be false, he owes a duty to the court to put the matter right."[2]

Anwar claims Shafee Abdullah using appeal to become next Attorney-General

Anwar's attack on Shafee Abdullah took another direction when he accused him of taking the deputy public prosecutor's role in the hope of becoming the next Attorney-General. He told the media that it was well known in Kuala Lumpur's political and legal circles that Shafee Abdullah had publicly stated his ambition to succeed Gani Patail as Attorney-General. He said "that explains why Shafee was so critical of Gani in the statutory declaration [of Mat Zain]".

The opposition leader added that Shafee Abdullah's interest to ensure the government succeeded in the appeal was so overwhelming that it overrode all his duties as lead DPP. He said: "Such a conflict of interest and duty will only undermine the administration of justice. It will certainly prejudice me during the hearing of the appeal."[3]

---

2   "Now Mat Zain wants Gani Patail to explain 'false' affidavits by Shafee, Ramli", *The Malaysian Insider*, Tuesday 17 December 2013; "Umno lawyer Shafee in HOT SOUP, accused of lying to the court by Mat Zain in latest police report", Malaysia Chronicle, 15 December 2013

3   *The Malaysian Insider*, 17 December 2013

Appeal relisted: 11 December 2013

The hearing resumed before the Court of Appeal on 11 December 2013 before the new panel of judges chaired by Justice Datuk Aziah Ali. The other presiding judges were Justices Datuk Rohana Yusuf and Datuk Mohd Zawawi Salleh.

On the morning of the hearing, however, Ramkarpal Singh, who was in Anwar's legal team, advised the court that his father had been admitted to hospital with a lung infection and was to remain there at least until the end of the week making it impossible for him to attend the hearing. He applied to adjourn the hearing to another date.

Shafee Abdullah told the court that while he wouldn't object to the application, he was anxious for the matter to proceed before the end of the year. He told the judges that he would push aside a busy calendar to make himself available for the hearing. He urged the judges to relist the appeal in the next two weeks, which he said was at a time when Karpal's health would be "at its best".

Another key person was absent too: Anwar, who was in Washington attending a seminar. In all criminal proceedings an accused person must attend the hearing, whether it is a trial or an appeal. My understanding is that the prosecution neglected to file and serve a notice requiring him to attend the appeal hearing and so he was not compelled to appear.

Justice Aziah Ali, after consulting her fellow judges, announced that the court would allow the application to adjourn, and would list the matter for a case management hearing on 19 December 2013, when it could be relisted. The court also requested Anwar to be present at that hearing.

Later that day, I visited Karpal at the Kuala Lumpur General Hospital. Although appearing to be a little weak, he seemed to be in good spirits. At the time he was often susceptible to infections of this type mostly because of being confined to a wheelchair and lacking mobility.

Court of Appeal hearing: 19 December 2013

The Court of Appeal, chaired by Justice Aziah Ali, convened again on 19 December 2013.

Anwar's lead counsel Tommy Thomas submitted to the court that it was inappropriate for Shafee Abdullah to be appearing that morning to argue the case against his own disqualification. The defence argument focused on his fitness to prosecute the appeal given the significant allegations made against him in Mat Zain's affidavit.

He submitted that Shafee Abdullah had committed serious misconduct by failing to report Mat Zain's allegations made against the Attorney-General concerning Anwar's "black eye" incident. He also submitted that taking the brief to prosecute in those circumstances amounted to professional misconduct under the Legal Profession (Practice and Etiquette) Rules 1978. He also submitted that the Attorney-General's Chambers had ample candidates who were experienced in handling appeal matters as a possible replacement.

Shafee Abdullah in reply submitted that the material that Anwar relied upon to bring his application — namely Mat Zain's statutory declaration — depended heavily on hearsay evidence and "frivolous allegations". He said that Mat Zain had not been examined in court or provided admissible affidavits for the court to verify the truth of the matter he had alleged. He submitted: "This application amounts to nothing more than a vexatious and frivolous application ... to delay and prolong the hearing of the main second sodomy appeal."[4]

The Court of Appeal delivered its decision the next morning. Justices Aziah Ali, Rohana Yusuf and Mohd Zawawi Salleh unanimously ruled that

---

4 *The Malaysian Times*, 19 December 2013; *The Malaysian Insider*, 20 December 2013

the second application to disqualify Shafee Abdullah from prosecuting the appeal "lacked merit".

Justice Aziah Ali, who delivered the court's decision, said that Mat Zain's statutory declaration, which Anwar relied upon, could not be used. She said that the central issue to be decided was whether Anwar's application was sustainable and it depended on Mat Zain's statutory declaration. "Our plain reading is that the statutory declaration is not relevant as it mainly related to the 'black eye' incident which had been decided on earlier," she said.

She also said the bench concurred with Shafee Abdullah that the statutory declaration was hearsay evidence and Mat Zain was "not available to ascertain the truth".

She also pointed to what the court regarded as latent defects in Mat Zain's statutory declaration. For example, it did not provide his identity card number and address, which had been blotted out in the document. She said: "There was no conceivable evidence as to why Mat Zain refused to give these details. For this reason, the statutory declaration cannot be accepted as cogent evidence and the application must be dismissed."

Justice Aziah Ali rejected Anwar's claim that he would not get a fair trial should Shafee Abdullah be allowed to prosecute the case. She said the verdict rested on the court, and since it was an appeal the court would rely on appeal records from the High Court (where the trial was held). She also made the point that Shafee Abdullah was not the sole person conducting the case, as two deputy public prosecutors would assist him.[5]

Justice Aziah Ali set 12 and 13 February 2014 for hearing of the main appeal.

---

5   *The Malaysian Insider*, 20 December 2013; *New Straits Times*, Punitha Kumar, 20 December 2013

Anwar reports Shafee Abdullah for professional misconduct

After leaving the Court of Appeal on 19 December 2013, Anwar told the waiting media that he intended to file a complaint against Shafee Abdullah with the Advocates and Solicitors Disciplinary Board for unprofessional conduct in failing to report the wrongdoing of the Attorney-General. He said he would act on the matter in a day or two.

Lawyer and opposition member of parliament Sivarasa Rasiah also spoke to the assembled media saying that there was a sound basis to believe that Shafee Abdullah had allegedly committed professional misconduct, which was unbecoming of a lawyer. Mr Rasiah said Mat Zain would have the opportunity to give evidence at the board's inquiry.[6]

Court of Appeal hearing: 12 February 2014

When the matter came before the court on 12 February, Karpal applied to call former Deputy Superintendent Jude Pereira, a key prosecution witness in the sodomy trial, over the issue of the retired investigating officer's credibility.

The court was told that Pereira's application to be admitted as a lawyer was rejected by a judge of the High Court in proceedings the previous month. The decision came after the Malaysian Bar Council objected on the basis that Pereira was not a fit and proper person to practice law. That, submitted Karpal, reflected adversely on Pereira's credibility as a witness during Anwar's sodomy proceedings and was directly relevant to the issue of whether his testimony could be accepted at all.

Justice Aziah Ali, speaking on behalf of the three-member panel, said the court unanimously rejected the application on the ground that Karpal had failed to prove the basis of his application was exceptional. She held that additional evidence would only be allowed if the court thought it was necessary.

The court found that Justice Mohamad Zabidin Mohd Diah, who presided over the sodomy trial, had not only relied on the evidence of Pereira, but also on evidence from the complainant and doctors who testified in the trial. Justice Aziah Ali said: "The recall of Pereira will not have important influence in the end of the prosecution's case."

However, the court granted Karpal's application to stay the proceedings pending an appeal of the decision to the Federal Court, but Justice Aziah also said: "We are conscious the court has to be fair and seen to be fair and we do not want to deprive the applicant [Anwar] of his remedies if there is any right to appeal, but we are concerned with the continuous delay [to hear the merits of the appeal]."

Commentary

(A) CORRECTNESS OF COURT OF APPEAL'S DECISION

The court's dismissal of the application, which was based solely on the affidavit of Mat Zain, was undoubtedly correct. His affidavit was not made for the purposes of this application, but was relied upon by Anwar, which meant that the allegations contained within the document were hearsay.

A brief explanation is needed. The legal rule against *hearsay* is one of the most fundamental rules of evidence. Simply put, it states that an out-of-court statement tendered for the purpose of directly proving the truth of what is contained in the statement is hearsay. Hearsay is inadmissible because it is unreliable. It is not something that has been tested in a court.

Anwar's affidavit in support of his motion relied on the allegations contained in Mat Zain's affidavit. He submitted that the allegations were true, and as such Shafee Abdullah was not a fit and proper person to prosecute the case against him. But he had no way of knowing whether the allegations were true or false because none of the information came from his direct knowledge.

It was open to Anwar's lawyers to call Mat Zain as a witness, but for whatever reason he wasn't called and therefore the truthfulness of his allegations could not be tested by the prosecution under cross-examination. Shafee Abdullah was quick to seize upon this deficiency.

(B) FOCUS OF ANWAR APPEAL SHIFTS TO PROSECUTOR'S INTEGRITY
The defence may well have lost the battle to remove Shafee Abdullah as prosecutor, but what took place at this point of the appeal hearing could only be described as extraordinary. The focus effectively shifted from the merits of Anwar's appeal to Shafee Abdullah's fitness to prosecute the case.

Shafee Abdullah's integrity was significantly challenged. The allegations also enveloped the Attorney-General Gani Patail, who some said must seriously have regretted his decision to appoint Shafee Abdullah to prosecute the appeal. Of course, the irony would not be lost on him that the man he appointed to prosecute the appeal — if Mat Zain's allegations were true — was actively campaigning against him alleging serious claims of corruption.

My local sources tell me that Shafee Abdullah has for a long time wanted to be the Malaysian Attorney-General, and made no secret of his ambition. Anwar alleged as much, suggesting that Shafee Abdullah has taken on the role of deputy public prosecutor against him to advance his ambitions to be appointed to that position.

During one of these court sessions, I recall, during a break in proceedings, being part of a courtroom conversation with former UN Special Rapporteur Dato' Param Cumaraswamy — also on Anwar's legal team — and Shafee Abdullah. Cumaraswamy teasingly suggested to Shafee

Abdullah that he still harboured ambitions to become Attorney-General. The deputy prosecutor just smiled and said, "Oh no, not at all." His denial wasn't very convincing.

Others have suggested that Prime Minister Najib foisted Shafee Abdullah on to Gani Patail as a means not only to attack his rival Anwar, but also to give the lawyer a high profile in prosecuting the case and so making it easier to appoint him as Attorney-General. They say that Gani Patail cannot remove Shafee Abdullah — even if he wanted to — because he is responsible for appointing him and also because of significant political pressure not to do so.

(c) should shafee abdullah have argued the disqualification application?

Mat Zain's allegations may not have been admissible at the hearing, but they seriously damaged the deputy prosecutor's reputation and in turn the prosecution service he represented. One can understand the prosecution opposing the application to disqualify its lead counsel in the proceedings, but given the serious nature of the allegations against Shafee Abdullah, it should have been argued by someone else.

That's what happened at Anwar's appeal against conviction in the Federal Court in 2004. The Attorney-General Abdul Gani Patail was the lead prosecutor at that hearing assisted by his deputy Datuk Mohd Yusof, who was later to prosecute Anwar at his second trial in 2010–12.

During the hearing, Gani Patail's integrity came under attack from one of Anwar's counsel Chris Fernando who alleged that Gani Patail had fabricated evidence against Anwar at his trial. Each time these allegations were made, I saw Gani Patail leave the court to allow his deputy to respond. It was the proper thing to do. And yet Shafee Abdullah not only remained in court, but argued the case. At the first attempt to disqualify him, he was at times giving evidence from the bar table about aspects of his conduct. That should not have happened.

It is one thing to argue the case on strictly legal grounds, but then to speak to the facts, which Shafee Abdullah did at the disqualification application, meant he was giving evidence from the bar table. That is not permitted at law, as evidence of the facts can only be given either by the filing of affidavits sworn on oath or by the witnesses testifying in court.

Affidavits were filed by the parties, including Shafee Abdullah, as part of the hearing of the fresh application, but again it was inevitable that when arguing the case he would go beyond the limits of his affidavit and speak to the facts, which meant giving evidence from the bar table.

It was surprising that the Court of Appeal should dismiss Anwar's preliminary objection that Shafee Abdullah should not be arguing the prosecution case, for it was well founded. What was more surprising is that neither Shafee Abdullah nor the prosecution service could see the inappropriateness of him doing so. Shafee Abdullah continued to act as the prosecutor with all this controversy happening around him and effectively acted for himself in defending these conflict allegations in court.

Prosecutors must be fair, independent and objective — and be seen to be so. All prosecution services must operate on this basis. The fact that Shafee Abdullah argued the case against his own disqualification raises serious concerns that these standards were not being met.

In this instance, there was a direct conflict of interest between the independence and impartiality of the prosecution service and the personal interests of Shafee Abdullah. For him to effectively appear on his own behalf to argue the prosecution's position had every potential to bring the law into disrepute. He may well have other prosecutors assisting him, but he was doing all the talking.

CHAPTER 15
A week of action

The prosecution appeal against Anwar's acquittal was last heard before the Court of Appeal on 12 February 2014. On that occasion, the judges refused Anwar's application to recall Deputy Superintendent Jude Pereira, the chief investigating police officer at Anwar's sodomy case, to testify at the appeal.

Karpal Singh immediately requested the Court of Appeal to stay the proceedings so that he might lodge a separate appeal against the decision to the Federal Court. The judges, led by Justice Aziah Ali, reluctantly agreed, but set a case management conference date of 28 February 2014 to appoint the new hearing dates.

It was expected that the new dates would be listed in early April 2014, as there had been no indication that there was any rush or need to list it for hearing before then. However, what happened at the case management hearing at the Court of Appeal on 28 February changed all that.

Karpal claimed to be ambushed and pushed into a timetable that effectively condensed everything into the space of one week. He concluded that the only possible explanation was that it was part of a political agenda to resolve everything before the Kajang by-election which was to be held on 23 March. Anwar had publicly announced he would be a candidate for that parliamentary seat, with the ultimate prospect that he would take over as Selangor Chief Minister.

Day 1: Case Management Conference (Friday, 28 Feb 2014)

The listing of criminal cases for hearing is managed through what is called a Case Management Conference presided over by the Registrar of the particular court in which the case is to be heard. Both parties attend and dates are appointed for the hearing.

Some time before the case management hearing, one of the court's registrars contacted Karpal and asked him to block off 7–10 April 2014 in anticipation of a listing within those dates. Karpal told the Registrar that he would be free to conduct the appeal during that period.

On 28 February, however, when Karpal attended at the case management hearing to deal with the listing, he found Justice Aziah Ali presiding instead of the court Registrar; she was the judge who had led the bench on the previous court hearing. In addition she told the parties that she intended to list the main appeal earlier, on 6 and 7 March. She also set the dates for two pending applications to be heard on 3 and 4 March as these had to be dealt with first before the substantive, or main, appeal could be heard.

The first concerned yet another defence application to disqualify Shafee Abdullah as prosecutor, this time relying on a finding against him of unprofessional conduct by the Malaysian Bar Council. The second was the prosecution application to strike out the appeal by the defence against the Court of Appeal's refusal to require DSP Pereira to testify.

Karpal protested to the new dates on the basis that he already had trials involving serious charges scheduled for that week, which he said could not be adjourned at such short notice. Justice Aziah Ali told him that the trial judges would be contacted and arrangements made for the trials to be adjourned.

It had been evident that the judges were determined to have an early listing for the main appeal. The fact that Justice Aziah Ali presided over the case management hearing, rather than the Registrar, seemed to confirm that the court was impatient about the delays and wanted the matter resolved.

Something else that confirmed the court's determination to hear Anwar's case on 6 and 7 March was the adjournment of Karpal's sentencing in the High Court, which had originally been listed for 7 March, to 11 March. He had been convicted of sedition for remarks he had made about the Sultan of Perak, and the date had already been set for sentencing. No explanation was given for this sudden switch though it was obvious to all that it was to ensure that Karpal was available to argue Anwar's appeal that week.

All of this gave every indication of a coordinated and determined effort to deal with Anwar during that week. The judges went to extraordinary lengths to do that, including instructing other courts to adjourn serious trials, hearing applications at no more than an hour's notice and waiving the service of appeal papers on the prosecution.

However there seemed to be no good reason for doing so. Anwar was not a sentenced prisoner awaiting trial, so he would not be prejudiced by any delay. He was not a person who had been convicted and waiting appeal, but was rather a person who had been acquitted and not in custody, so there was no need for haste. The appeal could have been heard at any time and it seemed that the dates were already allocated in early April. Something had changed and Karpal believed he knew the answer — which to him seemed obvious.

Day 2: Third application to disqualify Shafee Abdullah (Monday, 3 March 2014)

Two previous applications to disqualify Shafee Abdullah had been rejected by the Court of Appeal.

The first application was based on a technical argument asserting that the Attorney-General Abdul Gani Patail had no constitutional authority to appoint Shafee Abdullah to represent him in this case against Anwar. It was dismissed by the Court of Appeal on 17 September 2013. A subsequent appeal to the Federal Court was also dismissed, the court saying it was without merit and ruling that Shafee Abdullah's appointment was within the law.

The second application was based on a statutory declaration made by a former police officer Mat Zain Ibrahim who claimed that Shafee Abdullah had involved him in a plot to discredit the Attorney-General. Mat Zain alleged in his 31-page statutory declaration that he had gone with Shafee Abdullah and former Commercial Crime Investigation Department director Datuk Ramli Yusof to the house of former Prime Minister Mahathir Mohamad, where they allegedly discussed the wrongdoings of the A-G. These "wrongdoings" included allegations of corruption and fabricating evidence. A panel of three judges led by Justice Aziah Ali unanimously dismissed the application ruling that Mat Zain's statutory declaration, which was used by Anwar to support the second application, was hearsay and could not be admitted as cogent evidence.

In the third application to disqualify Shafee Abdullah, the defence again returned to his fitness to prosecute the appeal and on this occasion based their argument on two grounds.

First, that he was not a fit and proper person to act as deputy prosecutor in the appeal because, they argued, he had recently been found by the Malaysian Bar Council to have acted unprofessionally in advertising himself in the newspapers and was fined RM5,000.

Secondly, that it was not appropriate for him to prosecute the appeal because of a conflict of interest. That came about, so it was argued, because he had been the chairman of a committee of the Malaysian Human Rights

Commission (Suhakam) that had found Deputy Superintendent Pereira not to be a witness of truth and who had lied under oath. Karpal argued that the conflict arose because Shafee Abdullah would undoubtedly rely upon Pereira's truthfulness in submitting that the forensic samples entrusted to him by the forensic doctors who examined Mohd Saiful had not been tampered with and could therefore be relied upon.

The court rejected the application, finding that it was an abuse of process by the defence to cause delay in the hearing. It refused an application by Anwar's lawyer to stay the main appeal pending an appeal of this decision to the Federal Court. More on that later, but it removed the first hurdle to hearing the main appeal later that week.

Day 3: Federal Court: Prosecution motion to strike out defence appeal to call DSP Pereira (Tuesday, 4 March 2014)

The next morning the parties assembled at the Federal Court to hear an application by the prosecution to strike out the defence appeal against the dismissal by the Court of Appeal of the application to call DSP Pereira to testify before it.

The Court of Appeal had rejected the application on the basis that Pereira had been questioned at the trial about the Suhakam finding and his credibility tested, all of which was before the trial judge.

It is to be recalled that Jude Pereira was the officer who was given custody of the forensic samples taken from the body of Mohd Saiful by medical examiners at Hospital Kuala Lumpur (HKL) when he went there complaining of having been sexually assaulted. These samples were a critical part of the prosecution evidence to implicate Anwar in the alleged crime. The government DNA analysis concluded that the samples, one of which was taken from semen found in Saiful's rectum, matched Anwar's DNA.

The defence challenged this analysis on the basis that the proper chain of custody had been compromised by Pereira's mishandling of the samples. The trial judge agreed, finding that he could not be satisfied that the integrity of the samples had been preserved.

The defence application was based on a finding by Suhakam that Pereira was not a credible witness during a human rights hearing in a case involving the arrest of five lawyers who were assisting those arrested during a candlelight vigil outside the Brickfields police station. At the time Pereira was head of crime division at the police station. The finding related to a matter unrelated to Anwar's sodomy case.

The Suhakam inquiry that found Pereira not a credible witness was chaired by then commissioner Muhammad Shafee Abdullah — now leading the prosecution team in the appeal against the acquittal.

The application was decided on a legal technical point. The court accepted the prosecution submission that the appeal should be struck out because it was not a final order of the court. That removed the second hurdle to the main appeal taking place later that week.

Day 4: Federal Court: Appeal against refusal to disqualify Shafee Abdullah (Wednesday, 5 March 2014)

As we know, on Monday 3 March 2104, the Court of Appeal dismissed the third defence application to disqualify Shafee Abdullah from prosecuting the substantive appeal against Anwar's acquittal. The court refused an application to stay the appeal against that refusal pending an appeal to the Federal Court.

Papers were filed on the morning of 5 March 2014. At 3.30 pm Anwar's lawyers went to the court to see the Chief Justice. The Registrar informed Karpal that the Chief Justice would not see him, but that he should be ready to argue the appeal at 4.30 pm.

Karpal responded that he had not served the papers on the prosecution and that he wasn't ready to argue it so soon. He was told that the prosecution would be at court and that he could serve the appeal papers on the prosecution lawyers then.

The court convened at 4.30 pm. Having no time to robe, Karpal and the other lawyers assisting him appeared before the Federal Court in civilian clothing. An hour later, after hearing argument, the court dismissed the appeal. That effectively cleared the way for the substantive appeal to be heard the next day. Senior and experienced lawyers have told me that what happened was simply unheard of in their experience.

Day 5 & 6: The Substantive Appeal (Thursday, 6 and Friday, 7 March 2014)

The Court of Appeal convened on Thursday 6 March to hear the substantive appeal. The bench comprised Justices Balia Yusof Wahi, Aziah Ali and Mohd Zawawi Mohd Salleh. Justice Aziah Ali had previously chaired the bench. It was now chaired by Justice Balia.

The case against Anwar effectively revolved around the DNA analysis. The government scientists claimed to have matched Anwar's DNA to samples taken from Mohd Saiful's body by medical examiners from HKL. More specifically, the scientists claimed that the match was made from DNA extracted from sperm cells found in samples taken from Mohd Saiful's upper rectum, which they claimed was consistent with anal penetration.

The defence challenged not only the integrity of the forensic samples, but also the government analysis.

The history of the forensic samples wasn't disputed. Once taken from Mohd Saiful's body, the samples were given to DSP Pereira to deliver to the government scientists for DNA analysis. Pereira not only cut open the sealed packaging to relabel the samples, he also failed to follow instructions to place the samples into a freezer. When he finally delivered the samples to the government scientists, more than 96 hours had elapsed since the alleged sexual assault.

At the conclusion of the prosecution case, the trial judge Justice Zabidin had to decide whether there was a case to answer by the accused. If there was no case to answer, the accused would be acquitted. If there was a case to answer, the accused would need to respond by calling evidence. At that stage in the proceedings, he only needed to be satisfied there was a *prima facie* case, which in my view there was, if only by relying on the complainant's allegation.

Justice Zabidin concluded there was a case for Anwar to answer saying that he was satisfied beyond a reasonable doubt of the DNA evidence. It was unnecessary for him to say that, and in any event he still had not heard the expert testimony of the defence. The prosecution and judges were later to rely upon that comment at the substantive appeal.

The ultimate question to be decided at the end of the trial was whether the judge could be satisfied beyond reasonable doubt that the prosecution had proved the charge against the accused. It was a different question, based not just on the prosecution evidence, but the whole of the evidence which included the defence evidence as well.

After examining all of the evidence at the trial, Justice Zabidin concluded that he could not be satisfied that the integrity of the forensic samples, from which DNA was obtained, was intact. He said that he "couldn't be 100 per cent certain" that the samples had not been tampered with. If that was so, it was evidence that could not be relied upon leaving only the uncorroborated testimony of the complainant. He correctly applied the law, which says that it would be dangerous to convict on that evidence alone.

Karpal at the hearing in March 2014. He is flanked by his son
Ramkarpal and his personal assistant Michael Cornelius.

The prosecution, led by Shafee Abdullah, submitted in support of
its appeal that there was no evidence of tampering. The samples, it was
argued, were always in police custody, and DSP Pereira simply opened
the main package without interfering with the seals to the receptacles that
held the forensic samples. Shafee Abdullah further submitted that the trial
judge had erred in relying upon the foreign experts to challenge the DNA
analysis and should have been satisfied with the results provided by the
government scientists.

Karpal responded challenging the prosecutor's reliance on the integrity
of the forensic samples, saying that Pereira was a man who he had previously
found to be an untruthful witness. He had completely disregarded specific
instructions from the medical examiners to preserve the forensic samples
— and observe police standing orders.

Shafee Abdullah in his submissions made something of the trial judge's
remarks that he "couldn't be 100 per cent certain", saying that the judge
had applied the wrong standard of proof. Karpal replied saying the judge

was not referring to the standard of proof, but the integrity of the samples. He also said that it was open to the judge to prefer the testimony of the defence experts.

Ramkarpal Singh, on behalf of Anwar, focused on the DNA results. He exhaustively examined the analysis and results, submitting that the trial judge was right to reject the analysis provided by the government scientists, which for several reasons could not be accepted.

Submissions were concluded on the second day of the hearing at around 4 pm and the judges retired to consider the verdict.

Waiting for the verdict

The time waiting for the decision was surreal in a way. The courtroom was packed with media, supporters and Anwar's family. Present were lawyers unrelated to the hearing, but who had come to observe the drama that was unfolding.

Special Branch officers were also present and seated at different locations. They were obvious because they were unsmiling and didn't talk to anyone. From time to time they spoke on their mobile phones. There were also a large number of uniformed police stationed at the main door.

Anwar was obviously tense, but characteristically measured and calm as he moved around the courtroom speaking to his lawyers and others. People chatted to each other in subdued tones, speculating as to what might happen.

At one point Anwar's daughters, who had not been in court earlier, attempted to gain entrance, but were refused entry by the police. After checking with their superiors, they were finally admitted.

As we waited in court, Anwar's brother told me that on that morning he had observed two police vans parked nearby and a police helicopter circling the court building. Areas outside the court building had been cordoned off and it had been obvious to all entering the Palace of Justice that police were stationed around it to control the crowd and prevent any trouble. Public entry to the courtroom was restricted to persons holding special security passes, which were only available from court staff sitting at a table at the main entry to the building. Those given security passes had to identify themselves and record their personal details in a book. On each day, I managed to gain entry with the assistance of a senior court official, who was most helpful.

One of the senior lawyers in the court also told me that he overheard the police superintendent in charge of court security telling his officers to prepare themselves to take Anwar into custody.

Fifteen minutes before the judges entered the courtroom, court staff indicated they were about to return. Everyone took a seat and there was little talking. The tension built as time went on.

The judges had retired for no more than an hour or so, which gave rise to some optimism that they might dismiss the appeal, particularly because of the interest they had shown in Ramkarpal's compelling submissions on the inherent unreliability of the DNA evidence.

Finally the usher called the courtroom to order and the judges took their seats. There was silence as Justice Balia began his remarks. He mumbled his early remarks, saying there were a number of issues which would be discussed in detail in written reasons to be delivered at a later date, but in the meantime he would give brief reasons.

He said that the trial judge had erred in fact and law in acquitting Anwar and that on the evidence his decision was not sustainable. He said the judge had failed to properly adjudicate and give sufficient weight to the evidence. In particular, he said the judge had misconstrued the evidence of the forensic samples by concluding there was tampering and thereby impeaching their integrity.

Justice Balia said the court was satisfied that the plastic bag containing the individual samples had been cut open by Pereira, but it was done merely to properly label them, and that there was evidence that the hospital sticker on the top of each receptacle was still intact when delivered to the government scientists. He said "...had the learned trial judge properly appreciated this evidence he would not have concluded there was tampering."

Justice Balia then turned to the issue of contamination of the samples.

To recall, the defence experts had concluded that the final DNA analysis demonstrated there was evidence of contamination. Their considered opinion was that:

1. there was evidence of an unidentified third person in the high rectal swabs that had not been explained, which meant that Mohd Saiful had either been penetrated to ejaculation by another male or someone had contaminated the sample by handling it.

2. the DNA analysis was inconsistent with the known history of the samples, meaning there was little, if any, evidence of degradation in circumstances where contrary to specific instructions the samples had not been properly preserved by DSP Pereira.

3. the DNA allegedly taken from sperm cells had survived for more than 96 hours from the time of ejaculation to analysis, which was highly improbable according to scientific experience.

4. the Differential Extraction Process (DEP), used to separate sperm cells from non-sperm cells, was incomplete, admitting the possibility that the DNA claimed to match Anwar's DNA did not come from semen, but rather from non sperm cells.

Justice Balia dealt with none of these issues in his remarks. He said that there was "no reason for the learned trial judge to depart from his earlier findings concerning the findings and experience of the prosecution experts." He was referring to the judge's reasons at the end of the prosecution case. He went on to say "...the judge erred in giving weight to the defence experts who were no more than armchair experts."

This was a hurried and superficial analysis. The defence experts were critical to the final issue of guilt because if what they said was accepted — even to a limited extent — it was material sufficient to raise a reasonable doubt in the prosecution case. It was not enough for the judges simply to brush aside the defence experts, each of whom had significant credentials and experience, in such a petty and disparaging manner.

Justice Balia concluded his remarks by saying that the prosecution appeal was upheld and that Anwar was accordingly guilty of the offence of sodomy as charged. It was then about 6 pm and it was expected that the court would adjourn and fix a date for sentencing. But that was not to be.

CHAPTER 16

Anwar convicted and sentenced to five years in prison

The sentencing of offenders after conviction is a serious business and a process that often takes time as the prosecution and defence make their respective submissions.

The prosecution will refer to facts relevant to the sentencing and the principles applicable to the offence. The defence will in reply refer to facts in mitigation of sentence and any factors relevant to the offender's personal circumstances. The defence may often rely on medical or psychological reports in support of a plea for leniency and a reduction of sentence.

Court gives Karpal one hour to prepare sentence submissions

It was late in the evening — near 6 pm on Friday, 7 March 2014 — and it was expected that sentencing would be postponed to another date when the parties could make their submissions.

Karpal Singh told the court that he needed time to prepare mitigation for his client and asked that the proceedings be adjourned for sentence to the following Friday. He told Justice Balia Yusof Wahi, who chaired the bench, that the King was to open Parliament on Monday and Anwar was required to respond as opposition leader on Tuesday.

Lead prosecutor Muhammad Shafee Abdullah opposed the application saying sentencing should be done immediately. Karpal protested saying that the whole process had been rushed throughout the week, with a late sitting the day before and that it was now also late in the day.

Justice Balia responded saying that he would give Karpal one hour to prepare mitigation, to which Karpal replied that one hour was simply "unreasonable" and asked him why they were rushing? The judges did not respond, but simply got up and left the court to the jeers and boos of the gallery.

At 6.50 pm the judges returned. There followed a heated and animated exchange between Justice Balia, Karpal and Shafee Abdullah. Karpal again asked for an adjournment so that he might obtain a medical report concerning Anwar's heart and blood pressure. It was a reasonable request given the serious nature of the offence and the delay being asked for was only one week. The response however was bizarre.

Shafee Abdullah suggested that Karpal could summarise his client's medical condition. Justice Balia agreed with the prosecutor that a summary would be sufficient for the purposes of sentencing. But Karpal shot back saying he wouldn't be able to effectively submit a proper plea in mitigation without a medical report. This exchange then followed:

Karpal: Is Your Lordship saying that medical report is not necessary?

Justice Balia: We shall take your word and account of Anwar's ailment. It is our view that you can proceed without a medical report and in that case we shall take it for what it is worth.

Shafee Abdullah: We are not challenging the medical condition.

Karpal: Not challenging what? What is the difference between this case and others? Your Lordship has been at the Bar and you know this is not reasonable.

Justice Balia: Proceed.

At this the gallery roared in disapproval.

While this was taking place, Anwar's supporters, who had assembled at the rear entrance to the building, could be heard shouting in unison: "Free, free, free Anwar", "*Reformasi*" ('Reform') and "Down with Najib".

Shafee Abdullah then commenced to set out the various factors the prosecution considered relevant to sentence. These included such matters as the offence committed was a breach of trust of a young employee; that Anwar had accused the complainant of lying; that Anwar had shown no remorse; that Anwar had behaved recklessly penetrating Saiful without a condom; and that it was a premeditated offence.

Shafee Abdullah then referred to other factors for sentencing. These were of limited relevance, but probably said for the benefit of the assembled media. He said that it was still part of the court record that when acquitted of the charge of sodomy by the Federal Court in 2004, one of the judges had still commented that Anwar had been "involved in homosexual activity". This comment caused uproar from those in the public gallery, with many shouting at him.

Karpal interjected saying that Shafee Abdullah well knew that an application to expunge that reference was pending in the Federal Court.

Shafee Abdullah then referred to Anwar's intention to stand for the forthcoming by-election at Kajang, saying that because he held such high office he was open to blackmail and extortion and therefore represented a threat to national security. He likened the situation to the Profumo Affair in the UK in the 1960s. This caused even more commotion. Justice Balia threatened to remove members of the public if they did not remain silent.

Anwar jumped to his feet shouting at Shafee Abdullah: "...this is no political speech. You got what you wanted. It is a court of law where there should be justice for the people."

Several Anwar supporters and robed lawyers walked out of the court, apparently in protest. Later, when outside, some of them told me that they couldn't remain and watch what was happening, saying it was a disgrace.

Justice Balia asked Karpal if he had anything to say in mitigation. He replied that he had nothing more to say and that he wasn't abandoning his right to mitigate, but without a medical report he was unable to reply.

Justice Balia immediately recorded a conviction and sentenced Anwar to five years' imprisonment. This took place at 6.46 pm. Anwar stood from his chair shouting at the judges: "...this is a travesty of justice. I expected that you would have some courage."

Court agrees to grant bail pending appeal

Karpal then applied for a stay of the sentence and bail pending an appeal to the Federal Court, which was opposed by Shafee Abdullah on the ground that to release Anwar would cause a breach of public order. He referred in support of his argument to the chanting of supporters gathered outside the court.

Heated exchanges continued between counsel. Kapal called Shafee Abdullah a "mercenary" for opposing bail. When Justice Balia asked the lawyers to have some respect for each other, Karpal replied that he had "no respect personally" for Shafee Abdullah.

Justice Balia relented and at 6.55 pm ordered that the sentence be stayed pending appeal. He released Anwar, setting bail at RM10,000 with a surety in a similar amount. He ordered for bail papers to be signed on Monday morning as it was so late and a court registrar wasn't available.

"A clear case of hurried justice"

Soon after, Anwar and Karpal emerged from the courtroom with cameras flashing from the assembled mass of press photographers and supporters and family surrounding him.

Karpal — flanked by Anwar, his wife Wan Azizah and daughter Nurul Izzah — told the media:

> "This is a clear case of hurried justice. And as I say justice hurried is justice buried. For the whole of this week we were honestly put under pressure, which has not happened before. For the first time the Federal Court has sat after 4.30 pm, at least as my experience is concerned. What has been done is under appeal now and I can't say very much as a lawyer, but what has been done is a travesty of justice."

As he said that, it was obvious that he recognised the need to be careful of his comments given the matter would go on appeal, but he continued saying further:

> "For the judges in this case who have said that a medical report is not necessary in the circumstances of this case for the purposes of mitigation is something unthought of. I hope that what has happened will not be repeated because the international community is watching."

Anwar then stepped forward to take up the issue saying:

> "This is clearly a blatant disregard for the facts of the case and the law. Unfortunately, the judges were not concerned about the facts and the law. Clearly they were working under instructions. Look at the way they managed and rushed through the case, and even having less patience with my counsel on the first day and shocking on plea of mitigation for him to state, perhaps

subconsciously, that the circumstances of this case are different and therefore we cannot wait for the medical reports for Anwar Ibrahim. We have Najib's personal lawyer Shafee Abdullah, referred to by counsel as a mercenary, viciously using the court to malign and not on the substantive argument of the law.

We will of course appeal, but I think it is a clear signal to the people of Malaysia that they are not interested in economic malaise or endemic corruption, rising crime, but they are focused on killing, literally assassinating, political opponents.

Today Anwar [is convicted] ... the eleventh [of March] Karpal Singh. So I think it is time we warn Najib and his team and the arrogant Umno leadership that they must face the wrath of the people ... it is the fear that once we get in [to Selangor] that is the end of Umno so they want to end Anwar's political career but they have underestimated the wrath of the people. I believe in God, *Insha Allah* and the will of the people."

Anwar told the media he would continue his campaign in Kajang even though he may no longer be the opposition Parti Keadilan Rakyat (PKR) candidate in the by-election. "This is a travesty of justice. This has been choreographed," he said. He also said he would "let the people show their wrath. But I will be there in parliament and we will shoulder on." Anwar ended his comments saying:

> "It is a clear signal to the people of Malaysia that the government is not interested in economic malaise but they are interested in killing their political opponents. All over again, after 15 years, they want to put me in the lockup and that is why they are rushing."

Why the rush? The Kajang by-election

Kajang is a parliamentary seat located in the State of Selangor about 21 kilometers southeast of Kuala Lumpur. A by-election had resulted from the sitting member's retirement.

Anwar is an MP in the national parliament (Dewan Rakyat) for the federal seat of Permatang Pauh, which is located in the State of Penang. Kajang is a state parliamentary constituency in the State of Selangor. Malaysians can be MPs for both state and federal parliamentary seats at the same time.

The importance of the seat of Kajang for Anwar was that it represented the springboard to becoming the Chief Minister of Selangor, the richest state in Malaysia. As Chief Minister he would become the administrator of a state with significant infrastructure, resources and capital that would provide the opposition PKR with a base for taking power nationally at the next election. It would also demonstrate that Anwar, by administering Selangor effectively, could do the same at a national level. A conviction before nominations closed for the Kajang by-election would disqualify him from standing for election.

Anwar's conviction was a significant blow to the opposition. Not only was he disqualified from standing for election for the seat of Kajang, it also meant that he was effectively out of parliament. He would have to serve two-thirds of the sentence of five years, in this case 3 years 4 months. He would not be eligible to stand for a parliamentary seat until after six years from the completion of his sentence, namely July 2027. That represented two elections.

Karpal believed that the timetable imposed by the court to deal with the appeal was not accidental, but designed to coincide with the Kajang by-election. Nominations were scheduled to close at 10 am on Tuesday, 11 March 2014, which was the very morning he was to be sentenced for a conviction for the offence of sedition.

If sentenced to a term of imprisonment of more than 12 months or a fine in excess of RM2,000, then Karpal would, subject to appeal, be ineligible to remain a member of parliament. After a fiery and emotional session in court on the morning of the 11th, the judge fined Karpal RM4,000. (See Chapter 17 for more on Karpal's sedition trials.)

So in the brief period of a week, the two most senior parliamentary members of the opposition coalition were, pending appeal, effectively out of parliament — one to serve a prison sentence.

The opposition has long held the belief that the government has manipulated the justice system against its opponents. What happened that week, and the way in which it happened, gave substance to that claim.

Reaction to Anwar's conviction

Reaction to Anwar's conviction and sentence was immediate.

(A) GOVERNMENT SPOKESMAN

A government spokesperson said: "Malaysia has an independent judiciary and the judges will have reached their verdict only after considering all of the evidence in a fair and balanced manner. This is a case between two individuals and is a matter for the courts, not the government."[1]

(B) BAR COUNCIL OF MALAYSIA

The Malaysian Bar Council said it was deeply troubled by the conviction and sentencing of five years' imprisonment of Datuk Seri Anwar Ibrahim by the Court of Appeal, for what was essentially consensual sex between two adults.

---

1   *Wall Street Journal*, 8 March 20014

Bar Council president Christopher Leong said these provisions criminalise sodomy and oral sex (fellatio). Conviction carries a sentence of between five and twenty years with whipping. These provisions make no distinction between heterosexual and homosexual consensual sexual acts, and are thus applicable to both. The United Nations Human Rights Committee has ruled it contravenes international legal standards and should be "abolished".

He said the Bar had "grave misgivings" with respect to the manner and timing in which the appeal was handled. He said: "We are shocked by the manner in which mitigation and sentencing proceeded and the haste with which the appeal proceeded in the Court of Appeal."

He said that Anwar's legal team was notified on 28 February that the substantive appeal would be heard on 6 and 7 March, and that Karpal had only seven days to prepare for a criminal appeal over a case that had gone through a lengthy trial and which involved 32 witnesses, including expert evidence. According to Mr Leong, prior to this, the Court of Appeal registry had informed Anwar's lawyers to reserve 7–10 April as the proposed hearing dates, to which the team agreed.

However, these dates were abandoned and replaced with earlier dates.

"If this is true, it raises the question as to why the Court of Appeal brought forward the appeal to be heard when the April dates had been agreed on. After all the defendant was facing a possible 20-year jail term and the April dates would have given the legal team more time to prepare," he said.

Mr Leong further said that while the hearing of the appeal, which extended until past 6 pm was not unheard of, it was a rare occurrence. Further to this, after hearing submissions on 7 March, the court had taken approximately 90 minutes to consider before giving a unanimous decision in reversing the acquittal by the High Court. The panel then rejected Karpal's request for an adjournment to the following week for the mitigation and sentencing for the purpose of obtaining a medical report on Anwar and instead gave the legal team one hour to prepare. It then sentenced Anwar to five years' jail that evening with proceedings ending only at 7 pm.

"These matters raise many questions, cause much speculation, and lend to the perception that justice may have been hijacked," Mr Leong said.

He said that questions that must be answered were whether the cause of justice was best served by the manner and timing in which this appeal was handled and whether the administration of justice was compromised or interfered with. "Justice and independence are not only facts to be established, it is imperative that they are seen to be so established."

(c) INTER-PARLIAMENTARY UNION

The Inter-Parliamentary Union quickly responded to the result of the proceedings saying: "IPU is deeply concerned by the rushed process of the appeal hearing involving Malaysian opposition MP and leader Anwar Ibrahim that ended with a five-year jail sentence on sodomy charges. The sentence will now prevent him from standing in a key by-election on 23 March in Selangor, which could have led him to becoming Chief Minister of Malaysia's richest state."

It said: "...the defence had requested for a delay to the hearing until the end of next week to allow lawyer Karpal Singh to work on other cases involving the death penalty, but this request had been denied. After the sentencing on 7 March, the defence was also only given one hour to prepare its case for a lower sentence."

"Anwar will remain free on bail while he appeals against the guilty verdict. This is the second time Anwar has been given a jail sentence on sodomy charges. He spent six years in jail until his release in 2004.

Four years later, he was also charged under a colonial era law (1938) that criminalises 'carnal intercourse against the order of nature' and that according to the UN violates the rights to privacy and non-discrimination," said the IPU.

The IPU also recorded its concern about opposition leader Karpal Singh who at that stage was to be sentenced on 11 March. We now know that he was sentenced to RM4,000 which, subject to appeal, means that he would lose his parliamentary seat.

The IPU expressed its "genuine concern that both of the two leading opposition figures in Malaysia could be banned from political life."

(D) LAWASIA

LAWASIA also responded saying that it was concerned to learn of the undue haste with which the appeal was conducted. President Isomi Suzuki said that it "recorded its concern for the way in which the administration of justice and the rule of law in Malaysia will be perceived both nationally and internationally as a result of how this matter is played out."

The statement expressed concern that Anwar was charged of a little-used offence under the Malaysian Penal Code, which prohibits sexual conduct against international norms and human rights.

Mr Suzuki also observed that fellow opposition leader Karpal Singh was sentenced on charges of sedition, derived from legislation already slated by the government for repeal, and which may see him unable to continue in his parliamentary role.

He went on to say: "LAWASIA is accordingly cautious in accepting that the pursuit of justice is a prime motivator in these prosecutions. It fears for the future of the rule of law in Malaysia under circumstances that outmoded provisions in the legal system may be used as a tool to hinder the democratic processes to which the Malaysian people have a right."

5. INTERNATIONAL COMMISSION OF JURISTS

The International Commission of Jurists (ICJ) condemned Anwar's conviction as a miscarriage of justice, saying "it casts doubts on the independence and impartiality of the Malaysian judiciary and tarnishes the reputation of the country's legal system."

Sam Zarifi, ICJ Asia-Pacific Regional Director, said: "The ICJ condemns the use of the colonial-era Article 377B of the Malaysian Penal Code, which prohibits consensual same-sex sexual conduct, in conflict with international standards regarding respect for the right to privacy. This Article is seldom used in Malaysia, but this is the second time it has been used to convict Anwar, and both times its use seemed clearly motivated to hobble his ability to challenge the government as a politician."

The ICJ's observer at the court was a former Australian Federal Court Justice Commissioner Elizabeth Evatt.

(E) LAWYERS FOR LIBERTY

Malaysia's Lawyers for Liberty said the conviction on a "clearly trumped up and politically motivated charge" reaffirmed "the return of iron-fist."

(F) HUMAN RIGHTS WATCH

Phil Robertson, deputy director, Asia division of Human Rights Watch, said Anwar's trial "was all about knocking him out of politics and the government was prepared to do whatever it took to make that happen."

Commentary

Malaysia has every right to be respected for its economic progress and parliamentary system. However, what took place at the Court of Appeal in that single week in March 2013 was nothing short of alarming. Anwar described it as a "travesty of justice" — many thought it was just that. A modern democratic nation is judged by how it administers its justice system and whether it abides by the principles of the rule of law.

The judges of the Court of Appeal spent much time in their judgement criticising the defence for what it described as delaying tactics. Whether that was true or not did not really affect the substantive issues for appeal, but it was used as some justification of why the court hurried the appeal process.

While it may be that to some extent Anwar's lawyers — as claimed by the prosecution and court — delayed the proceedings, it was only because Anwar exercised his rights as an accused under threat of prosecution for an offence carrying a 20-year sentence.

But that is not the issue. Of concern was the unnecessary haste in which the court of appeal conducted the proceedings. Why the haste? Anwar's lawyers were given only one week to prepare for the hearing. That forced them to abandon serious capital cases of a more deserving nature.

Critical applications relating to the fitness of the prosecutor to conduct the appeal and a prosecution appeal to strike out another appeal against a court ruling were disposed of three days later.

The Federal Court listed an appeal to be heard with an hour's notice, and without documents having been served on the prosecution. The court hearing the main appeal sat into the early evening on each day of the actual hearing.

When the judges returned late in the evening around 6 pm with their decision to convict Anwar, Karpal requested an adjournment until the following week so that he might obtain an expert report concerning Anwar's medical condition — which was surely relevant to the sentence to be imposed.

It was a reasonable request, but was immediately refused by Justice Balia Yusof Wahi who maintained there was no rush. Yet he allowed Karpal only one hour to prepare mitigation. When Karpal asked why the process was being rushed he was brushed aside despite his complaints that he was unable to effectively mitigate on behalf of his client. Anwar was sentenced to five years' imprisonment at 6.55 pm. So again why the rush?

Some commentators say it was to prevent Anwar standing for a parliamentary seat, with nominations closing only days away. I don't know about that, and surely the legal process couldn't be subverted to that extent. But I do know what I saw that week and it was disturbing for any lawyer to witness.

Malaysia claims it conducts its affairs according to law, but on this occasion it fell way below the international standards expected of a modern democratic nation.

CHAPTER 17
Karpal convicted of sedition

Karpal Singh was twice charged with acts of sedition, first in January 2000 and again in March 2009. These charges spanned a turbulent decade in Malaysia's history. The sedition trials — a decade apart — provide some insight into the means by which the government has, since 1948, used the legislation to stifle free speech and peaceful assembly. They also illustrate how Karpal, both as a lawyer and politician, continued to challenge the government and assert his right to free speech.

The Sedition Act — a relic of colonial rule

The Sedition Act is a relic of British colonial rule. It was enacted in 1948 to deal with a perceived communist insurrection, but remained in force after Malaysia attained independence in 1957, having been preserved under Article 162(1) of the Federal Constitution, which kept pre-existing statutes and gave the Malaysian government the power to amend and repeal them.

During the political unrest of 1969, a state of emergency was declared. Not only was Parliament suspended, but also the Act was amended so as to broaden its scope (Modification of Laws (Sedition) (Extension and Modification) Order 1969 Emergency (Essential Powers) Ordinance No. 45, 1970). Effectively, the Act has over the past 50 years been adapted and extended well beyond the intended scope of the original legislators.

The Sedition Act provides that a person can be convicted on the basis that what they said had a "seditious tendency" — which is an extremely vague phrase. It includes any words spoken which would "bring into hatred or contempt or to excite disaffection against" the government or engender "feelings of ill-will and hostility between different races". It doesn't matter if the words spoken are true or false. The defendant doesn't need to intend that the words spoken had one of the results identified in the Act. Legislation of this type hardly seems appropriate in a modern democratic nation, which Malaysia claims to be.

July 2012: Government announces intention to repeal Sedition Act

On 11 July 2012, Prime Minister Najib Razak announced his intention to repeal the Sedition Act and replace it with a National Harmony Act, which he claimed would balance freedom of expression with the protection of Malaysia's different cultural and religious groups.

Despite his pledge to repeal what he declared to be outdated legislation, the current prosecution against Karpal proceeded to his ultimate conviction and sentence on 11 March 2014. It was just three days after Anwar Ibrahim was convicted of the offence of sodomy and sentenced to five years' imprisonment.

At the same time the Sedition Act continued to be used against opposition members of parliament, academics and student activists to silence dissent. If anything, prosecutions for sedition have become more frequent in the last two years.

The first sedition charge

The first charge of sedition brought against Karpal came about because of his representation of Anwar, when he was deputy prime minister, during the opposition leader's first trial on allegations of sodomy in 1998.

During the course of the trial, Karpal raised the prospect that Anwar was being poisoned while in custody. That revelation had come about after his lawyers obtained a report confirming that traces of arsenic had been found in Anwar's blood. He submitted to the trial judge that he suspected "people in high places" to be responsible for the poisoning; the clear implication was that he meant Prime Minister Dr Mahathir Mohamad.

He was subsequently charged in January 2000 with the offence of sedition, which stirred the anger of the international legal community. It was the first time that a lawyer in any Commonwealth country had been charged with sedition for remarks made in court defending a client.

The prosecution eventually fizzled out when the newly appointed Attorney-General Abdul Gani Patail withdrew the charge on the morning of the trial, but not before Karpal had launched a broadside at the presiding judge Justice Augustine Paul — who had also presided at Anwar's first trial.

Karpal told Justice Paul that he had acted more as a prosecutor than a judge in Anwar's trial and that he should be "observed" by the international observers who were at court — which included myself and other foreign lawyers.

Karpal's remark enraged Justice Paul who claimed that it was an attack on his integrity and impartiality, and he threatened Karpal with contempt of court. Karpal refused to back down and continued to provoke the judge. Despite his threats, however, Justice Paul refrained from charging Karpal with contempt of court. Instead he referred the matter to the Bar Council disciplinary tribunal. The complaint eventually fell away when Justice Paul refused to attend the hearing.

Karpal later told me that he wasn't going to miss the opportunity of taking the judge to task for what he believed was inappropriate behaviour in the Anwar trial and to "keep him in check".

Augustine Paul died in January 2010. Both he and Karpal had been students at the University of Singapore. Some people criticised Karpal for speaking graciously of him after his death, but Karpal was not one to carry grudges.

The second sedition charge

The second charge of sedition brought against Karpal arose from comments he made at a press conference at his offices on 6 February 2009 about the Sultan of Perak, Sultan Azlan Shah.

The Sultan had intervened to remove the Perak Menteri Besar (Chief Minister) after making personal inquiries as to whether the state government still enjoyed a majority in the Parliament following declarations by three government members that they had resigned from the ruling party.

Karpal said during the press conference that the Sultan's removal of the Chief Minister and appointment of another to fill the office was beyond his constitutional powers and could be questioned in a court of law.

The prosecution immediately jumped on these remarks and claimed the words had a "seditious tendency" by bringing hatred or contempt or exciting disaffection against the Sultan. Karpal said he was doing no more than offering a legal opinion that the Sultan was subject to the Malaysian Constitution. Karpal was charged under the Sedition Act, a few weeks later in March 2009.

The charge was dismissed when tried before the High Court on 11 June 2010. The trial judge ruled that the prosecution had failed to prove a *prima facie* case against him. The Court of Appeal later reversed the acquittal and the trial was ordered to continue with Karpal required to enter his defence to the charge. (See Pendakwa Raya v Karpal Singh a/l Ram Singh Criminal Appeal No. W-05-233- 2010 delivered on 20 January 2012)

Resumption of second sedition trial (2 November 2012 – 11 March 2014)

The trial resumed, some 30 months later, on 2 November 2012. Karpal's lead counsel, his son Gobind Singh, called him to testify. Karpal was first asked whether the transcript of the press conference taken from the media recording was accurate, and he conceded that it was correct.

Gobind then asked Karpal what had motivated him to release the press statement. Karpal replied that it was his duty as a member of parliament to comment on the political crisis in the state of Perak and to inform the public of the legal reasons for it. He described his press release as "legal opinion backed up by legal authority. I thought the public ought to know." He also made it perfectly clear that he was "not questioning the Sultan's prerogative, but the manner in which he exercised it."

He went on to say that the Parliament was supreme under the constitution and not the courts or the executive. "Even rulers are subject to the constitution. The constitution is supreme and nothing else. In my mind what I said didn't amount to sedition," he said.

The trial was adjourned part-heard to resume on 8 November 2012. When it resumed on 8 November, Karpal was asked by his counsel to read from the transcript recorded by the media at the press conference and explain his intention in making these statements.

Karpal explained the background of what had happened at that time. He told the court that three state assemblymen, who were members of the government, had tendered their resignations. That called into question whether the state government continued to enjoy a majority in the state assembly. He said that under section 33 of the Perak State Constitution, it was for the Assembly to determine whether the letters of resignation were valid and until that happened there was no basis for the Sultan to exercise his prerogative.

Karpal explained how the Sultan had telephoned each of the three assemblymen and asked them where their allegiance lay. He said: "...there was no constitutional provision which allowed the Sultan to do that. He could not usurp the powers of the state assembly. In the state of Perak everyone — including the ruler — is subject to the constitution. Again I wasn't questioning the Sultan's prerogative, but only saying that the situation in Perak at that point of time didn't warrant his intervention."

Karpal went on to say that the Sultan could only exercise his prerogative under Article 18 of the State Constitution in circumstances where a vote of no confidence had taken place in the Parliament. "He had no right to intervene. It was for the Parliament to decide if there was a majority or not."

He explained: "I was an MP commenting on a political crisis that affected one of five governments held by PKR. It was a legal opinion. I had no intention whatsoever of committing sedition. The last thing on my mind was sedition."

Karpal alleges selective prosecution

Karpal claimed that the Attorney-General Abdul Gani Patail had been "influenced by irrelevant considerations. There is no basis for him to exercise his discretion to bring prosecution. It is selective prosecution. There has been discrimination against me. The acts and words of the former PM Mahathir in 1993 to clip the wings of the sultans by setting up a 'special court' was unadulterated sedition. No decision was made at that time to prosecute him and others for clear acts of sedition. I suppose there was no one there to skin the cat."

Karpal then read extensively from Hansard (the transcripts of parliamentary debates), quoting extracts from several speeches made in Parliament in 1993. The excerpts concerned the Malaysian Parliament's move to remove the legal immunity accorded to members of the royal family, and included speeches made by government officials as well as Dr Mahathir himself. Karpal said all this demonstrated how the prosecution against him was selective.

Before the amendments were made, the Constitution granted rulers who had violated the law the right not to be prosecuted by the criminal court unless they voluntarily wished to surrender their legal immunity. The amendments also proposed removing the power of the rulers to pardon offences committed by family members. Naturally the rulers opposed the proposals, but the government used a two-pronged approach of persuasion and coercion to obtain their assent. The amendments were implemented in March 1993.

The trial was again adjourned. When it resumed on 25 January 2013, Karpal continued his testimony by reading from a speech by Dr Mahathir. Karpal then said: "There is no doubt in my mind that comments made by Mahathir and others were seditious going beyond mere discussion about power of the rulers, but concerning alleged criminality, including assaults upon the public and rape. This was unadulterated sedition committed by them, particularly against royal family of Johor."

He was referring to the notorious case where in a fit of rage the Sultan of Johor was alleged in 1987 to have beaten his caddy to death with a golf club. He reminded the court that there had been other instances of alleged assaults by members of the royal family against members of the public, which were referred to in the parliamentary debates.

Karpal returned to his assertion that the prosecution against him was selective and made for political reasons. "I have been denied equal protection of the law under the Constitution," he said. "There has been a selective prosecution in my case. The comments made by Dr Mahathir and others even if justified — which at law they could not — would have warranted the intervention of the Attorney-General of the time and even now by the current A-G Gani Patail because there is no statute of limitations. Mahathir and others could still be prosecuted."

He pointed out that in 1993 many members of the opposition had been charged with sedition for a range of issues for comments made in various publications, but that no action had been taken against government members.

Karpal criticises Attorney-General for not discontinuing prosecution

In July 2012 the government announced its intention to repeal the Sedition Act. Prime Minister Najib Razak declared that this would "mark another step forward in Malaysia's development".[1]

The only basis on which it could repeal the law was because it considered the legislation to be no longer relevant or appropriate in contemporary Malaysia, but why then did the Attorney-General continue to prosecute Karpal under that Act?

During his trial, Karpal criticised the A-G for failing to discontinue the prosecution, but there was no response from his office.

The Attorney-General has a very wide discretion over the control and direction of all criminal prosecutions. Not only may he institute and conduct any proceedings for an offence, he may also discontinue criminal proceedings that he has instituted, and the court cannot compel him to institute any criminal proceedings that he does not wish to institute or to go on with any criminal proceedings that he has decided to discontinue.

The general principle that the Attorney-General must act in the public interest applies with particular force to his powers under clause 3 of Article

---

1   *The Guardian*, AAP in Malaysia, 12 July 2012

145 of the Malaysian Federal Constitution and section 376(1), Criminal Procedure Code, which states:

> "In deciding whether to institute or discontinue a prosecution against an accused the Attorney-General is always guided by legal principles, but the public interest shall also be the paramount consideration."

Given the circumstances, one would have thought that public interest justified discontinuing the prosecution. However, the Attorney-General chose not to do so. While he was prepared to withdraw a similar charge against Karpal ten years earlier in 2002, when he thought it was not in the public interest to continue the prosecution, for some reason he did not think it was in the public interest to do so in this case.

Some commentators say it is because the opposition was not the threat then as it is today. His failure to act gave support to Karpal's claim that the prosecution was politically motivated.

Karpal convicted for sedition

The trial continued on throughout the year with several adjournments. In the last part of 2013 Karpal was cross-examined at length by the prosecutor. These sessions were particularly volatile.

Karpal disagreed with the prosecutor Noorin Badaruddin that the wording in his statement, especially the word "firm reminder" could be construed as giving an ultimatum to the Sultan, but that it was just a reminder based on two case laws.

When she contended the facts of the two case laws cited by him in the press conference were totally different from the political crisis of Perak he responded saying: "Right or wrong, that was my view. As a lawyer, you can't be always right. But never accuse any lawyer of misleading the public".

When the trial concluded on 21 February 2013 the judge returned a verdict of guilty as charged. He listed the hearing for sentencing for 7 March 2014, but at the last minute the dated was changed to 11 March.

The events surrounding the prosecution appeal against Anwar's acquittal the previous week in the Court of Appeal suggested the change of date was made to ensure that the appeal hearing would proceed with Karpal as counsel and provide no excuse for delay.

Sentencing hearing, High Court, 11 March 2014

The sentencing hearing took place at the Kuala Lumpur Court Complex at Jalan Duta, located about 10 minutes from city. It is a huge structure in the Islamic style only completed in 2008. It is where Anwar stood trial in the proceedings known as Sodomy II, and where he was acquitted.

Outside the court building was a small group of supporters from the Democratic Action Party (DAP), of which Karpal was at the time chairman, holding banners declaring "Justice for Karpal Singh" and "Why No Charge Mahathir 4 Sedition? AG is Hypocrite".

At 10.15 am, the courtroom located on the 4th floor of the Complex was packed with supporters, lawyers and political allies. In the gallery were veteran DAP MP Lim Kit Siang, Anwar's MP daughter Nurul Izzah Anwar, deputy president of PAS Mat Sabu, and former UN Special Rapporteur for the Independence of Judges and Lawyers Dato' Param Cumaraswamy. There were at least 40 persons standing, while another 50 or so filled the seats in the public gallery.

Anwar came late after attending the ceremony for nominations of candidates for the by-election for the parliamentary seat of Kajang. He had been disqualified from nominating because of the conviction for sodomy and sentence of five years' imprisonment imposed upon him by the Court of Appeal the previous Friday.

Sitting at the bar tables were members of Karpal's legal team, which included his sons Gobind and Ramkarpal, and also his daughter Sangeet Kaur — all of them lawyers.

Present too were also lawyers with watching briefs for organisations including Malaysian Bar Council President Christopher Leong, Dr Cyrus Das of the Commonwealth Law Association, and Ranjit Singh of LAWASIA.

Noorin Badaruddin continued to prosecute, assisted by two other lawyers.

Sangeet Kaur spoke to written submissions that had been filed on her father's behalf. Essentially, the submissions relied upon a number of factors to mitigate sentence:

1. That the particular sub-section [s. 3(1)(f)] of the Sedition Act, under which Karpal was charged, had since been repealed and it was the Government's stated intention to repeal the whole of the Act;

2. Karpal's intention was to give a legal opinion on the matter. There was no intention whatsoever to question the prerogative of the Sultan, but only to express the view that he was subject to the Constitution, which was a matter of public interest;

3. Karpal wanted no more than to be treated equally under the law, but there were many instances of persons committing more serious acts of sedition where no action had been taken against them, including the former Prime Minister Mahathir Mohamad and other senior members of the government;

4. The circumstances of the offence were not serious, but of a technical nature; and

5. Karpal was a man of good character and reputation, who suffers from significant and permanent spinal injuries as a result of a traffic accident in 2005, and that to impose a penalty that would disqualify him from Parliament would be an excessive penalty.

Gobind, who is also a member of parliament for Puchong, Selangor, then addressed the court. He described his father as a "national figure and towering Malaysian" who had been prosecuted under legislation, which courts had described as "limiting the freedom of speech."

He told the judge that Karpal was being prosecuted for "giving a legal opinion in good faith, not in intemperate language, but couched in legal terms pointing out the Sultan's legal obligations. He was doing exactly what the King in opening his speech to Parliament insisted MPs should do, and that is defend the Constitution."

Gobind told the judge that this case had stirred lawyers internationally, and many of them had expressed shock that a lawyer could be prosecuted for providing a legal opinion on a matter of public interest. He then pointed out the several representatives of the organisations present in court. Two of them — Christopher Leong and Dr Cyrus Das — asked to address the judge, but he refused to allow them to do so.

The prosecutor Noorin Badaruddin then addressed the court on behalf of the Attorney-General's Chambers. She submitted that Karpal was more culpable because of his experience as a constitutional lawyer and "should have known better" — and he knew he was "questioning the Sultan's prerogative."

She emphasised that deterrence was an important factor, and that the Sultan had been offended by Karpal's remarks and that a proper sentence "would include imprisonment."

As she said this, the gallery erupted jeering and shouting at her.

Gobind then jumped to his feet exclaiming: "This nonsense must stop. She is threatening the court that unless it imposes a significant sentence it would send the wrong signal to the Sultan." He kept going saying: "If only the prosecutor had the same fire in defending the Constitution. Who is going to defend the Constitution if the AG's Chambers doesn't?"

This comment brought cheers of support from the packed gallery prompting the prosecutor to stand and shout at the judge in order to be heard: "Why is he attacking our Chambers?"

Anwar called out: "Because you deserve it."

Gobind was not to be stopped. The atmosphere in the courtroom was more like a political rally. He continuing his impassioned remarks saying: "The people are sick and tired of this selective prosecution. It happens every day. Do not be threatened by the prosecution service that a light sentence would insult the rulers. Where do we go for justice? We have a duty to defend the Constitution and the courts must defend us. It's the law [the Sedition Act], but a terrible law. It is still your role [the judge] to sentence but don't send Karpal Singh to jail for doing his duty".

The judge put up his hand to still the courtroom, which it did. He then quickly announced his decision, convicting Karpal of sedition and imposing a fine of RM4,000. He immediately got up from his chair and exited through the wood-paneled door behind him. The conviction, sentence and fine (which was over the limit of RM2,000) meant that, subject to appeal, Karpal would have to vacate his parliamentary seat.

Karpal immediately lodged an appeal against the decision, but his sudden death five weeks later interrupted the process. His sons vowed to continue the appeal to clear his name, which they believe had been unjustly tarnished.

On 24 March 2014, the Malaysian Bar Council wrote to the Attorney-General requesting that he takes disciplinary action against the prosecutor for professional misconduct. It complained that it was evident that Noorin Badaruddin attempted to threaten or pressure the court into imposing a heavy penalty on Karpal. It also claimed that she had strenuously argued for a custodial sentence despite knowing Karpal's medical condition. "In her submission, she had stated that his physical disability was not a relevant factor to be considered [in sentencing Karpal Singh]. As such, she failed to uphold the sanctity and dignity of her office and failed to act justly," said the Bar Council, adding that she had violated her duties as DPP.[2]

The Attorney-General declined to take any action against Noorin Badaruddin and on 20 June 2014 she was appointed as a Judicial Commissioner of the High Court, which in Malaysia means that she has the powers of a full judge but without the security of tenure being appointed for a term of two years. Karpal's supporters claimed this was a reward for her efforts in prosecuting him.

So in the short space of one week, the opposition parties effectively lost its two most senior members. Opposition members of parliament and supporters have long believed that the government has resorted to the criminal law to rid the political system of the main opposition players. After what had happened, it seemed they may be right. And if they were right, then politics finally destroyed the independence and diminished the reputation of the Malaysian judiciary and prosecution service.

CHAPTER 18
Failure to expunge 'homosexual' remark from record

On 20 September 1998 Anwar Ibrahim appeared at a rally of more than 30,000 people protesting his dismissal as deputy prime minister a few weeks earlier and demanding the resignation of Prime Minister Mahathir Mohamad. The massive crowd of demonstrators that had gathered in Merdeka Square in the heart of Kuala Lumpur must have been viewed as a serious threat to Dr Mahathir's rule.

Later that evening, while Anwar was in the middle of an international press conference, a contingent of 250 armed and masked security police forced their way into his home smashing doors and manhandling a large number of supporters who had gathered there.

He was immediately arrested under the Internal Security Act (ISA) and taken from his house. He was kept in solitary confinement in police custody for nine days, interrogated and severely beaten by the Inspector-General of Police Rahim Noor. When finally brought before a court, Anwar was charged with several offences of corruption and sodomy.

Two others were also charged with Anwar. They were Dr Munawar Anees, Anwar's former speechwriter, and Sukma Darmawan Sasmita Atmadja, Anwar's adopted brother, who were arrested under suspicion of engaging in homosexual acts.

Five days later, on 8 September 1998, they were given a jail sentence of six months after pleading guilty to "unnatural sex" with Anwar. They later recanted their confessions, and appealed the sentence, claiming to have been coerced into pleading guilty. Anees made a statutory declaration to that effect, but his appeal was rejected by the High Court on 29 October 2008 and the guilty sentence upheld. Sukma later appealed his conviction with Anwar in 2004.

After a lengthy trial lasting many months, Anwar was convicted on 14 April 1999 for acting corruptly in using his office to interfere with the police investigation of the sodomy allegations and was sentenced to six years' imprisonment.

At the culmination of a second trial on 8 August 2000, he was also convicted of various acts of sodomy allegedly committed on his wife's driver, Azizan Abu Bakar. He was sentenced to an additional term of nine years' imprisonment.

Both trials attracted considerable international attention with complaints made of procedural unfairness and allegations that trumped-up evidence had been used to convict him.

Appeal against the sodomy conviction — 10 May 2004

On 10 May 2004, the Federal Court commenced to hear arguments on the appeal against Anwar's convictions for sodomy. He was joined in the appeal by his adopted brother Sukma Darmawan, who became the second appellant in the proceedings.

The application was heard in the courtroom located on the first floor of the newly constructed Istana Kehakiman (Palace of Justice) at the administrative city of Putrajaya located 30 kilometres from Kuala Lumpur.

Together with other international observers and foreign embassy officials, I attended the hearing representing both the Australian Bar Association and the Geneva-based International Commission of Jurists. By 9 am the public gallery was filled with international observers, members of the national and international media, Anwar's family and supporters.

Security was particularly heavy both inside and outside the court building where a crowd of about 1,000 people had gathered to express their support for Anwar. At one stage on that first day, supporters breached security and invaded the large entry hall of the building chanting slogans and calling out *"Reformasi"* and "Free Anwar". Security officers soon dispersed the crowd and thereafter supporters were kept outside on the steps of the building. A few were admitted, but only after obtaining a pass from court staff.

After hearing argument, the court reserved its decision, reconvening on 2 September 2004.

Appeal against conviction upheld — 2 September 2004

On 2 September by a majority of 2:1, the Federal Court upheld the appeal overturning the conviction and ordered Anwar's immediate release from prison.

Justices Datuk Abdul Hamid Mohamad and Datuk Tengku Baharuddin Shah Tengku Mahmud (Justice Datin Paduka Rahmah Hussain dissenting) upheld the appeal because of what they considered to be significant deficiencies in the prosecution's case. They found the complainant Azizan Abu Bakar, on whose testimony the prosecution was based, to be an unreliable witness.

Given the various inconsistencies and contradictions in his testimony, the judges concluded that it was not safe to convict on the basis of his uncorroborated testimony alone. They found that Anwar should have been acquitted without having to enter a defence.

The primary thrust of Anwar's attack was on the credibility of Azizan on whose testimony the prosecution for the most part relied. At the trial, Azizan maintained during examination-in-chief that Anwar had sodomised him, but when cross-examined by Anwar's counsel he conceded that it did not happen. And when pushed in re-examination by the prosecution he changed his mind yet again. He also changed the dates on which he alleged the offences had occurred, but was unable to explain why he had changed his mind. At one stage he said that he changed the dates at the request of the police.

Justice Abdul Hamid Mohamad said in the majority judgement:[1]

"... even though reading the appeal record, we find evidence to confirm that the appellants were involved in homosexual activities and we are more inclined to believe that the alleged incident at Tivoli Villa did happen, sometime, this court, as a court of law, may only convict the appellants if the prosecution has successfully proved the alleged offences as stated in the charges, beyond reasonable doubt, on admissible evidence and in accordance with established principles of law.

We may be convinced in our minds of the guilt or innocence of the appellants, but our decision must only be based on the evidence adduced and nothing else. In this case Azizan's evidence on the 'date' of the incident is doubtful as he had given three different 'dates' in three different years, the first two covering a period of one month each and the last covering a period of three months. He being the only source for the 'date', his inconsistency, contradiction and demeanour when giving evidence on the issue does not make him a reliable source, as such, an essential part of the offence has not been proved by the prosecution.

---

1   *Dato' Seri Anwar bin Ibrahim v. Public Prosecutor* (2004) Federal Court of Appeal No. 05-6-2003 (W)

We also find the second appellant's confession [Sukma Darmawan] not admissible as it appears not to have been made voluntarily. Even if admissible the confession would not support the 'date' of the commission of the offences charged.

We have also found Azizan to be an accomplice. Therefore corroborative evidence of a convincing, cogent and irresistible character is required. While the testimonies of Dr Mohd Fadzil and Tun Haniff and the conduct of the first appellant [Anwar] confirm the appellants' involvement in homosexual activities, such evidence does not corroborate Azizan's story that he was sodomised by both the appellants at the place, time and date specified in the charge.

In the absence of any corroborative evidence it is unsafe to convict the appellants on the evidence of an accomplice alone unless his evidence is unusually convincing or for some reason is of special weight which we find it is not. Furthermore, the offence being a sexual offence, in the circumstances that we have mentioned, it is also unsafe to convict on the evidence of Azizan alone.

For all the above reasons, we are not prepared to uphold the conviction. Since the applicable law in this case requires that the prosecution must prove its case beyond reasonable doubt before the defence may be called, the burden being the same as is required to convict the appellants at the end of the case for the defence, we are of the view that the High Court has misdirected itself in calling for the appellants to enter their defence. They should have been acquitted at the end of the case for the prosecution.

We therefore allow the appeals of both appellants and set aside the convictions and sentences."

Justice Hamid described Azizan as an 'accomplice'. The adverse impact that had upon the court's assessment of Azizan's credibility needs some explanation. Azizan admitted that he actively participated in the act of sodomy with Anwar and Sukma. By doing so, he became an accomplice to the offence.

The law has found from experience that accomplices are a class of witness whose evidence is inherently suspect because their involvement in the crime with which they are charged may incline them to falsely implicate another person, either to exculpate themselves or with a view to minimising their own role or perhaps with a view to currying favour with the police. As such, it says that is dangerous to act upon that evidence in the absence of corroboration, that is independent evidence, of which the majority in this case found there was none.

The acquittal was a relief for Anwar not only because it vindicated his claims of innocence, but it also resulted in his immediate release from prison. However two weeks later, on 15 September 2004, the same court refused to overturn the convictions on the corruption charges.

Still, for Anwar, the court's decision was the culmination of a six-year struggle for justice after pleading his innocence through the various tiers of the Malaysian court system.

During his lengthy period of incarceration, Anwar Ibrahim became the symbol of political opposition to the Mahathir regime. Amnesty International declared him to be a prisoner of conscience, stating that he had been arrested in order to silence him as a political opponent.

Yet, it was a bittersweet decision. Justice Abdul Hamid Mohamad (who became Chief Justice of Malaysia in 2007) when delivering the decision of the court remarked that even though the court was of the view that homosexual activity had taken place, by necessity it had to strictly apply the law and as such a conviction could not be sustained.

For Anwar, these were the offending words: "...even though reading the appeal record, we find evidence to confirm that the appellants were involved in homosexual activities and we are more inclined to believe that the alleged incident at Tivoli Villa did happen..."

These remarks were to haunt Anwar over the years. For example, on 17 September 2013 Justice Tengku Maimun Tuan Mat was forced to withdraw from presiding at the prosecution appeal against Anwar's acquittal in the Court of Appeal when she was challenged by Anwar's lawyers for citing these remarks with approval in dismissing a defamation claim brought by him against Dr Mahathir in 2004.

Anwar was determined that the suggestion that he had engaged in "homosexual activity" should be removed or expunged from the judgement of the court. He, therefore, brought an application in the Federal Court to remove that reference from the court's decision.

Anwar's lawyer, Karpal Singh, when bringing the application, told the media that political opponents, especially those from Umno, were using the judgement to discredit the opposition leader's character.[2]

PKR Legal Bureau chairman Latefa Koya said at the time that apart from politicians, Umno-owned newspaper *Utusan Malaysia* had also been relying on the judgement as a defence of justification every time Anwar filed a defamation suit against the newspaper. She said they were using the judgement to prove that Anwar's character was tainted. "This practice has gained intensity over the past few years and we want to put a stop on the reliance of a paragraph which is hidden behind an unsubstantiated passing remark," she said, adding the application was filed out of necessity and that Anwar was not time barred from making the move.[3]

---

2   *The Malaysian Insider*, 16 September 2013

3   *The Malaysian Insider*, 18 September 2013

Federal Court rejects application — "judge entitled to his opinion"

On 25 March 2014, a five-member Federal Court panel, chaired by Chief Judge of Malaysia Tan Sri Zulkefli Ahmad Makinuddin, unanimously dismissed Anwar's review application to have the remark removed from the majority judgement delivered by Justice Abdul Hamid Mohamad.

"We are of the view that the majority judgement accepted that the sexual incident forming the crux of the charge did in fact occur, but were doubtful as to when it in fact took place," said Justice Zulkefli when reading out the unanimous judgement of the five-member panel. He said then Federal Court judge Abdul Hamid Mohamad was entitled to his opinion that the sexual act had taken place.

He went on to say: "We agree that the comment is part and parcel of the analytical process undertaken by the learned judge in arriving at the decision which the majority judgement did. In our view, the conclusion arrived at by the majority judgement in the impugned paragraph was in fact based on evidence found in the appeal record. It, therefore, cannot be termed as a personal opinion of the judge who delivered the decision."

CHAPTER 19
"A good lawyer dies in the saddle"

Karpal Singh was one of Malaysia's most prominent lawyers and a controversial figure both in the law and politics. He was an outspoken advocate of human rights in Malaysia for more than 40 years.

Often these distinct roles seemed to merge. That may be because politics and the law are inextricably linked in Malaysia. He is regarded as a true Malaysian 'patriot' who had a direct and progressive influence on his country's political and legal process.

Except for a short period out of office, Karpal was a member of parliament for more than 30 years. He was the National Chairman of the Democratic Action Party (DAP), one of the component parties of the opposition alliance known as Pakatan Rakyat (PKR).

In 2008 when Anwar Ibrahim was again charged with an offence of sodomy, his former political opponent became his fiercest advocate. Anwar claimed that the charge was politically motivated and an attempt to again damage him politically upon his successful return to politics. Anwar was found not guilty on 9 January 2012, almost two years after the trial started.

Karpal successfully led the defence team during an often-gruelling process despite being wheelchair-bound and relying on his son to handle the legal papers. He was more than once threatened by the judge with contempt, but he casually shrugged off those threats.

At one stage during the hearing, he claimed that one of the judge's threats of contempt had 'intimidated' him. I thought at the time that this must surely be no more than a bit of theatre because I could never imagine Karpal Singh being intimidated by anyone, let alone a judge.

Karpal was to argue the final appeal before the Federal Court, following Anwar's conviction and sentence, but his sudden death meant that others — including his son Ramkarpal — would argue the case.

His sudden death at such a critical time left the ship rudderless as Anwar's lawyers struggled not only to emotionally come to terms with his sudden death, but also to frame a series of effective arguments to support the appeal. He was, after all, Anwar's fearless champion and it seemed for a time that his shoes could not be filled.

A fatal collision

The accident which killed Karpal happened on the North-South Expressway near the town of Gopeng about 20 kilometres south of Ipoh (or about 180 kilometres north of KL) at around 1.10 am on 17 April 2014.

Karpal was en route to Penang for a court hearing scheduled for later that morning. The vehicle in which he was travelling was a Toyota Alphard MPV with the private number plate KS9898. The vehicle had been equipped with a mechanism to lift him from his wheelchair into the front passenger seat, which is where he was seated at the time of the collision. Apart from the driver C. Selvam, others in the vehicle included his faithful and long-time assistant Michael Cornelius, his Indonesian maid and his son Ramkarpal.

The Toyota apparently collided with the rear of a slow-moving five-ton lorry carrying steel and cement. The vehicle was badly damaged, its passenger side ripped apart. Karpal died instantly as did Michael Cornelius, who was seated right behind him. While Karpal's domestic helper was seriously injured, Ramkarpal and Selvam escaped with slight injuries.

The lorry driver Abu Mansor Mohd was not injured and was later tested positive for cannabis use. Police later charged Selvam with dangerous and reckless driving; there was a suggestion that he fell asleep at the wheel.

Karpal was taken to the Kampar Hospital mortuary. The mood was highly emotional as members of his family arrived in the early hours of that morning. His elegant wife Gurmit Kaur was inconsolable asking "why, why!" as her son Gobind escorted her to the mortuary to view the body. It was a question many were to ask.

Karpal's movements that night

At a memorial service on 24 April 2014, Anwar told of his last conversation with Karpal on that fateful night. The telephone conversation took place at around 6.30 pm.

Anwar recounted how Karpal was worried about the pending Federal Court appeal saying he was particularly troubled by the "unprecedented speed at which the appeal records were sent to his office". Anwar said Karpal started to sound agitated and worried, but immediately "switched back to his usual cool and confident self, no doubt intending to put me at ease." He said their long chat ended with the words: "Anwar, you carry on. Don't worry. I'll do my best." He says those words were still ringing in his ears when several hours later he heard the news of Karpal's death.

Later that night Karpal visited his son Gobind at his home in Kuala Lumpur before he left to travel to Penang. Even at that late hour he was anxious to get moving to be ready the next morning to represent a client at a trial. He left his son's home at about 10.30 pm. At 2 am Gobind was told there had been an accident and that two members of his family had died. He telephoned his mother and brother and they rushed to the hospital in Ipoh. As they drove at speed he was telephoned by a fellow MP who told him his younger brother had survived, but not his father and Michael Cornelius.

Reaction to Karpal's death

The reaction to Karpal's death was swift with politicians from opposing sides using the social media to respond to the news.

PM Najib Razak said on Twitter: "I have just landed at Ankara when I heard the news that YB Karpal Singh died in a road accident. My condolences to the family." His office later issued a statement saying: "I am shocked to hear of Karpal Singh's tragic passing. In a career that spanned five decades, Karpal's abilities made him a formidable opponent. In politics, he was an implacable leader; in law, a committed advocate."

Anwar wrote on his Facebook profile: "We've lost a colleague; an indefatigable fighter for justice; the legendary Karpal Singh! Our sincere condolences to the family. RIP."

Many others expressed their sorrow at his sudden death.

"A man who fought for us and this country"

Karpal's funeral was conducted with full state honours on 20 April 2014 in Penang. Tens of thousands of people attended his funeral and chanted prayers as his body, in a casket covered with a Tiger skin, was taken to the Batu Gantong crematorium at George Town.

Along the way, stops were made at the Penang High Court, the State Assembly and his former school St. Xavier's Institution. The cortege had to make several other unscheduled stops as mourners crowded onto the streets to pay their respects. His body was cremated after the family had completed the final rites. His ashes were later scattered into the sea.

There were a series of memorial tributes to the Bukit Gelugor MP. The seventh and last was held on a rainy evening on 5 May 2014 in Penang. Karpal's son, MP Gobind, in an emotional speech to the assembled crowd spoke of his father's legacy and told them that it was important to remember "how he lived because he was a man who fought for us and this country, believing that this country can change one day ... a Malaysia where all Malaysians are equal and treated fairly by our government. If there was darkness, Karpal was the light."

Gobind continued: "If there was weakness, it was him who gave us strength. But now that he is no longer with us, are we going to back down now because he is no longer with us? Do we stop our fight because he is no longer here with us? Or do we remember the fighting spirit that the Tiger of Jelutong has left behind?"

The crowd roared with approval.

Karpal Singh was truly a significant figure in Malaysia. He was a larger than life character not only because of his involvement in politics, but also the law. He appeared as counsel in most of Malaysia's significant cases over the last 44 years or so. But it is not just the big cases that mattered to him. His reputation for defending the 'little man' was well deserved.

For Karpal there was no question of retirement. In a CNN interview with Talk Asia in 2002, interviewer Lorraine Hahn asked him whether he had considered retirement, and that perhaps is was time to call it quits and hand over the baton to maybe one of his children.

Karpal responded saying: "I don't think the question of handing over the baton arises actually because a good lawyer dies in the saddle and that's what it will be as far as I am concerned. To keep going, I think a lawyer has to keep going. I have to go on as long as I can mentally and physically do so."

Karpal's life reflects the modern history of Malaysia and the events that have shaped it as a nation since Independence more than 50 years ago. Karpal is very much an integral part of that history.

Before he died, Karpal said that when he is no longer here then "100 Karpals would take my place". If that were only true, but he really is irreplaceable.

CHAPTER 20
Sedition crackdown
to silence dissent

A few weeks before his death on 17 April 2014, Karpal Singh was sentenced in the High Court of Malaysia for the criminal act of sedition, for having expressed a legal opinion about the constitutional power of the Sultan of Perak over the state parliament.

Had he failed to overturn the conviction on appeal, the conviction and sentence (with its fine of RM4,000) would disqualify him from the right to sit as a member of parliament. Karpal's conviction happened on 11 March, four days after Anwar's conviction of the offence of sodomy and sentence of five years' imprisonment.

Karpal saw these convictions as a contrived two-pronged attack on the opposition leadership, which effectively removed both of them from the federal parliament.

Of course, both appealed the convictions, but only Anwar lived to challenge his conviction and sentence. Not only did Anwar have to challenge his conviction and sentence, but he also had to face a prosecution appeal to increase what it claimed was a lenient sentence of five years in prison.

A wave of sedition charges

As this was happening, the government's sedition crackdown was widening as opposition members of parliament and officials, academics and student activists were charged with having committed acts of sedition. According to Lawyers for Liberty, a legal NGO, as at September 2014, some 25 cases were then going through the courts.

A sedition conviction had the potential to result not only in a sentence of imprisonment for those charged, but also for members of parliament the prospect of being banned from public office for five years.

Anwar was not immune, at least from investigation. On 26 September 2014, police went to his party headquarters to take a statement from him in answer to a complaint that he committed sedition in a speech he gave at a political rally in Gombak in 2011. It is believed that the alleged seditious words spoken by him related to the 2006 murder of a Mongolian model named Altantuya Shaariibuu, who was alleged to have had close links to the then Deputy Prime Minister Najib Razak. Anwar apparently told those assembled to "fight the evil government".

Speaking at a press conference at the Pakatan Rakyat HQ soon after the police left, he said: "Some of the leaders present at the talk, Selangor Menteri Besar Mohamed Azmin Ali and Selangor assemblymen Saari Sungib and Aminuddin Shaari gave statements that same year, but mine was postponed under the direction of the Attorney-General and Putrajaya."

"My stance has consistently been opposed to the use of the Sedition Act to suppress the voice of the people whether political leaders, academicians, students and civil societies," he said.[1]

It was difficult to reconcile what appeared to be a concerted use of the sedition law against those opposing and critical of the government, with the prime minister's announcement in 2012 that the law would be repealed. The wave of sedition charges was roundly criticised by several groups including the independent Malaysian Bar Council, which called

---

1   TPR News, "Anwar claims Sedition laws being used to pressure him politically", 26 September 2014

it "an intense period of oppression against the citizenry and regression in the rule of law".

One of the lawyer's in Anwar's legal team, N. Surendran, was on 19 August 2014 himself charged with sedition for commenting on the Court of Appeal decision to convict Anwar. He was charged for a statement saying the decision was "flawed, defensive and insupportable". He claimed the crackdown was a "sedition blitz" and "clearly an attempt to stifle dissent".[2]

Prominent lawyer and electoral reform activist Ambiga Sreenevasan called the sedition surge an "attack on parliamentary democracy", saying Umno was clamping down to stave off eventual electoral defeat. "It is absolutely shocking, worrisome, and legally wrong. Some of these charges are so tenuous. They have obviously decided that critics are a nuisance and must be silenced," she said.[3]

"The easiest offence to satisfy"

The Sedition Act was enacted in 1948 to deal with a perceived communist insurrection, but remained in force after independence in 1957. During the political unrest of 1969, a state of emergency was declared. Not only was parliament suspended, but the Act was also amended so as to broaden its scope. Effectively, the Act of 1948 has over the past 50 years been adapted and extended well beyond the intended scope of the original legislators.[4]

Before the wave of prosecutions in 2014, Malaysian Bar Council constitutional law committee chief lawyer Syahredzan Johan noted a trend for the authorities to cite the Sedition Act as an early measure in

---

2   Channel News Asia, 18 August 2014

3   Channel News Asia, 3 September 2014

4   *Modification of Laws (Sedition)(Extension and Modification) Order 1969; Emergency (Essential Powers) Ordinance No. 45, 1970*

their investigations and prosecution because "it is the easiest offence to satisfy".[5]

"They don't have to prove that there is sedition, only to show there is a tendency," Mr Syahredzan said, pointing to Section 3(1) of the Sedition Act, which lists six sub-clauses defining a seditious tendency. It includes "to bring into hatred or contempt or to excite disaffection against any Ruler or against any Government."

He said there was tendency for the government to go on the offensive and use the laws as weapons when it was being hit by criticism. He cited as an example the prosecution of Karpal for publicly saying the Sultan of Perak could be questioned in a court of law.

Relevant provisions of the Sedition Act 1948

An examination of the relevant provisions of the legislation is informative, because it shows how difficult it is for any person charged with the offence to avoid conviction given the need for the prosecution to prove only that the words uttered had a "seditious tendency" — not that they actually were seditious or that the person intended them to be so.

Section 4(1)(b) of the Sedition Act 1948 creates the offence of sedition, providing that any person who "...utters any seditious words ... shall be guilty of an offence".

The penalties provided for on conviction are: "...for a first offence to a fine not exceeding five thousand ringgit or to imprisonment for a term not exceeding three years or to both, and, for a subsequent offence, to imprisonment for a term not exceeding five years..."

Section 2 of the Act defines the meaning of the word "seditious" to include any "...words ... capable of ... having a seditious tendency".

The phrase "seditious tendency" is dealt with in Section 3(1). This is the key section of the Act. Essentially, the words, which are the subject of complaint, must be proved to have a tendency to produce any of the consequences described in that Section. Six categories of "seditious tendency" are described in Section 3(1)(a)–(f):

1. to bring into hatred or contempt or to excite disaffection against any Ruler or against any Government;

2. to excite the subjects of any Ruler or the inhabitants of any territory governed by any Government to attempt to procure in the territory of the Ruler or governed by the Government, the alteration, otherwise than by lawful means, of any matter as by law established;

3. to bring into hatred or contempt or to excite disaffection against the administration of justice in Malaysia or in any State;

4. to raise discontent or disaffection amongst the subjects of the Yang di-Pertuan Agong or of the Ruler of any State or amongst the inhabitants of Malaysia or of any State;

5. to promote feelings of ill-will and hostility between different races or classes of the population of Malaysia; or

6. to question any matter, right, status, position, privilege, sovereignty or prerogative established or protected by the provisions of Part III of the Federal Constitution or Article 152, 153or 181 of the Federal Constitution."

There are aspects of Section 3(1) of the Act that deserve mention. First, it should be noted that it is immaterial whether the words used did or even could have produced one of the six categories of "seditious tendency". Secondly, it is also immaterial whether the words used were true or false. Thirdly, an accused by uttering the words alleged to be seditious does not have to intend that they result in one of the six categories of "seditious tendency".[6]

Defences under the Sedition Act

The Act provides defences to an allegation of sedition. For example, Section 3(2)(b) of the Act provides that the "words" do not have a seditious tendency only where they criticise "error or defects" in the Government or Constitution or the administration of justice with a view to their being remedied. The authorities suggest that the Act tolerates *bona fide* and fair criticism, but only so it seems to the extent that it does not have a tendency to produce any of the consequences set out in subsection 3(1).[7]

Unfulfilled promises

Prime Minister Najib Razak promised on 11 July 2012 to repeal the Sedition Act. He said the legislation would be replaced by a National Harmony Act, which he claimed would "balance freedom of expression with the protection of Malaysia's different cultural and religious groups." He described the Sedition Act in the following terms:

> "The Sedition Act represents a bygone era in our country and with today's announcement we mark another step forward in Malaysia's development. The new National Harmony Act will balance the right of freedom of expression as enshrined in the Constitution, while at the same time ensuring that all races and religions are protected."

---

6   *Public Prosecutor v Ooi Kee Saik & Ors* [1971] 2 M.L.J. 108;
    Public Prosecutor v Fan Yew Teng [1975] 1 M.L.J. 176

7   *Public Prosecutor v Fan Yew Teng* [1975] 1 M.L.J. 176 per Abdul Hamid J.

He added: "Our country's strength lies in its diversity. The new Act underlines my commitment to nurturing the spirit of harmony and mutual respect that has been the foundation of our stability and success."[8]

The prime minister did replace some repressive laws, such as the Internal Security Act, but his reforms seemed to stall after the May 2013 national election. And two years after making his promise to repeal the Sedition Act, it is still firmly in place and being used effectively against the opposition, academics and political activists to silence dissent.

Despite this apparent about turn, the Prime Minister's Department continued to maintain that the Sedition Act would be repealed and replaced with different legislation, possibly in late 2015. PM Najib also continued to affirm his promise to repeal the legislation as part of his plan to modernise and reform laws relating to public disorder.

At the same time, however, some of his ministers were publicly denying the government had ever promised to repeal the legislation, only that it would be reviewed.

Datuk Seri Shahidan Kassim, Minister in the Prime Minister's Department, said that the PM's previous remarks that new laws would replace the Sedition Act did not mean the colonial-era law would be abolished. He said: "The prime minister never promised to repeal it, he only pledged to review it. This means the Sedition Act may be replaced with the National Harmony Act but it might not be repealed."[9]

Of course, his statement was a direct contradiction of the prime minister's announcement, which was reported widely by both the mainstream and online media, and what he had continued to say about it.

---

8   FMT News, 11 July 2012

9   *The Malaysian Insider*, 5 September 2014

It was also common knowledge that home minister Datuk Seri Zahid Hamidi was contradicting Mr Najib both in private and publicly. There were confusing messages. Some saw it as a deliberate attempt to undermine the PM, encouraged by Dr Mahathir, and an attempt to advance his own ambitions for the leadership. Others saw it as an attempt to deflect criticism away from the prime minister.

On 7 October 2014, in reply to a question from the opposition leader in the Dewan Rakyat (Parliament), the *de facto* law minister Nancy Shukri said the government was studying how best to address the weaknesses of the 1948 legislation and that it could be "complemented with new laws instead of being repealed".[10]

Anwar had questioned the consistency of the government's public commitment to make Malaysia a more democratic country with the action taken to prosecute some Pakatan Rakyat leaders, including a few MPs, activists and intellectuals for sedition.

It is difficult to know whether these statements were official party policy, but if so it meant that the government was clearly in the process of retreating from its promise to reform the public order laws. The large-scale prosecution of opponents for offences of sedition was certainly more consistent with an official about turn. There was evidence that the conservative forces within the government were pushing a harder line against the opposition, particularly after the electoral gains it made at the 2013 General Election.

Saifuddin Abdullah, a leading Umno moderate involved in pushing the replacement legislation forward, said it was being opposed by forces who "still believe in a sledgehammer approach" on free speech. Speaking at the

---

10 *The Malay Mail*, 7 October 2014, "Minister: Putrajaya may complement, not replace Sedition Act", by Pathma Subramaniam

launch of a national campaign to repeal the sedition law on 15 September 2014, he said: "I am very concerned with the recent [sedition] cases. It does not show that the government is in the process of repealing it. The prime minister has intentions to abolish the [Sedition] Act, but those around him don't want to agree to the idea ... they don't want to let him".[11]

Some political observers thought the contradictory statements reflected a power struggle that was taking place within the ruling party. They thought this definite change of direction indicated that traditionalists in the long-ruling ethnic Malay party appear to have gained the upper hand.

Former Prime Minister Mahathir Mohamad, still an influential conservative within the ruling party, publicly withdrew his support from PM Najib in September 2014 over his reformist promises, fuelling speculation that the prime minister could be replaced.

It should be recalled that Dr Mahathir also undermined PM Najib's predecessor Abdullah Badawi by resigning from the ruling party until he stepped down as prime minister. That brought about Badawi's resignation on 2 April 2009.

Walk for Peace and Freedom, 16 October 2014

On 19 September 2014, the Malaysian Bar Council convened an Extraordinary General Meeting (EGM) to discuss what had become the frequent use of the sedition law against opposition members of parliament, journalists, academics and student activists who were considered hostile to the government.

The Bar Council is a conservative organisation representing about 16,000 members throughout the Malaysian peninsula. In recent years it has become more publicly critical of what it believed was the infringement

---

11 *Malaysia Online*, 16 September 2014

of human rights within Malaysia. For example, the Bar Council in 2012 played a major role in monitoring the Bersih 3.0 street protests when thousands took to the streets advocating electoral reform. Its president Lim Chee Wee was highly critical of police conduct at that time saying that while the police may have been provoked by some demonstrators there was unjustified human rights violations and widespread brutality by them.[12]

Lim's successor Christopher Leong was equally forthright in his criticism of human rights violations. The widespread prosecution of persons for alleged acts of sedition was a matter of serious concern for the Bar Council. At the EGM, he proposed a motion on behalf of the Bar Council, which was entitled: *Resolution against the Sedition Act, other laws and actions taken which stifle speech and expression, and matters in connection therewith.*

It was a lengthy motion, but it characterised the Sedition Act as "an archaic and repressive law that was the antithesis of democracy, rule of law, justice and human rights."

The government was criticised for failing to keep its promise to repeal the legislation and the Bar Council protested that it had been used to selectively arrest and prosecute academics, journalists and members of parliament. It resolved to call upon the Malaysian Government to repeal the Sedition Act and the Attorney-General to withdraw all pending charges, cases and appeals then before the courts brought under the Act. The Bar Council finally resolved to organise a peaceful protest in the form of a walk to promote its stand against the sedition law.

---

12   *The Malaysian Insider*, "Police Brutality more widespread during Bersih 3.0, says Bar Council", by Shazwan Mustafa Kamal, 1 May 2012

The meeting almost did not go ahead when police turned up just as it was about to start saying they were responding to a bomb threat. The police were told they could search, but the members opted to continue with the meeting. Of course, they would have had no choice had the police insisted on an evacuation of the building. As the meeting continued, the crowd watched as police together with bomb sniffer-dogs searched the main room's mezzanine. No bomb was found.

It was resolved that the protest march, called "Walk for Peace and Freedom 2014", would be held on 16 October 2014. Foreign lawyers expressed their support for it including bar associations from Australia, Taiwan, South Africa, the United States, South Korea, Germany, New Zealand, Sri Lanka and Nepal.

(It was just the fourth 'Walk' in the Malaysian Bar's 67-year history. Recent marches were the 2007 "Walk for Justice" over a judicial appointment scandal and the 2011 "Walk for Freedom to Walk" protesting against restrictions on public assembly.)

On 16 October, a crowd of about 2,000 lawyers gathered at the Pedang Merbok carpark before walking together to the Dewan Rakyat where PM Najib had arranged for a delegation from the Bar to be received by the Minister in the Prime Minister's Department to present its views.

Watching the event were many international observers including a team from LAWASIA led by President Isomi Suzuki and General Secretary Janet Neville. The president-elect of the Law Council of Australia, Duncan McConnel, was there and acting as an observer for the Law Society of England and Wales and the Union Internationale des Avocats. The Commonwealth Lawyers Association was also represented in an observer capacity, as was the International Commission of Jurists. Others present also included members of diplomatic missions in Malaysia.

Malaysian Bar president Christopher Leong told the crowd: "We are here this morning in the sun, in the car park, in the heart of Kuala Lumpur not for ourselves alone. We do this not for our friends alone, we do this not for our families alone, we do this not for our fellow Malaysians alone but for the future generations of Malaysia. We are here to claim back democratic public space. We are here to say as much as you try, you can't stifle speech. You can't stop expression of thought by thinking Malaysians."

He then turned to the sedition law saying: "The Sedition Act is a law specifically designed to shut you up and we have seen the unprecedented use of this abusive act in the last three months against students, law professors, lawyers, journalists, members of civil society, members of parliament and members of state parliaments. We demand the government to abide by its pledge to repeal the Sedition Act."

Government 'flip-flops' on pledge to abolish Sedition Act

If there was any doubt of a change of direction by the government it was resolved at the 65th Umno General Assembly on 27 November 2014 when PM Najib bowed to pressure from conservative forces telling delegates that the sedition law would be retained and even enhanced.

In his policy speech at the start of the annual convention, he said the decision was made after consultation with party leaders, NGOs and grassroots members. "As prime minister, I have decided that the Sedition Act will be maintained," Mr Najib told the 2,700 delegates gathered at Putra World Trade Centre at Kuala Lumpur. [13]

Mr Najib said he would also add more clauses to the act to protect the sanctity of Islam, prevent insults to other religions, and take action

---

13   *Daily Express, Saturday*, 29 November 2014

against anyone who calls for the cessation of the Borneo states of Sabah and Sarawak.[14]

Anwar responded by accusing the PM of "caving to rightists and racists" in ruling the establishment who were "instilling a culture of fear" in order to cling to power. "Is it not embarrassing to the Malay community? To save the Malays, laws are needed so they can arrest and abuse others? This is the start of authoritarian rule by Najib," said Anwar.[15]

Rights groups also condemned Najib's latest move, with Human Rights Watch calling it a "major reversal on human rights". Phil Robertson, the group's deputy Asia director, said: "Since the Sedition Act gives the government the discretion to declare almost anything seditious, social activists and political opposition figures are likely to face a renewed crackdown that will be discriminatory and politically motivated."[16]

"They are sending a strong signal to non-Malays and to the Chinese that if you don't support Umno, Umno will keep moving to the right and you will regret it," said James Chin, a political analyst with the Jeffrey Cheah Institute, a Malaysian think tank.[17]

In the run-up to the Umno Conference, Mr Najib had been under immense pressure from conservative forces within his own party to retain the Sedition Act. Dr Mahathir had publicly withdrawn his personal support for PM Najib, which provided a rallying call for his supporters to demand the prime minister's resignation.

---

14   BBC, Jennifer Pak, News Asia, 27 November 2014

15   AFP, 'Malaysia reverses vow to scrap controversial sedition law' 27 November 2014; *Malay Chronicle*, 28 November 2014

16   AFP, "Malaysia reverses vow to scrap controversial sedition law", 27 November 2014

17   Ibid.

Mr Najib repealed the draconic Internal Security Act in 2012, but it was obvious that to also repeal the sedition law would leave the government without any effective weapon to use against its political opponents and silence dissent.

The call to retain the law was dressed up as necessary to maintain racial harmony and protect the Malay culture, the Malay rulers and the "sanctity of Islam". Najib needed to appease the forces challenging his authority. If Anwar was right, the prosecution against him was part of an attempt by the PM to shore up his support base. Najib's policy reversal on the sedition law left his claim to be a liberal reformist in tatters.

Shortly after Mr Najib's announcement, Phil Robertson with Human Rights Watch tweeted that this meant the death of human rights and freedom of expression in Malaysia. "Opposition politicians and activists watch out," he wrote.[18]

The Americans also expressed their concern at what was plainly a reversal of policy and the government's use of the legislation against political opponents. These comments caused a diplomatic furor with Malaysia.

It happened when on 5 December 2014 the U.S. Vice President Joe Biden raised concerns about the rule of law in Malaysia and the ongoing prosecution of Anwar on his Twitter account.

First, Mr Biden tweeted that "amid growing U.S.-Malaysia ties, [the] Malaysian government's use of the legal system and Sedition Act to stifle opposition raises rule of law concerns." This was followed with another tweet a minute later: "Anwar Ibrahim's appeal gives Malaysia a vital chance to make things right and promote confidence in its democracy and judiciary."

18   BBC, Jennifer Pak, News Asia, 27 November 2014

The next day the U.S. Ambassador to Malaysia Joseph Yun said in an interview with an online news portal that the U.S. was "puzzled" about the reversal of policy. "We were a little bit puzzled why the government announced recently that actually it would not be repealed, rather it probably should be strengthened. So what has changed between 2012 and now?"[19]

The ambassador's comments caused him to be summoned to the Malaysian Foreign Ministry to explain. One government minister — Home Minister Ahmad Zahid Hamidi — reacted angrily to Biden's tweets telling him to "mind his own business" and stay out of Malaysian affairs. "Do not disturb our sovereignty and dignity. Our political situation is different from others," he added.[20]

Tourism and Culture Minister Nazri Aziz said the United States should first resolve its own problems with racial discrimination against African-Americans, adding that Malaysia "will not hesitate to sever ties" with Washington if it continues to meddle in its internal affairs. Meanwhile, Youth and Sports Minister Khairy Jamaluddin drew attention to America's record of torture in Guantanamo Bay.[21]

This tension between them came at a time when Malaysia was very near to assuming both the Asean chairmanship as well as the UN Security Council non-permanent seat for two years from 2015.

19 The Diplomat, Asian Beat, Prashanth Parameswaran, 12 December 2014

20 *The Malaysian Insider*, 7 December 2014

21 The Diplomat, Asian Beat, Prashanth Parameswaran, 12 December 2014

CHAPTER 21
The final appeal –
Federal Court of Malaysia

Case Management Hearing: 8 August 2014

There was a false start to the listing of the Federal Court Appeal. It was well known that Anwar's lead counsel Datuk Sulaiman Abdullah was unwell. Proceedings were delayed because of his ill heath, and this led to another delay when the Federal Court attempted to list the appeal for hearing on 8 and 9 September 2014.

Anwar's lawyers protested to the deputy registrar, Mohd Izzudin Mohamad, at a case management hearing on 8 August 2014 saying it seemed to be an attempt to again rush the appeal and that these dates were unsuitable because Sulaiman Abdullah would be on medical leave until 13 October. Mohd Izzudin relented and rescheduled the listing to an open court hearing before the Court of Appeal president Tan Sri Md Raus Sharif to 14 August 2014. At that hearing, new dates were fixed for 28 and 29 October 2014.

Anwar's lawyer charged with sedition

Ten days later, on 18 August 2014, one of Anwar's legal team was charged with sedition for criticisms he made about the Court of Appeal's judgement of conviction against Anwar.

Lawyer N. Surendran, who is also the opposition MP for Padang Serai, was charged with saying the court judgement was "flawed, defensive and insupportable". He said that he was merely giving his views on the appellate court's decision as Anwar's legal counsel, which would also form the basis of defence submissions to be made at the forthcoming appeal.

As if that wasn't enough, on 27 August 2014, Surendran was charged a second time for comments he made on a YouTube video on 8 August 2014, in which he claimed that the prosecution against Anwar was a "political conspiracy" involving the government. Again, that was a claim he was later to make in the Federal Court.

Surendran's counsel, Latheefa Koya — also a member of Anwar's legal team — said the authorities had gone too far in charging Surendran with a second sedition charge, arguing that it was a clear attempt to interfere with his duties as Anwar's counsel. She stressed that the speed at which the authorities decided to charge him was a clear indication that they intended to "undermine Anwar's defence and deny him a fair hearing".[1]

Executive director Eric Paulsen of Lawyers for Liberty (LFL) was reported as saying that the government had targeted Surendren because he was Anwar's counsel.[2]

Call by PKR to rally at Federal Court in support of Anwar

The PKR leadership issued a nationwide circular to its members and supporters to assemble at the Palace of Justice at Putrajaya to rally under the banner of "Rakyat Hakim Negara" ("People's Justice") and to show their support for Anwar at his appeal.

Professor Chandra Muzaffar a well-known academic and Islamic activist, criticised the proposed rally as an attempt to apply political pressure on the judiciary.[3] He was supported in the same newspaper article

---

1   *The Malay Mail*, 27 August 2014

2   *The Rakyat Post*, "Sedition Act, the new ISA", 27 August 2014

published in the *New Straits Times* by former DAP vice-chairman Tunku Abdul Aziz Tunku Ibrahim who was quoted as saying the planned rally was "tantamount to criminal intimidation" of the judges.[4]

Tunku Aziz joined the DAP following the 2008 election, but fell out with the party over the Bersih street protests, disapproving of what he regarded as their unlawful nature at times. Secretary-General of the DAP Lim Guan Eng rebuked him for not accepting the party line on Bersih, and when his endorsement as a senator was questioned by the party, he resigned.

When Anwar arrived at the start of the appeal on Tuesday 28 October, he greeted his supporters who were assembled outside the court building, but kept at a distance with a 300-metre barricade erected by the police to prevent entry to the court precinct. Police had also closed off the section of the road passing in front of the court building. As we left the court on the evening of the 29 October we passed seven trucks used to transport police officers who had earlier been mobilised to ensure security.

The media gave various estimations of the crowd, but it seemed to me to be in the vicinity of around 500 or more. There was an incident that occurred on Wednesday 29 October when Anwar supporters attempted to get past the barricade, but they were stopped by the police.

Assembled nearby were a hundred or so supporters for Mohd Saiful — mostly young men — waving signs condemning Anwar. From time to time the two groups exchanged insults.

---

3   *New Straits Times*, 27 October 27 2014, page 10

4   Ibid.

5   *The Malaysian Insider*, 14 May 2012

Appointment of Datuk Seri Gopal Sri Ram as lead counsel

Originally, senior lawyer Sulaiman Abdullah was to lead Anwar's team at his appeal. However, it became increasingly obvious that his health had not improved sufficiently to allow him to appear. Hearing dates had already been vacated once before because of his ill health.

Gopal Sri Ram was a controversial appointment. His reputation was mixed. Some thought him too close to the ruling party, and yet others considered that in later years he had become critical of the judiciary and what he described as political interference by the executive government.

In a reported speech given shortly after his retirement on 17 September 2010 at the National Conference on Integrity, Sri Ram said that that the judiciary had failed in its duty to defend minority rights. He said that he thought because the judiciary had become so "executive-minded" that judges had become creatures of the government. He believed that such interference by the executive was clearly a breach of the doctrine of separation of powers, and the executive should never have usurped the power of the judiciary to convict and sentence. He was concerned that given the deteriorating condition of the judiciary since the 1988 crisis, when PM Mahathir sacked the Lord President (now called the Chief Justice) and other senior judges for not favouring the government, that Malaysia was failing as a nation.

When Sri Ram returned to private practice as a lawyer, his right to appear on behalf of a party at trial was challenged by his opponent who claimed that his appearance before his former peers would undermine the administration of justice. The Court ruled that the Legal Profession Act 1976 did not prevent a retired judge from appearing in court. (See the decision of *Innovations Construction Sdn Bhd v MTM Millenium Holdings Sdn Bhd* (2013) Civil Appeal No: W-02 (NCC) (A)-248-01/2013)

That same complaint was raised against him when he appeared at the Federal Court appeal hearing for Anwar, but it really came to nothing and Sri Ram abruptly dismissed any complaints.

The defence case

(A) ANWAR'S GROUNDS OF APPEAL

With a new team of lawyers conducting his defence came additional grounds of appeal. These were more extensive than the grounds argued earlier before the Court of Appeal, which essentially had focused on the unreliability of the DNA evidence and break in the chain of its custody. These were still very much key issues in the appeal, but amongst other things more attention was given to Mohd Saiful's lack of credibility as a complainant.

The defence claimed there was insufficient evidence to even require Anwar to reply to the prosecution case. It also asserted that errors were made not only by the trial judge, but also the Court of Appeal in overturning Anwar's acquittal.

(B) THE OPENING OF ANWAR'S CASE

In opening Anwar's case, Sri Ram informed the court that the appellant's submissions would be divided between several counsel who were members of Anwar's team.

He told the judges that he would make preliminary submissions that would focus on key issues relating to Mohd Saiful's credibility. He explained he would submit that Mohd Saiful's evidence was so unreliable that the trial judge should have dismissed the charge at the conclusion of the prosecution case rather than calling on Anwar to enter his defence. He then identified the topics on which each counsel would make submissions.

Gopal Sri Ram conferring with lawyers in the defence team as Anwar looks on; Sri Ram with his assistant Lim Choon Kim.

N. Surenden would submit the prosecution was part of a conspiracy to fabricate evidence against Anwar and deal with criticisms by the appeal court of the dock statement made by Anwar at his trial.

Sangeet Kaur would deal with an obvious error made by the trial judge in reversing his decision to admit a DNA analysis of items taken from Anwar's cell shortly after he was arrested. She would also submit there was insufficient evidence to prove that the items taken from Anwar's cell — which were used to extract DNA — had actually been used by Anwar.

Finally, Ramkarpal Singh would deal with the DNA analysis, exposing once again what he claimed were improbable results obtained from the samples taken from Mohd Saiful by the medical examiners. He would also explore the possibility that there was interference and contamination of the forensic samples such that they could not be relied upon at all.

(c) MOHD SAIFUL'S CREDIBILITY

Having identified the key issues at the appeal, Sri Ram launched his attack on Mohd Saiful's credibility. He submitted that Mohd Saiful could not be believed as a witness and that the trial judge erred in finding him to be credible. He submitted further that the trial judge should not have called upon Anwar to answer the prosecution case. He listed several facts, which he claimed directly affected Mohd Saiful's credibility. These included Mohd Saiful's:

- purchase of lubricant to take to the condominium when he knew that sex would take place without his consent. It was, said Sri Ram, a "highly improbable" explanation.

- production of a tube of lubricant at the trial claiming Anwar used it when committing the alleged sexual act (Exhibit A8). It was the first the defence knew of its existence because no mention of the tube was made in the original police report nor had it been listed in the police exhibits. When asked for an explanation, Mohd Saiful claimed he had offered it to the investigating officer Jude Pereira but was told by him to "hang on to it". Sri Ram submitted that was a nonsense explanation and the production of the tube was "clearly an afterthought".

- claim that when the sexual act occurred, some of the lubricant spilled onto a rug that was on the floor. However no evidence of lubricant was ever found on any floor coverings examined from the condominium.

- affair with a junior member of the prosecution team, which compromised the integrity of the trial by providing him direct access to confidential information in the possession of the prosecution.

- conduct after the alleged sexual assault, which was "inconsistent with a man roughly sexually assaulted the day before", when he was photographed the very next day

at a meeting with Anwar and others without showing any
obvious sign of distress.

- claim that he delayed reporting the sexual assault to
  police because he was fearful and embarrassed at what
  had happened. However, only days before the incident,
  he had met with DPM Najib and a senior police officer to
  complain about Anwar sexually penetrating him. He had
  also spoken with the Inspector General of Police.

- care to preserve any evidence that may have been on his
  body by not washing himself for two days before the
  medical examination. However, he washed the underwear
  he had worn on the day he claimed to have been sexually
  assaulted.

- presence in the condominium complex on the afternoon
  of the alleged offence. However, there was no evidence
  — apart from his account — that he was ever where he
  claimed he was sexually assaulted.

- meeting with DPM Najib and senior police officers
  only days before the alleged offence, which gave rise to
  the suspicion that the whole scenario was contrived and
  planned before the alleged offence occurred.

(D) ERRORS BY TRIAL JUDGE

Sri Ram then listed a series of errors made by the trial judge, which
included:

- ruling at the conclusion of the prosecution case that a
  prima facie case had been made out and that Anwar was
  required to enter his defence.

- finding that Mohd Saiful was a credible and truthful

witness and ruling that his complaint of sexual assault had been corroborated by evidence of the uncharged acts.

- relying upon the uncharged sexual acts to bolster the credibility of Mohd Saiful's complaint when he had already ruled to exclude that evidence from the trial.

- ruling that Mohd Saiful's complaint to the medical examiners at Hospital Kuala Lumpur was a "recent complaint" when it was clear on the evidence that it was not. (A recent complaint of a sexual offence is an exception to the hearsay rule and while not proof of the offence, it may be admitted into evidence and used to bolster a complainant's credibility). Mohd Saiful's complaint to the medical examiners was not the first complaint he had made because he complained to Dr Mohd Osman at Puswari Hospital when he presented himself for medical examination some hours before.

- ignoring the testimony of Dr Osman who said that when he examined Mohd Saiful he was told that a plastic object had been inserted into his rectum — which Mohd Saiful later denied saying — but this was never considered in the context of assessing his credibility.

- refusing to allow the defence to have access to the original statements given by Mohd Saiful to the police when it was clear that it was "expedient for the purposes of justice to do so" particularly when there was a sufficient legal basis to require disclosure under section 113 of the Criminal Procedure Code.

- ruling that Mohd Saiful could corroborate himself by making a complaint of sexual assault, when that could only go to his credit and was not independent evidence of the offence.

(E) ERRORS BY COURT OF APPEAL

Sri Ram next turned his attack to the decision of the judges of the Court of Appeal, who unanimously had reversed Anwar's acquittal, sentencing him to five years' imprisonment. He submitted that:

- the appeal court "went beyond its duties" when it criticised Anwar's decision to abandon his alibi. Anwar gave his reason for doing so in his dock statement saying that his main alibi witness (the owner of the condominium in which the alleged sexual assault occurred) had refused to testify having been intimidated by the police who had interviewed him for more than 30 hours. "It was not an issue for the trial judge nor a ground of appeal," said Sri Ram, but the appeal court wrongly used it to justify the conviction, which amounted to a serious misdirection.

- the appeal court should not have been critical of Anwar's failure to testify under oath. Anwar chose at the trial to make a dock statement, meaning that he read a prepared statement to the court. Sri Ram submitted that it was Anwar's legal right to choose that option and it was inappropriate for the judges to draw an adverse inference against him for doing so. While it was true that the dock statement had not been tested by cross-examination that simply went to the issue of the weight that should be given it.

- the appeal court dismissed the expert testimony of the defence experts concerning DNA and the procedures necessary to ensure the integrity of forensic samples without having proper regard to their expertise and sufficiently analysing the key issues raised by their testimony.

- the appeal court made no finding as to Mohd Saiful's credit by having regard to the evidence, which was a factor critical to the case, but simply agreed with the trial judge's finding.

(F) CONSPIRACY TO FABRICATE EVIDENCE AGAINST ANWAR

N. Surendran was the next counsel to address the court and he submitted that the allegation of sexual assault wasn't a coincidence, but rather "part of a pre-arrangement" to destroy Anwar politically. It is clear the judges were not comfortable with that submission and effectively ignored it.

He then turned to a more specific analysis of the dock statement. He said there was no basis to criticise Anwar's decision to rely on it and it was a "serious misdirection". He rejected the Court of Appeal's characterisation of it as no more than a "mere denial".

He also said there was no basis for the court to be critical of the fact that Anwar had not subjected himself to cross-examination, as if that was something from which they could draw an adverse inference. He said the law provided three options for an accused standing trial: make a statement from the dock, testify, or remain silent. A dock statement may have less weight than direct testimony, but it was still evidence to be considered by the court, which it failed to do.

(G) REVERSAL OF JUDGE'S DECISION TO EXCLUDE THE DNA EVIDENCE

Karpal Singh's daughter Sangeet Kaur followed next. Her primary focus was on the ground of appeal relating to the trial judge's reversal of his decision to exclude DNA evidence obtained by the police.

At the trial, Anwar's lawyers challenged the admissibility of the DNA samples taken from items seized by police from a cell where Anwar had spent the night after his arrest. These items included a hand-towel, toothbrush and water bottle, which the police claimed were used by Anwar.

The DNA profile extracted from these items was used by the police as a 'reference sample' of Anwar's DNA to compare with the samples taken by medical examiners from Mohd Saiful's rectum and anus. The government chemists claimed the DNA extracted from the forensic samples matched the reference sample and thus directly implicated Anwar.

This was a critical submission because if the samples taken from the lockup were excluded, then there could be no link to the forensic samples taken from Mohd Saiful. If that happened, then the whole of the DNA evidence against Anwar would collapse.

The challenge by Anwar's lawyers to the admissibility of this evidence at trial was twofold. First, that the police had unlawfully seized these items because Anwar had already exercised his right to refuse providing a forensic sample for DNA analysis.

Secondly, that it would be unfair to admit the DNA evidence derived from those items because they had been seized after his refusal. Sangeet said that when Anwar refused to supply a DNA sample, the police "resorted to trickery" to obtain a sample by collecting these items from his cell and thus undermining his right to refuse.

She explained that after having heard submissions from counsel the trial judge accepted that it would be unfair to admit the evidence and ruled that it should be excluded. He was later asked by the prosecution to reconsider his ruling, which he did, and then reversed his earlier decision finding that it had been lawfully obtained.

Her key point was that the judge's first ruling excluded the evidence on the basis of unfairness, but he reversed his decision on a completely different ground, namely that it was lawfully obtained.

Finally, she submitted that there was simply no evidence before the trial judge that Anwar had ever touched these items. There was nothing in the lockup diary to say that he did and no police officer testified that he had been seen to touch them.

(H) INHERENTLY UNRELIABLE DNA EVIDENCE

Ramkarpal Singh was the next counsel to address the court. He commenced his submissions by reminding the court about what he described as the 'prosecution fallacy' when it came to dealing with DNA evidence.

He explained that DNA is a purely statistical probability. It is a fallacy to reason that simply because a person's DNA is found at a crime scene the person is thereby guilty of the crime. "That may or may not be so. It is an incriminating piece of evidence," he said, "but whether an inference of guilt can be made will depend on whether it is supported by other evidence."

Ramkarpal attacked the DNA evidence on a number of grounds, reiterating the defence experts' conclusions that were submitted at the Court of Appeal hearing in March 2014:

- There was evidence of an unidentified third person in the high rectal swabs that had not been explained, which meant that Mohd Saiful had either been penetrated to ejaculation by another male or someone had contaminated the sample by handling it.

- The DNA analysis was inconsistent with the known history of the samples, meaning there was little, if any, evidence of degradation in circumstances where contrary to specific instructions the samples had not been properly preserved by DSP Pereira.

- The DNA allegedly taken from sperm cells had survived for more than 96 hours from the time of ejaculation to analysis, which was highly improbable according to scientific experience.

- The Differential Extraction Process (DEP), used to separate sperm cells from non-sperm cells, was incomplete, admitting the possibility that the DNA claimed to match Anwar's DNA didn't come from semen, but rather from non-sperm cells.

Ramkarpal made other criticisms of the extraction process and analysis conducted by the government scientist. He submitted that the government scientists had failed to meet "minimum international reporting thresholds", which meant in this case that they had been "selective" in identifying reportable findings. In fact, he said, Dr Seah Lay Hong's report did not accurately reflect the material she provided to support her analysis and she was at a loss to explain the inconsistencies.

He was also highly critical of the way the appeal court judges dealt with the expert evidence called by the defence at trial. The judges, he said, simply "brushed aside" the expert witnesses without properly analysing their testimony and dismissed them as "arm-chair experts".

Finally, Ramkarpal submitted that the evidence was such that the identity of "Male Y" — which was alleged by the prosecution to be Anwar — had not been proven beyond a reasonable doubt.

The prosecution reply

(A) SCANDALOUS ATTACK ON JUDICIARY — THE DOCK STATEMENT

Chief Prosecutor Shafee Abdullah's primary attack was on Anwar's dock statement. He described it as amounting to an allegation of a "total conspiracy", which he said was a "scandalous attack on the trial judge, the police, the chemists, the prosecution and the courts."

In his dock statement Anwar had given reasons why he did not testify, but in doing so, said Shafee Abdullah, he opened himself up to attack. It was nothing but a "mere denial' and failed effectively to respond to the facts of the case.

(B) ALIBI ATTACK UNFOUNDED — DUTY TO CALL WITNESSES

At the trial, Anwar had abandoned his defence of alibi, and justified doing so saying the owner of the condominium refused to testify after having been interrogated by police for several hours. Yet, said Shafee Abdullah, the police were doing no more than carrying out their duty to investigate an alibi.

Shafee Abdullah submitted that Anwar had listed several persons in his notice of alibi and having done so had a duty to advance his defence. But he failed to call any of them. Having abandoned this defence, it was open for the court to make adverse inference against him.

(C) MOHD SAIFUL AN HONEST AND CREDIBLE WITNESS

Shafee Abdullah defended the complainant Mohd Saiful describing how Anwar had attacked him in a "terrible way" and yet at the close of the prosecution case the trial judge found him to be an honest and credible witness. He said that Mohd Saiful was cross-examined for "many, many days" and he was "believable, consistent and very credible".

He then focused on the nature of the relationship between Anwar and Mohd Saiful. The latter may have been a "university dropout", said Shafee Abdullah, but yet he was given "special treatment". He described how Anwar had "groomed him" by giving him preferential treatment and gifts and exercised a "dominance" over him. When Anwar asked Mohd Saiful for sex, said Shafee Abdullah, there was no attempt at seduction;

he simply said, "Can I fuck you?" That indicated, said Shafee Abdullah, that it had "happened before" and that Anwar "took it for granted" that he would comply.

Shafee Abdullah submitted that Anwar's lawyers had questioned Mohd Saiful's conduct after the alleged incident submitting that it was inconsistent with a person who had been sexually assaulted. Shafee Abdullah said that Mohd Saiful had resigned shortly after this incident, which indicated that he wanted to leave his employment with Anwar.

Mohd Saiful met with then DPM Najib Razak and spoke with senior police officers, said Shafee Abdullah, "but no one seemed to care about this young man until the final act occurred." He delayed reporting the incident because he did not want to "spoil his future".

(D) MOHD SAIFUL'S COMPLAINT OF OTHER SEXUAL ACTS

Shafee Abdullah submitted that evidence of uncharged sexual offences was admissible as 'relationship evidence'. It was relevant to understanding the context in which the offence charged was committed and in assessing Mohd Saiful's credibility.

For example, he said, it may explain why Mohd Saiful did not resist and brought lubricant to the apartment. It may also explain why Anwar's request for sex was so direct. It was, said Shafee Abdullah, because Mohd Saiful had become "familiar with his predicament" and offered little, if any, resistance. It wasn't a jury trial — where the risk of prejudice would be high — so the court was entitled to consider the evidence without prejudicing the accused.

(E) PROSECUTION DECISION NOT TO CALL DR OSMAN

Shafee Abdullah responded to criticism that the prosecution had chosen not to call Dr Osman who was clearly a material witness. He justified not calling him, detailing several facts, which he claimed satisfied the prosecution that Dr Osman could not be regarded as a reliable and truthful witness. If that view was soundly based, the prosecution was entitled to exercise its discretion not to call him. One factor the prosecution relied upon was the doctor's failure to record in his medical notes, at the time of the physical examination, Mohd Saiful's mention that a plastic object had been inserted into his anus.

That point was added later, said Shafee Abdullah, and gave rise to the suspicion that it was because someone had asked him to include it. "He was clearly a witness who was lying and his statement was not credible," said Shafee Abdullah.

(F) THE "ARM-CHAIR" EXPERTS

Shafee Abdullah launched a major attack against molecular geneticist Dr Brian McDonald, who is a specialist in the field of DNA testing and analysis. He was a key witness for the defence at the trial and substantially damaged the DNA evidence relied upon by the prosecution.

(Curiously, he made no mention of Professor David Wells, who was also a defence expert witness and critical of the prosecution forensic evidence. Perhaps it was because he was less of a target.)

He submitted that Dr McDonald had been discredited in other court cases in Australia and was "not an expert to rely on". He was "knocked about" in Anwar's trial when questioned over a range of issues. He said the Court of Appeal had correctly described him as an "arm-chair expert" and "every Australian court had said that about him". He submitted that the testimony of the government chemists was to be preferred.

(G) NO THIRD MALE IN DNA SAMPLE

First, Shafee Abdullah dealt with the potential finding from the DNA extraction that a third male had contributed to the sample taken from Mohd Saiful's perianal swab (Exhibit B5).

He submitted that as this result happened only once that it might have been no more than a "drop-in" or an "aberration". Shafee Abdullah speculated that it might even have come from contamination by Dr Osman when he examined Mohd Saiful at Hospital Puswari.

He said: "Dr Osman washed his hands after examining Saiful. There is a possibility that he was not using gloves. We do not have a statement that he used gloves or sterilised the proctoscope. So it was possible that the third DNA is from Dr Osman."

(H) SUFFICIENT DNA IN FORENSIC SAMPLES TO IDENTIFY ANWAR

Secondly, Shafee Abdullah responded to the defence submission that the DNA profile analysis was inconsistent with the known history of the forensic samples.

He rejected the claim that the DNA could not have survived for 96 hours or more after the alleged incident saying there had been cases where DNA had survived for many years. He cited as authority a murder case in Australia where a rapist's DNA had been extracted from a beach towel after more than 13 years.

He attempted to introduce medical literature that he claimed recorded the experience that DNA cells could survive well beyond the time frames stated by the defence experts. In a rather comic scene he produced an article in the Thai language to support his claim. He was relying on the brief summary, which was the only part of the article that was in English.

One of the judges suggested that it wasn't very helpful, and for all they knew the article could be about KFC chicken. This brought howls of laughter from the gallery. The Chief Justice upheld Ramkarpal's objection that it be excluded.

Shafee Abdullah rejected the claim that the government DNA expert, chemist Dr Seah Lay Hong, ever said the DNA samples were "pristine", but only that the quality of the sample was sufficient to allow an analysis to be undertaken.

He said that a sample may be degraded, but so long as it can be read it is still sufficient to match a donor. The analysis strongly identified Anwar in each of these samples.

(I) CHAIN OF EVIDENCE INTACT

Shafee Abdullah criticised the defence attack upon the chain of custody of the forensic exhibits. He said no challenge was made at the trial, which he said was unfair as it deprived the prosecution of the ability to respond.

He submitted there was no basis to challenge the continuity of the forensic samples. He said the samples were always in the custody of DSP Pereira from the time they were handed to him by the medical examiners until he delivered them to the government chemist for analysis.

(J) NO PROOF OF FABRICATED EVIDENCE

Shafee Abdullah was also critical of complaints Anwar made about the conduct of the police claiming amongst other things that they had fabricated evidence against him. "How," he asked rhetorically, "could they obtain fresh semen from Saiful's rectum? Somebody must explain it, I can't."

In any event, he continued, the plastic bag containing the forensic samples wasn't tamper-proof, but simply sealed with a tag. In that large bag were some plastic containers into which the swabs taken by the medical examiners were placed. The lid of each of the plastic containers was sealed with an adhesive tag upon which was written the chief examiner's signature.

He emphasised that DSP Pereira did not hide the fact that he had cut the large plastic bag open to relabel the exhibits given to him by the medical examiners. Unfairly, he said, the allegation of "fabrication" was never put to the investigating officer.

(k) NO EVIDENCE OF CONTAMINATION OF FORENSIC SAMPLES

Thirdly, Shafee Abdullah responded to the allegation that the forensic samples had been contaminated. He said the medical doctors examining Mohd Saiful took care to avoid contamination of the swabs taken from Saiful by using gloves and sterilised instruments. The only possibility of contamination was from Dr Osman.

He submitted that while DSP Pereira opened the main plastic bag containing the forensic samples, there was no evidence whatsoever that he touched the swabs in the sealed hospital containers.

(l) DID ANWAR USE ITEMS RECOVERED FROM HIS CELL?

Shafee Abdullah submitted that while there may have been no direct evidence of Anwar using the items recovered from his cell, from what police officers said and recorded in the lockup diary there was an irresistible inference that he used them.

He pointed out that none of the officers were cross-examined about this at the trial. If there was a conspiracy to implicate Anwar then it would have been an easy thing for Pereira to say he had seen Anwar use these items, but he did not, which debunked the claim of conspiracy.

The trial judge was right to reverse his ruling and admit evidence obtained from these items, said Shafee Abdullah, because there was nothing unlawful in the way they had been seized by the police.

Anwar was lawfully detained after his arrest and his rights were fully explained to him, which meant that the evidence obtained from these items

Anwar addressing supporters and the media immediately
after the Federal Court hearing on 8 November 2014.

was admissible. And in any event, the probative value of the evidence far
outweighed the prejudicial effect of its admission.

(M) TRIAL JUDGE APPLIED WRONG STANDARD OF PROOF

Finally, Shafee Abdullah claimed that the trial judge had misapplied the law.
When he said that he could not be "100% certain" that the forensic samples
had not been compromised he applied the wrong standard of proof. Rather
than "100% certain", it should have been "beyond a reasonable doubt".

The defence submitted in the Court of Appeal that the trial judge
was not talking of the general standard of proof, but only that he could
be satisfied the integrity of the samples was intact. As such, there was no
substance to this ground of appeal.

The parties completed their submissions on Friday, 7 November 2014 at
which time the court reserved its decision to a date to be fixed.

CHAPTER 22
The final verdict –
10 February 2015

It was the morning of Tuesday, 10 February 2015 and still dark when I left the hotel at 7.15 am. The journey to the Palace of Justice at Putrajaya would take about 40 minutes. The Federal Court was to announce its verdict at 9 am. I thought it prudent to leave early as large crowds were expected to be there in support of Anwar Ibrahim and security would be tight.

I had flown to Kuala Lumpur the afternoon before. I checked my email messages when I arrived at the hotel and was relieved to find that the Secretary General of LAWASIA, Janet Neville, had sent me a copy of the Chief Justice's authority to attend the hearing as an international observer. Chief Justice Tun Arifin Zakaria had previously been most helpful in accommodating international observers at the proceedings. It was a relief, as his written authority would at least guarantee me entry to the courtroom. I hadn't come all this way to stand in the corridor.

As the taxi drove with the fast-moving traffic along the freeway towards Putrajaya, there was plenty of time to reflect on what I had observed in the last decade. I had been an international observer at Anwar's successful appeal against his first sodomy conviction at the Federal Court in 2004. Now, eleven years later, I was returning to that same court to witness the conclusion of proceedings for a second charge of sodomy. It was hard to believe that it was happening all over again.

Nothing had really changed. Anwar was still fighting a criminal charge that threatened to return him to prison. If the Federal Court upheld the conviction he would be removed from the political arena and, given his age, was most unlikely to make a political comeback. Yet just less than two years earlier he had come within a whisker of winning at the 2013 General Election. The opposition coalition which he led won the popular vote, but the gerrymander of parliamentary seats denied it victory.

After his release from prison in 2004, Anwar brought three disparate groups into the opposition coalition and for the most part kept them together despite the occasional conflict. The opposition was now stronger. New leaders had emerged so there was hope for the future — where before there had been none.

The government, however, was now weaker. The conservative elements led by former Prime Minister Mahathir Mohamad had turned against the incumbent PM Najib Razak. The ruling party was severely shaken after having come so close to losing government, and fearing electoral defeat it had abandoned any pretext of liberal reform. Over the previous 12 months the government had resorted to using the repressive sedition law against its opponents to intimidate and silence opposition members of parliament, journalists and university students.

There had also been dissent. The conservative Malaysian Bar — representing some 15,500 lawyers throughout the peninsula — marched in protest against the sedition law and voiced its opposition to the selective prosecution of Anwar. Students defied the university administration and brought Anwar onto campus grounds to deliver a speech. Student activism is a new phenomenon in Malaysian politics and it is moving to support Anwar. The mood of the country had changed and it wouldn't be the same again. Convicting and jailing Anwar wasn't going to stop the quest for change.

The sky began to lighten as we got closer to Putrajaya. Police helicopters could be seen heading for the area and we came up behind a police armoured personnel carrier that was slowly lumbering along with its own escort. We passed it quickly.

When we arrived at Putrajaya the police had already sealed off a wide perimeter surrounding the court precinct. A large number of huge passenger buses were pulled up on the side of the road disgorging Anwar supporters who were gathering to march to the court building. My taxi driver was familiar with the area and he took all sorts of detours to get me close to the building.

I collected an entry pass at a table at the front door and then walked to where Anwar's supporters were massing and waving flags and banners. They were all very much contained by metal barriers and a large police presence. Uniformed officers were spread out in lines along the barriers to prevent trouble. Not wanting to miss out on a seat, I walked back to the Palace of Justice and went through the massive domed entry hall up the stairs to the courtroom on the first floor. Outside the courtroom there was a throng of media and supporters.

I entered the courtroom and saw familiar faces. Anwar's family were already seated in the reserved seats and waiting expectantly for the judges to arrive. The public gallery at the rear of the courtroom was full and included foreign and local media, international observers, embassy staff and supporters.

Anwar was walking around the courtroom shaking hands, joking and chatting with the crowd.

The verdict and Anwar's immediate response

At around 9.40 am, the judges entered the courtroom. The courtroom was called to order and the judges took their place on the bench while Anwar quickly went to his seat in the dock, which was located immediately in front of the public gallery. Chief Justice Tun Arifin Zakaria, who led a five-member panel[1], immediately began to read from a summary of the court's unanimous decision.

The judgement took two hours to read, but it was apparent early on just what the outcome would be from the way it was reasoned. The conclusion was inescapable: the court intended to uphold Anwar's conviction. Anwar sensed that as well, and from time to time would turn around to look at his lawyers and supporters for confirmation. Finally, the Chief Justice concluded his remarks confirming Anwar's conviction and it was all over.

Anwar's lead counsel Gopal Sri Ram then struggled to his feet — as he suffers from an arthritic hip — and pivoting on a walking frame asked the court to hear his client. The Chief Justice agreed.

Anwar stood, and in a soft voice started to read from prepared notes. But as he read his voice became louder and the pace quickened. His was not a statement of acceptance of guilt or remorse, but a condemnation of the verdict and the judges:

> "I maintain my innocence of this foul charge.
>
> This incident never happened. This is complete fabrication coming from a political conspiracy to stop my political career.
>
> You have not given proper consideration to the case presented by my counsel from day one — that this incident never happened at all.
>
> I can go on and on but I see from your statement today that it will be fruitless, it appears, as I have been condemned again,

---

1   The other judges were Court of Appeal president Tan Sri Mohd Raus Sharif, and Federal Court judges Tan Sri Abdull Hamid Embong, Tan Sri Suriyadi Halim Omar and Datuk Ramly Ali.

as I was in the Court of Appeal. Only here we went through a facade of an eight-day hearing!

It is not a coincidence how the PM was able to release a full written statement on your decision barely minutes after you handed your judgement today — even before sentencing.

In bowing to the dictates of the political masters, you have become partners in crime for the murder of judicial independence and integrity. You have sold your souls to the devil, bartering your conscience for material gain and comfort and security of office.

You had the best opportunity to redeem yourselves — to right the wrongs of the past and put the judiciary on a clean slate and carve your names for posterity as true defenders of justice.

But instead you chose to remain on the dark side and drown your morals and your scruples in a sea of falsehood and subterfuge. Know you not that you are now wallowing in filth and foulness and the stench of your injustice will permeate through every nook and cranny of this so-called Palace of Justice and I do pity you all.

Yes, you have passed judgement on me — and I will, again for the third time, walk into prison, but rest assured my head will be held high. The light shines on me.

But the shame is on you for you will be judged by history as the great cowards of humanity. Sitting on that high horse of judicial power, you have stooped so low to become the underlings of the political masters.

Students of law and professors of jurisprudence will scrutinise your judgements, and as they dissect your reasoning and your decision your credibility and integrity will be torn to tatters. And you will be exposed as the fraudsters who don the robe of judicial power only to pervert the course of justice.

Do not forget that, as all of us will have to, you too will have to answer to your Maker. You will have to answer why you turned your backs on the principles that you had so solemnly sworn to uphold.

People who come into your court have to bow their heads and address you as 'My Lords' but don't you know that you too will have to answer to your Lord one day? By then you will need more than bowing and prostration to justify why you wilfully transgressed Allah's command as ordained in Surah an-Nisaa, verse 58:

'Indeed, Allah commands you to render trusts to whom they are due and when you judge between people, judge with justice. How excellent is that which Allah instructs you. Indeed, Allah is ever Hearing and Seeing.'"

The judges moved uncomfortably in their seats and were clearly agitated at what Anwar was saying. The Chief Justice turned to Gopal Sri Ram, who was seated in the front row of the tables reserved for lawyers, exclaiming this was "not mitigation". Sri Ram replied that Anwar was simply exercising his right to speak. It was obvious the Chief Justice could tolerate it no longer, and after a brief discussion with his fellow judges together they left the courtroom.

All the while, Anwar kept reading.

There was no doubt that Anwar was determined to continue. He knew that he would get only one chance and he wasn't going to miss it. He kept on reading with his voice rising in defiance:

Anwar giving his statement in court after the verdict was announced.

"Going to jail, I consider a sacrifice I make for the people of this country. I have fought most of my life on behalf of the people of this country. For the people I am willing to go to jail or face any other consequence.

My struggle will continue, wherever I am sent and whatever is done to me.

To my friends and fellow Malaysians, let me thank you from the bottom of my heart for all the support you have given me. And Allah is my witness. I pledge and I will not be silenced, I will fight on for freedom and justice and I will never surrender."

With the cry of "never surrender", Anwar's supporters chanted in unison the catchcry of his party: "*Reformasi, Reformasi*". It was chaotic in the courtroom as the police and court ushers attempted to restore order.

Anwar worked his mobile phone giving interviews and telephoning key supporters.

Anwar comforts his wife after the verdict was announced.

The judges returned some 30 minutes later and the hearing resumed. The Chief Justice announced that the court would not uphold the prosecution appeal for a higher sentence, and reaffirmed the five-year sentence of imprisonment imposed by the Court of Appeal.

With that the court adjourned, but it did not seem that anyone was in a hurry to leave. Anwar walked around thanking his legal team and supporters and hugging his family who were clearly distressed. Forty minutes later (by then it was almost 1.40 pm) he was led out of the courtroom through a side door in the custody of several police officers.

Meanwhile, Anwar's supporters had moved to the rear of the building where Anwar would emerge, and gathered along the road that leads from the court exit to bid farewell to their leader. Regular police officers dressed in navy blue uniforms lined the roadway and kept the crowd under control.

By then the police had already cleared a path to allow troops from the Federal Reserve Unit (FRU, a riot control force that deals with civil unrest) to leave the court building in their red armoured vehicles. But instead of doing so, the FRU decided it would confront the supporters with a

Police and troops from the Federal Reserve Unit outside the courthouse.

phalanx-like formation of riot officers armed with shields and batons. They marched down the road towards the crowd banging their riot shields with their batons. High-pressure hoses were used to disperse the crowd, but only very briefly and probably as a warning more than anything else. On this day some were armed with automatic firearms.

It was very dramatic, but all quite unnecessary as one senior regular police officer admitted to me. It provoked a few minor skirmishes and taunts from the crowd, but that was all. It soon became apparent that Anwar had been taken away from the court building by another exit and the crowds slowly drifted away.

Commentary

The unanimous judgement of the Federal Court on 10 February 2015 dismissing Anwar's appeal and upholding the sentence of five years' imprisonment will no doubt be discussed and dissected in detail by others. However, I should provide at least some brief impression of the judgement. What I say about the judgement is by no means an exhaustive analysis of every point discussed by the court, but focuses on the key issues.

Frankly, the judgement was unconvincing and lacked a detailed analysis of the facts on which it was based. It rested on two conclusions:

- Mohd Saiful was a credible witness and should be believed.
- Mohd Saiful's allegation was corroborated by independent evidence and in particular the DNA material which proved he had been anally penetrated by Anwar.

In reaching these conclusions, the court rejected or ignored evidence that raised serious doubts about the credibility of the complainant and the reliability of the evidence upon which the prosecution relied.

Credibility of Mohd Saiful

The Federal Court endorsed the finding of the trial judge — which the Court of Appeal had also accepted — that Mohd Saiful was an honest and credible witness. While the trial judge may have been of that view at the close of the prosecution case, it had come at a time *before* the defence presented its evidence. Importantly, it was also *before* the defence experts raised significant doubts in their testimony about the reliability and integrity of the DNA evidence.

When all of the evidence was before the court and the trial judge had to decide the ultimate question of whether the prosecution had proved Anwar's guilt, he correctly cautioned himself of the need to look for independent evidence to support Mohd Saiful's allegation. He found it could not be relied upon. For that reason, he acquitted Anwar because he could not be satisfied of his guilt.

The Court of Appeal could add nothing more because, as the Federal Court had observed, the trial judge was in the best position to assess Mohd Saiful's credibility. But that assessment had to be based on the whole of the evidence.

The Federal Court was convinced that Mohd Saiful was credible and should be believed because "he could not have described [the sexual acts] unless he was there and had gone through the ordeal." The judgement went further saying that the "minute details testified by PW1 [Mohd Saiful] gave his testimony the ring of truth, as, unless he had personally experienced the incident, he would not be able to relate the [facts] and the sexual act in such minute details."

That is a possible explanation, but it is not the only one. There are many ways in which a person may have knowledge beyond their experience. In modern times, a person has access to a wide range of information. For example, the Internet is full of pornographic websites that explicitly show all kinds of sexual activity. Who better than a young person to explore this readily available source of information? Young persons today are also well informed and ready to discuss what their parents would never talk about. Furthermore, a young person may be more sexually aware and experienced than persons of an older generation.

There was also the possibility that Mohd Saiful may have had previous sexual experiences with other males. The high rectal samples taken from him by the medical examiners gave a mixed DNA profile. Apart from DNA identified as belonging to Anwar ("Male Y"), the sample also contained the DNA profile of an unidentified third male, which suggested that Mohd Saiful had anal sex with that male before the samples were taken.

The Court accepted the explanation of Dr Seah Lay Hong, the government chemist, that the result showing a third male was no more than a "stutter"; in other words, an aberration. But it was not accepted by the defence expert Dr Brian McDonald. The mixed DNA profile raised the prospect that Mohd Saiful was no stranger to the experience of anal sex, and if that were so, he would have been able to convincingly describe the sexual act.

The Federal Court was also convinced that Mohd Saiful was telling the truth because "it takes a lot of courage for a young man, like PW1, to make such a disparaging complaint against a well-known politician like [Anwar]. Knowing that such an allegation might taint him, we cannot ignore the life-long negative effect such a serious allegation would have on PW1 and his family even if the allegation were proven to be true."

The court seemed to be saying that making an allegation in those circumstances made it more likely to be true. Well it does take courage to complain, and to see it through, but experience tells us that complainants at times bring false accusation and their accounts are sometimes rejected.

Bringing a complaint of sexual assault may bolster a complainant's credibility, but the law says it doesn't make the accusation true. Making allegations of sexual assault are the easiest accusations to make — and most difficult to refute. That is because the alleged sexual act usually happens in private without any independent witnesses so the case effectively becomes "word-against-word". It is for that reason that the law cautions a judge to look for independent evidence to support the accusation.

The court touched upon a few points raised by the defence at the appeal, which it decided were not relevant or critical "in light of other compelling evidence". That clearly was a reference to the DNA evidence. However, while particular facts singly may not have been conclusive, together with other facts they adversely affected Mohd Saiful's credibility.

Consider the following, which directly affected his credibility:

- No mention was made by the court of Mohd Saiful's affair with a member of the prosecution team during the trial. This was a glaring omission. The affair raised the prospect they had collaborated. It tainted the prosecution case and adversely affected his credibility.
- The meetings between Mohd Saiful and DPM Najib Razak at the latter's home, as well as secret meetings and communications with

senior police officers only days before the alleged sexual assault, raised the prospect of collusion to fabricate evidence against Anwar.

- Mohd Najwan Halimi (PW6) was a university friend of Mohd Saiful. He testified that during his student days Mohd Saiful was pro-Barisan and "hated Anwar". He told of seeing a photograph of Anwar, uploaded on social media by Mohd Saiful, with the caption *"Pemimpin Munafik"* ("Hypocrite Leader"). While the court alluded to his testimony at the trial, which suggested a motive to make false accusation, it took no account of it in assessing Mohd Saiful's credibility.

- Mohd Saiful testified at the trial that he had brought a tube of KY-Gel to the condominium expecting that he would have sex with Anwar. He described how it was used during the sex act and produced a tube of the lubricant, which he claimed was the one used on the day. It was the first the defence knew of it. It had not been on the list of police exhibits, and when challenged about it he claimed that DSP Jude Pereira had asked him to hold on to it until later. This seems a fanciful explanation given the strict police procedure relating to exhibits.

- Mohd Saiful further testified that reacting to the pain of being anally penetrated he had squeezed the tube of lubricant. He thought this might have caused some of the contents to spill onto the rug (P49A). However no rug was found in the condominium in which the assault was alleged to have taken place, but in another unit. The Federal Court found that the prosecution never explained why that was so, but it thought it was "not a critical piece of evidence ... in light of other compelling evidence." It also found there was "no conclusive evidence the lubricant in fact spilled onto P49A." Not once was the rug forensically tested for the presence of lubricant. It was potentially an important piece of evidence because if lubricant was found it would corroborate Mohd Saiful's account. The fact that it wasn't tested suggests that the first the police or prosecution knew of it was when Mohd Saiful mentioned it at the trial.

- Mohd Saiful claimed that he did not wash his body for 54 hours after the sexual assault to "preserve the evidence" of sexual penetration. Yet he washed the clothes he had worn on that day. Furthermore, he claimed to be a devout Muslim, which required him to perform ablutions before praying or reading from the Quran. Dr Mohd Razali Ibrahim found Mohd Saiful's lower rectum to be empty of faeces when he examined him at Hospital Kuala Lumpur. He explained that might not necessarily indicate that he had defecated, but it potentially contradicted Mohd Saiful's claim not to have defecated at all. The court made no mention of these apparent inconsistencies.

- Dr Mohd Osman, the doctor who first examined Mohd Saiful at the private Puswari Hospital, was a material witness. But he wasn't called by the prosecution because he was not thought to be a truthful witness. It was no doubt because he had recorded Mohd Saiful as saying that a plastic object had been inserted into his anus. The defence called Dr Osman, but the court rejected his evidence. It did so, said the judgement, because Mohd Saiful had denied saying that to Dr Osman; it was not something he told doctors at HKL, and it was not in his police statement. As I have said in an earlier chapter, there was no apparent reason why Dr Osman would lie. The prosecution never put to him in cross-examination a motive to lie nor was anything suggested to him that would even give rise to a suspicion that he wasn't telling the truth.

- The absence of any bodily injury to the anus and rectum doesn't mean that penile penetration had not taken place, but it was inconsistent with the violent forcible anal penetration described by Mohd Saiful as being "*laju dan rakus*" ("fast and vigorous").

- Mohd Saiful's demeanour the day after the alleged sexual assault was a fact that, if accepted, was inconsistent with his claim to have been sodomised without his consent, yet the court simply mentioned the fact that the defence had raised it as an issue, but took no account of it at all.

'Corroboration' (independent evidence)

In the words of the court's judgement: "Corroboration is independent evidence which implicates the accused by connecting or tending to connect him with the crime." In sexual offence cases it means some fact independent of the accusation made by a complainant.

The law does not require the evidence of a complainant in a sexual offence case to be corroborated, but it is a matter of practice and prudence that corroboration is normally required. Of course, whether it is required or not will depend on the circumstances of each case and there are instances where an accused may be convicted simply on the testimony of the complainant. But in this case the trial judge thought it necessary to direct himself on the dangers of relying upon the uncorroborated testimony of a sexual complainant.

The Federal Court in its judgement listed the so-called independent evidence the trial judge relied upon to support Mohd Saiful's testimony. It concluded that the trial judge was correct in relying upon these facts — as was the Court of Appeal — and that it had no reason to disagree with that finding.

In my view, it should have disagreed with at least some of them. The problem is that some of the facts relied upon by the trial judge could not amount to corroboration. These included:

- The opportunity for Anwar to have committed the offence. Anwar, through his chief of staff, had asked Mohd Saiful to bring an envelope to him at the condominium complex on 26 June 2008. The CCTV security recordings confirmed that they were both there on that afternoon, but there was no evidence that Mohd Saiful was ever in the condominium (Unit 11-5-1) where the alleged act was said to have occurred. Furthermore, the law says that mere opportunity alone does not amount to corroboration.

- The account given by Mohd Saiful to the medical examiners at HKL that he had been sexually penetrated by a well-known public figure and there was ejaculation. Mohd Saiful could not corroborate himself. It wasn't independent evidence because it was based on what he said and not on material evidence independent of him. The most it could be used for was 'recent complaint' — an exception to the hearsay rule — which could only bolster his credit.

- The findings by the medical examiners that the absence of scarring, fissure or any sign of recent injuries to the external areas of Mohd Saiful's anus was consistent with his claim that lubricant was used. The absence of injury was a neutral fact and could not be used to prove that lubricant was used or that it was the reason why no injury was found. For the same reason the defence could not reason that the absence of injury proved there was no penetration. It was all too speculative.

There were facts which the Federal Court also relied upon and if proved were capable of corroborating Mohd Saiful's account:

- The taking of rectal and anal swabs by the medical examiners and the presence of semen were undoubtedly corroborative that sexual penetration had taken place.

- The matching of Anwar's DNA taken from the items that he used while in the lockup with the DNA profile of "Male Y" developed from samples taken from Mohd Saiful's rectum. Again, there is no doubt this would corroborate his account of having been penetrated by Anwar.

The DNA evidence

The DNA evidence was the key factor relied upon by the Federal Court to convict Anwar and which it found proved the act of sodomy. If proved, it was independent evidence capable of connecting Anwar to the crime and corroborating Mohd Saiful's complaint of sodomy.

The court relied upon the expert testimony of the chief government chemist Dr Seah Lay Hong who conducted the analysis of the forensic samples provided to her by DSP Jude Pereira and matched them to the DNA profile extracted from the items taken from Anwar's cell.

The reliability and integrity of the DNA evidence was challenged by the expert testimony of Professor David Wells and Dr Brian McDonald. They raised serious concerns about the way in which the forensic samples had been handled and stored; how the government chemist had performed the DNA extraction process; and given the known history of the forensic samples how Dr Seah interpreted the results,

(A) DEFENCE EXPERT OPINIONS REJECTED

The court dismissed the testimony of Professor Wells and Dr McDonald because neither of them performed any tests on the forensic samples nor had they undergone proficiency tests for some years.

This response was disingenuous because the defence experts were not laboratory technicians. They were called to testify because of their expertise and experience in the extraction and analysis of DNA and to comment on the adequacy and reliability of the tests conducted by the government chemist.

Both experts raised serious issues that were not adequately addressed by either of the appeal courts. The Federal Court did not dismiss Professor Wells and Dr McDonald as "arm-chair experts" — which the Court of Appeal did — but the effect was the same. It was an unconvincing response to their expert evidence.

(B) DEGRADATION OF SAMPLES

The Federal Court viewed the defence challenge to the DNA analysis as being that a DNA reading could not have been obtained because of the degradation of the samples, which it said had come about because of the time taken to analyse the samples and the conditions under which they were kept.

Remember that the forensic samples were not analysed until at least 96 hours after ejaculation and they had not been kept in a freezer to prevent the samples degrading. That meant the samples should have degraded significantly, and according to Wells and McDonald the chances of finding any semen cells was extremely remote, if at all possible.

The Federal Court found that the DNA was readable despite the degradation. It said that it agreed with the prosecution that "it was incorrect and misleading to conclude that because of the degradation the DNA profiling is rendered unreliable. It is thus our finding that the degradation has no effect whatsoever on the DNA profiling in this case."

But that wasn't the point. DNA may be extracted from a degraded sample, depending on the extent of its degradation, but in this case the samples when analysed were shown to be in a "pristine" condition. The defence experts thought this was inconsistent with the known history. It raised the prospect they were not the samples taken from Mohd Saiful.

(c) BREAK IN CHAIN OF CUSTODY OF EXHIBITS

The police handling of the samples taken by the medical examiners was sloppy and unprofessional. The containers with the swabs were kept by the investigating officer DSP Jude Pereira in a filing cabinet for 43 hours contrary to the clear instruction of the doctors to freeze them.

Pereira admitted during the trial that by not placing the swabs in the police station freezer and taking a storage number, he violated the Inspector-General's Standing Orders (IGSO) which were the same standing orders the court relied upon to justify his opening of the sample bag.

In reply to a question about that by Anwar's lawyer Sankara Nair at the trial he said: "Yes, it [the samples] should be kept in a store. I broke the law, but it was my decision to do so." But there was more.

Before taking the samples to the government chemists he opened the sealed package containing the containers and relabelled them. The trial judge was correct when he found that this was "not necessary since the receptacles were already packed and labelled by the experts who collected them. The whole purpose of packing and labelling and sealing by the experts who collected the specimen was to maintain the integrity of the samples and the chain of custody."

There was also an issue relating to Pereira's integrity that was relevant to assessing his conduct in handling the forensic samples. During the earlier appeal hearing, the defence informed the Court of Appeal that an adverse finding had been made against him at a hearing before the Human Rights Commission of Malaysia (Suhakam) in 2009 which found him to be an untruthful witness. No mention was made of that fact in the Federal Court judgement.

Nevertheless, the Federal Court justified Pereira's conduct, saying he did no more than follow the IGSO to "put proper markings and labelling to exhibits for the purpose of identification in courts". It found that the way he opened the sample bag showed "transparency in his action" and the government chemist "did not detect any tampering of the seals of the exhibits".

It is my view that by his actions Pereira compromised the integrity of the samples and risked contamination. He broke the chain of custody. His actions should have been sufficient to completely exclude the DNA evidence. Whether the DNA evidence could be accepted would depend on the integrity of the forensic samples, the reliability of the extraction process and the interpretations of the results. The expert testimony of Professor Wells and Dr McDonald put all that evidence into contention and to my mind was sufficient to raise a reasonable doubt.

(D) EVIDENCE OF A POLITICAL CONSPIRACY?

The defence submitted at the appeal hearing that the prosecution for the offence of sodomy was politically motivated. The Federal Court accepted that neither the trial judge nor the Court of Appeal explicitly considered what it called "the political conspiracy defence", and which it said, "if accepted, or believed, would have entitled Anwar to an acquittal."

However, the court said that the only evidence of a political conspiracy was that alleged in Anwar's unsworn dock statement, which was "no more than a mere denial". As such, it did not amount to a credible defence and the Court found that "the defence of political conspiracy remains a mere allegation unsubstantiated by any credible evidence."

But there was evidence apart from Anwar's dock statement that was capable of suggesting collusion. The judgement particularised meetings and communications between Mohd Saiful and "prominent persons, including adversaries of [Anwar]" before and after the alleged sexual assault.

These particulars came from Mohd Saiful's testimony at trial.

He testified that he met with then DPM Najib Razak at his home on 24 June 2008 having been taken there by the DPM's special officer. Also present at the house was Mr Najib's personal lawyer Shafee Abdullah, who claimed not to have spoken with Mohd Saiful, but to have been in the kitchen giving legal advice to the DPM's wife about another matter.

That same evening, Mohd Saiful secretly met with Senior Assistant Commissioner Rodwan Mohd Yusof in a hotel room at Kuala Lumpur. The next day he contacted the Inspector General of Police Musa Hassan who was accused by Anwar of fabricating evidence against him when he led the police investigation in 1998.

The sexual assault was alleged to have occurred on the afternoon of 26 June 2008. The day after, he met with a senior MP and officials of the ruling party. All of these meetings and conversations happened before his complaint to the police, which was not made until 28 June 2008.

Mr Najib initially denied meeting with Mohd Saiful, but he was later forced to admit that he had done so after a photograph emerged showing Mohd Saiful with one of his senior staff. He then attempted to pass it off as an inquiry about obtaining a scholarship, but finally three days later on 3 July 2008 he conceded that Mohd Saiful did go to his house, at which time he revealed to him he had been sodomised by Anwar.

I have no idea whether there was a political conspiracy or not. That is for others to decide. But the circumstances surrounding the alleged sexual assault were all very suspicious. The meetings and communications with senior politicians and police before and after the assault obviously had everything to do with Anwar.

There was also another curious aspect. Why did Mohd Saiful, after making his complaint to these people, go back to his employment with Anwar when there was every expectation he would be sexually assaulted again? He didn't need to return because he had already reported what was happening. It just doesn't make sense.

Karpal Singh told me that these meetings were to ensure that there was sufficient evidence to convict Anwar. He said it was all contrived and arranged so that the false accusation would stand up under the scrutiny that would surely follow once Mohd Saiful made the police complaint.

However, suspicion is not enough. The true test of whether the offence occurred was whether the evidence was sufficient to prove the charge beyond a reasonable doubt. For the reasons briefly explored in this report, my view is that it was not sufficient to that standard of proof and that Anwar should have been acquitted.

Epilogue

The options available to Anwar to contest his conviction and imprisonment are limited.

His family have lodged a petition for a royal pardon to the Yang di-Pertuan Agong. But the odds are against him. The petition is not based on any concession by Anwar that he is guilty of the offence, but rather that his incarceration is a result of a miscarriage of justice. Given the Federal Court's decision, that is most unlikely to succeed.

Anwar must serve at least 40 months of his sentence, which is two-thirds of five years. He can then be released on parole, but the release is discretionary and will depend on the parole board. He cannot become a member of parliament for another five years after that, so effectively he will be excluded from politics for a decade.

Then there is Rule 137 of the Rules of the Malaysian Federal Court which empowers the court to review its own decision. Anwar's lawyers have indicated that they will make such an application, obviously based on what they believe is a miscarriage of justice. However, the Federal Court has considered the limits of its power to review previously in the Anwar case, when the defence sought to have the court review its decision to uphold the prosecution's appeal against disclosure at the trial. The court dismissed the application, ruling that even if it had the power to review its own decision it was not satisfied there were exceptional grounds to justify the review. It also thought it was not a suitable case for review and there needed to be some finality to the proceedings.

So Anwar's lawyers will need to satisfy the court that there are exceptional circumstances to review the guilty verdict and prison sentence, which is a difficult task given that the court has previously taken the view that where its findings are questioned, whether in law or facts, that is not a matter for review. Anwar's roller-coaster ride through the Malaysian legal system may seem to have come to an end, but he has been in tight corners before and seems to manage to come back even stronger.

There is one final legal hurdle for Anwar to jump. He must defend Mohd Saiful's civil action against him for damages of RM50 million (USD13.5 million) for "physical trauma and agony since 2008". That claim is to be heard in the High Court in mid-August 2015.

The pattern of intimidation and arrests escalated in the weeks following Anwar's imprisonment. The government reacted swiftly to suppress any dissent by launching another crackdown on opposition MPs using the sedition law. At least six MPs and party officials were arrested and detained after joining public protests in support of Anwar. One of those was Anwar's eldest daughter Nurul Izzah who was arrested on 16 March 2015 for reading out parts of a statement made by her father in a speech she gave in Parliament. She was later freed on bail. The next day police arrested senior PKR MP Chua Tian Chang for sedition over his involvement in the #KitaLawan march a few days earlier. It is difficult to know where this will all lead, but in the opposition claims it will not be silenced.

Conservative members of the government no doubt expected that Anwar's jailing would, after the initial reaction of dissent and protest from his supporters, help usher in a period of political stability for the ruling coalition, but rather it has only brought continued turmoil in Malaysia. Anwar may be locked up in prison, but his long shadow still hangs over the political landscape, and it will not easily be lifted. How this all plays out is yet to be seen.

Interview with Anwar Ibrahim
(9 July 2014)

Trial observers often do just that — observe. They report on what they see and hear in court so as to maintain independence and objectivity, but it can also mean that insight is limited to just what is happening at that moment. I know because I have been observing trials on behalf of several international organisations.

Observers might get a quick comment here and there from key players, but seldom do they get the chance to interview the person at the centre of the controversy. It seemed to me that readers of this account would gain a better insight by hearing Anwar's views about his predicament and the several issues confronting him with the ongoing prosecution in the Malaysian courts.

Dato' Seri Anwar Ibrahim was gracious to spare time from a busy schedule to be interviewed at his office in Petaling Jaya on 9 July 2014. It was also the same week that a case management hearing was held to list his appeal against the conviction and sentence imposed by the Court of Appeal three months earlier.

Independence of the Malaysian judiciary

Anwar first stood trial over 15 years ago, in 1998. He was convicted and sent to prison for acts of sodomy and corruption. It wasn't until 2004 that the sodomy conviction was overturned on appeal, but by then he had spent six years in prison.

The conduct of these trials met with international condemnation given what many thought were substantial instances of procedural and judicial unfairness. There had also been allegations of corrupt conduct by the police and the prosecution.

Did he think the judiciary had in any way changed for the better since his first series of trials in 1998?

Anwar acknowledged his acquittal by a judge of the High Court in January 2012, saying that was obviously a reflection of how some judges of that court were prepared to be independent, but he saw no real change in political trials at higher levels.

He further explained: "In the lower court, judges ... a few of them ... tend to be fiercely independent, but the Court of Appeal and Federal Court seem to be more submissive because of the prospect of elevation and the position accorded to them and the guarantees of lucrative office after retirement."

Asked if he thought the decisions made in cases affecting the government were predictable, he replied: "If you go to the higher court, then people can anticipate fairly well what the result will be and which is not necessarily based on the facts or the law." So he didn't think that the judiciary — except in the lower courts — had shown much independence in recent times.

Appointment of Muhammad Shafee Abdullah as prosecutor

The Attorney-General Tan Sri Abdul Gani Patail was a long time foe of Anwar. He successfully prosecuted Anwar at his first sodomy trial in 1998, and also appeared against Anwar at his appeal against conviction in 2004. Anwar had in the past made serious allegations against Gani Patail alleging that he was guilty of grave misconduct and had even fabricated evidence against him.

Gani Patail appointed private lawyer Tan Sri Muhammad Shafee Abdullah to prosecute the appeal against Anwar, when he could easily have appointed a prosecutor from his own office. Shafee Abdullah had for many years represented senior Umno officials and parliamentarians, often against Anwar, and was known to be a confidant of Prime Minister Najib Razak. Would Gani Patail be satisfied with Shafee Abdullah's appointment, given the controversy that surrounded it and the serious allegations of corruption Shafee Abdullah allegedly made against him?

Anwar paused, reflecting on the question, then replied: "He is still edgy, and now worse with the appointment of Shafee Abdullah who's known as an Umno lawyer."

Was he surprised at the appointment, I asked? "I am not surprised, but I did not anticipate that they were prepared to go this far. I mean they could have just secured a conviction if the instruction had gone to the judges, as it did. They did not need to verbally exacerbate or worsen the case by putting someone known ... it's public knowledge ... as an Umno lawyer, who has over the years viciously attacked the opposition."

Anwar described the appointment of Shafee Abdullah to prosecute the case against him as the "height of arrogance". He said, "They are now prepared to adopt the crudest form of attack, and are completely oblivious to the concerns of others or international observers."

Anwar may have been right about that. While the international observers, which included such distinguished persons as former Justice Elizabeth Evatt of the Australian Federal Court, were shown every courtesy by the court, the judges behaved as if they were oblivious to their presence.

Did Anwar think the Court of Appeal was biased in favour of Shafee Abdullah? Anwar responded saying "...they gave blanket support to Shafee, and were so blatantly biased against the defence. There was no attempt even to appreciate some of our legitimate concerns."

Did Anwar blame Shafee Abdullah for the way the case was conducted? "No," said Anwar, "it's not Shafee, it's the system."

He explained that Shafee Abdullah's appointment as prosecutor fitted in with his plans to replace the existing Attorney-General. His ambitions were widely known "as far back as '98, when he was lobbying for that position." But why would he want to be the A-G given he had a lucrative legal practice? "Now he has all the money, he needs the power. And with that power, he can get more money," replied Anwar.

Has Malaysia changed since Anwar's first conviction in 1998?

We had discussed development of the legal system since his conviction in 1998, but had he noticed any other changes in Malaysia in that time? This was a more general question, and he responded to it saying: "Not the electoral process, not the media, not the traditions, probably some pronouncements. In some areas it's not as crude as in the past, but there are the same laws, which are still draconian."

He also commented on the state of the national media, where you didn't find any "dissenting news" about the government, but there had been a major change in coverage by the social network media, which Anwar thought had been "most helpful" to the opposition.

Loss of 13th General Election

The next series of questions related to the 13th General Election — held on 5 May 2013 — in which the opposition parties won on the popular vote, but failed to win the majority of seats. There had been many claims of fraudulent conduct during the election, which Anwar later publicly claimed was anything but fair and that the result had been stolen from the opposition.

Did Anwar think it was ever going to be a fair election given what was at stake for the government parties? "No, but still we thought that given the level of discontent and anger, people would register a protest at the ballot box and I think they did, but because of the fraud we lost. We were surprised at the extent of the fraudulent conduct."

How certain was he that there had been fraudulent conduct? He said: "We produced enough evidence to support the case, but it didn't get us anywhere. The Electoral Commission was complicit in the crime. We took it to the courts, but lost and we were stuck with substantial costs."

Using the law as a means of oppression

At the time of the interview, many opponents of the government were being charged with the criminal offence of sedition, including not only opposition members of parliament, but also academics and student activists.

Did Anwar believe that the law was being used as a weapon against free speech and dissent? He was quick to respond saying, "That's what happens with any authoritarian or semi-authoritarian rule."

He elaborated and spoke about the means by which the government kept control. "Control the media, control the courts ... that is the ultimate. Normally the courts will be the last to be questioned. If they can be clear, confident, and successful, then the courts can be independent, but when the government resorts to the courts there is no justice," he said.

Did Anwar think that the government could continue to maintain such control indefinitely? He thought not, saying that what he found reassuring was that even in his case people understood "it was just political". He gave an example: "Last night I went to the mosque, and if there was any bit of suspicion that I was involved, they would not ask me to give a sermon, or lead the prayers, but they did."

No regrets for a life of politics

Anwar's ambition to lead his nation ended abruptly with his conviction and imprisonment in 1998, but he had fought back after his release in 2004 to bring together disparate political parties into a coalition that won the popular vote at the 2013 General Election. Of course, after his release from prison and return to politics he again had to endure further allegations of sexual impropriety, which ended in his acquittal in 2012. Yet, the prosecution would not let go, and so the process continued until his conviction at the Court of Appeal in March 2014.

Had it all been worth it? Did he have any regrets about his political and personal life? He admitted that it had been a "heavy price to pay, but no regrets." What about the impact on his family, for whom it must have been very hard, particularly during the years of his imprisonment?

He paused, no doubt reflecting on that aspect of his political commitment, then replied: "It's been painful for the children and the family. Even now, you have to imagine, I have to endure this again, at this age, in my condition, but I am resigned to the fact that if you are fighting a corrupt and unjust system then there is no easy way. And you are reassured by the fact that when you go around ... the massive sentiments of public support ... that people are not that gullible or easily duped."

He especially regretted missing the prime years of his daughters' upbringing, particularly the youngest. "She was in the kindergarten or Standard One when I was sent to prison. By the time I was released, she was already in secondary school, so I missed those critical years of development," he said.

Had he discussed with his family what might happen if he was again imprisoned? He said that he had spoken to all of them about that, and they had been "very supportive". "I have a remarkable family," he said, "my wife may look fragile on the surface, but she is very strong."

Thwarted ambition

Anwar's political rise was meteoric. He morphed from firebrand student activist to government minister to deputy prime minister in Dr Mahathir's regime. However, he eventually came into conflict with the prime minister, which ultimately led to his dismissal on 2 September 1998.

Some observers thought that Anwar's ambition had been too obvious, but Dr Mahathir was not ready to be replaced and so he acted swiftly and ruthlessly to eliminate a potential rival.

Did Anwar think that if he had been more patient, if Mahathir did not see him as a threat, it might have turned out differently? Wouldn't it have been better to allow an orderly succession to take place?

Anwar quickly replied: "No, well there was a limit. I was known to be a Mahathir loyalist and worked reasonably well with him. But there were tensions, for example, the issue of the marginalisation of the poor, the fight against corruption ... these are the things that I had to do. It wasn't a matter of patience."

He added: "Can you be patient when billions are stolen? Should you be patient when he asked for two billion ringgit to bail out his son? People say 'you need to be patient'. What they mean is that you must approve. I said 'I can't approve' and I told Mahathir that. When he decided to use Petronas funds, that was beyond me; when he asked for the Treasury, I said no."

The Malays and Islam

Anwar had been critical of the government for using race and religion to maintain its power. Was it legitimate for an essentially Malay government to protect its people and religion?

Anwar replied saying there was nothing wrong with the government being pro-Malay, but "if it is pro-Malay, it should actually help the common people. The poorest are the Malays. The most marginalised are the Malays and the indigenous people. But the government is corrupt and an elitist club, which does little to help the poor Malays."

He also spoke critically about the way Umno promoted itself as the sole embodiment and protector of Islam. "But that isn't true," said Anwar, "when they talk about Islam, to me the notion of justice is absent. What is religion? It's to promote peace. It must be this strong passion for justice, but for them it is absent. It doesn't matter to them."

"Good for Malaysia"

Anwar wasn't surprised that the Court of Appeal convicted him in March 2014. But his reaction was surprising because when he was moving around the courtroom after the verdict we shook hands and he said to me: "This is good for Malaysia." What did he mean by that?

"Well," he said, "as a consolation what else can I do? This is the only way the people can be alerted and understand what took place. Azizah [Anwar's wife] said earlier, in '98 or '99 when she was campaigning, 'We have to endure this and it is very tragic, very difficult for the family, but this is something good for Malaysia.' So in the same way, by this verdict the people can understand that our major institutions, including the judiciary, are rotten, corrupt and decadent."

Karpal Singh

We turned to discuss the importance and loss of Karpal Singh. He had been a political opponent when Anwar was part of the ruling party, but had then become his stalwart defender against the ongoing campaign to convict him of sodomy.

Anwar recalled with affection a time when he was, in his own words, "this radical Muslim youth leader that at that time was a major movement with about 40,000 members." Anwar was invited to a DAP conference by Lim Kit Siang in 1980 in Cameron Highlands. The topic for discussion was Islam in a multiracial society. It was a major DAP retreat of MPs, state assemblymen and all the party leaders.

Anwar went with his wife Dr Wan Azizah Wan Ismail and when he got there was surrounded by "over 20 very experienced political giants". He recounted: "I said, oh my God! I was quite nervous because I was in their terrain. Of course Kit Siang was very reassuring. He said, 'Look, just say whatever you want and then answer some questions.' The first question came from Karpal Singh. He said, 'Anwar, you sound impressive, you talk about justice and fairness. If that's what you mean, tell me, can a non-Malay, non-Muslim be the prime minister of this country?' "

"Well what could I say?" Anwar laughed as he recalled the moment, saying "That's Karpal."

Anwar described the opposition he faced from his own supporters when he decided to use Karpal as his main lawyer. They were against Karpal because of his DAP status and because they regarded him to be anti-Islam and anti-Malay. For Anwar, however, Karpal was the "right choice".

He said people "missed the point" and that was why he had a huge argument with senior lawyer Raja Aziz Addruse, who was his lead defence counsel at his corruption and first sodomy trial. Anwar said that Raja Aziz wanted to appeal based "strictly according to the procedure. I said no, there are things to say, and that you are always trying to avoid the media who have been smearing you for years."

Anwar said that at times he was worried whether Karpal was fully prepared, but at the last minute he would "come straight through". Anwar acknowledged that it was very difficult for Karpal because of his medical condition. He said, "Karpal's frustration because of his disability was at times obvious."

Raja Aziz subsequently withdrew from Anwar's team claiming ill-health as the reason, but he and others on the original team, which included Chris Fernando and Haji Sulaiman, may well have been put out by Karpal's appointment and they too withdrew from the team. Karpal, of course, was a one-man team on his own.

Yet Anwar was confident he had chosen the right man for the job, saying he found that Karpal became his "greatest defender". He said they developed a "genuine affection" for each other. He described their growing relationship as they had "long chats into the wee hours in the morning, in his office, and even in prison. We would go on for hours, and we chatted about a number of issues, which he didn't do normally."

He also spoke about how comforted he was by Karpal's reassurances that he would take care of things, and who would say such things as "We will fight them." "Don't be distracted." "You carry on with your politics." He recalled they were Karpal's last words to him on the night of his death.

Anwar then told a story which he thought exemplified Karpal's character: "I remember when I was in prison and my family and friends put together what they could for Karpal's legal fees. My brother collected 200,000.00 ringgit (about US$62,000) and went to see Karpal with it. Karpal threw him out of his office for offering him the money. Karpal later said to me, 'What is this brother trying to do?' Then he explained. He said, 'Anwar, you gave your life and now you are in prison, for a cause that we all believe. I've been fighting this for decades and you are there, you sacrifice your life. You mean to say I am doing this for money? What sort of a person am I?' So that was the way he reacted. Again that was Karpal."

Sedition

Anwar was very critical of the way the government had prosecuted Karpal for sedition. He was supportive of Karpal's family continuing the fight to clear his name saying, "They have to do it. It's not just a matter of innocence, but fighting against an unjust law."

He was also critical of the way the prosecution against Karpal was justified in terms that appealed to "the Malay crowd, with the message don't touch the Malay rulers, this is a Malay country." But he made it clear that he supported the constitutional provisions that recognised the Malay rulers as part of the structure of a constitutional monarchy, and that they should be respected.

However, he thought that Umno was not being consistent at all, for as Karpal had reminded the judge at his trial, it was Prime Minister Mahathir and his government who had removed the powers of the rulers.

Expectation of Federal Court decision

Anwar's appeal against conviction had not at the time of this interview been heard, so his future was unknown. What happens, I asked him, if the Federal Court upholds the appeal?

"Well then," he said, "I go to jail." He added: "There are some books I have not finished and I'll probably read Mark Trowell's latest book and make copious notes, as I did for the *Complete Works of Shakespeare*." He explained: "I've had 12 years of our prison system. I speak to friends in Indonesia, or even Philippines ... we talk about Suharto's son or Estrada ... they thought, you know, it was like a house arrest. They don't know that this is actually high-level security prison, solitary confinement, and 13 steel doors to get to my blinking cell! That's not easy."

"Gong glang, gong glang, gong glang. You know, when you get out of prison there are a few things you hate. One is the sound of bells and keys.

The other is that everything is closed. You get to my house and everything is glass. Openness. I hate to see keys," he said.

Future of the opposition

Anwar was confident about the future of the opposition should he be imprisoned. He said: "We have a competent younger team. Of course it takes time, but then, I think they will take up the issue of leadership of the coalition opposition. They will probably have to take rotation, chairing the meeting, things like that."

He then outlined the experience that he considered the opposition now had: "We have gone through 15 years and the relationship is well cemented. The policy guidelines are there so there is no dispute over the issue of Islam in the constitution, or the issue of the Bible, or the issue of Allah ... we have resolved that. There have been more complex issues, such as Chinese education, poverty, inequality. These issues are quite resolved and that has made things easier. There are daily issues to confront, but I think we can manage."

Anwar accepted my suggestion that he had played a pivotal role in keeping the three opposition parties together at times of potential conflict, saying: "I probably facilitate things a bit even over the more contentious issue like the *hudud* (Islamic penal law), which was tough. That day I remember, was very, very fragile at that time and I managed to avoid a break-up. I spent my time going back and forth between the DAP and PAS offices, you know back and forth until I said, look, I've done enough, it should get resolved and it did."

Acknowledgements

The author wishes to thank the organisations that sponsored his role as an observer at the trial and the appeals of Anwar Ibrahim. Without their support this book would not have been possible. The organisations include the International Commission of Jurists, the Commonwealth Lawyers Association, the Union Internationale des Advocates, the Law Council of Australia and LAWASIA. Special mention must be made of the Inter-Parliamentary Union that maintained its financial and personal support over the life of the court proceedings, which was a period of almost three years. (The opinions of the author expressed in this book do not necessarily reflect that of the views of these organisations.)

There are also those who helped make this book possible: Ingeborg Schwartz and Rogier Huizenga of the Human Rights Programme of the Inter-Parliamentary Union; Janet Neville, General Secretary of LAWASIA; Chris Newson, the former general manager of Marshall Cavendish; and Lee Mei Lin, the senior editor of Marshall Cavendish, who transformed several, disjointed reports into a proper narrative. Her deft touch in guiding the general form and structure of the manuscript is very much evident and appreciated.

About the author

Mark Trowell is a leading criminal lawyer from Perth, Western Australia. He was appointed Queen's Counsel in 2000. Despite some time in commercial and common law, he was ultimately attracted to the challenge of the criminal law.

He has prosecuted criminal cases for the Director of Public Prosecutions and has also appeared as counsel at two Royal Commissions. In December 2006, he was appointed by the Australian Government to undertake a review of the legislation governing the *Australian Crime Commission*.

He is co-chair of the criminal law standing committee of LAWASIA. In recent years, he has been an international observer reporting on behalf of LAWASIA, the Australian Bar Association, the International Commission of Jurists, the Commonwealth Lawyers Association and the Union Internationale des Advocats. He has also represented the interests of the Geneva-based Inter-Parliamentary Union at the criminal trials and appeals of opposition leaders Anwar Ibrahim in Malaysia and General Sarath Fonseka in Sri Lanka.